Contents

Preface

In the last two years appraisal has been put back on the agenda of schools and classroom observation is to play an important part. This time there is a considerable base of theory, research and practice upon which the system can be based.

The three general purposes of appraisal – promotion, reward and professional development – are all under consideration again. In this book the main emphasis is on methods of classroom observation for professional and school development. However, a range of appraisal techniques are reviewed in Chapter 1 which can be used for a variety of purposes. Questions are raised about whether the 'instruments' used for assessing performance for promotion and reward can be the same as those used for development.

In Chapter 2 the range of techniques available for classroom observation are discussed and in the final section a professional development method is presented which can be used to consolidate the performance of good teachers and retrieve the performance of failing teachers or those in difficulties.

This method and evidence for its effectiveness are presented in Chapter 3 in both quantitative and qualitative terms and then illustrated through a series of primary and secondary case examples.

In Chapters 4 and 5 an analysis of the nature of effective learning and teaching is undertaken and a range of methods and examples are given to support professional and school development plans.

Diane Montgomery
Maldon, Essex
April 1999

Positive Teacher Appraisal Through Classroom Observation

DIANE MONTGOMERY

David Fulton Publishers
London

David Fulton Publishers Ltd
Ormond House, 26–27 Boswell Street, London WC1N 3JD

First published in Great Britain by David Fulton Publishers 1999

The right of Diane Montgomery to be identified as the author of this work has been asserted by her in accordance with the Copyright, Designs and Patents Act 1988.

Copyright © Diane Montgomery 1999

British Library Cataloguing in Publication Data
A catalogue record for this book is available from the British Library

ISBN 1–85346–607–7

Typeset by FSH Print & Production Ltd
Printed by The Cromwell Press Ltd, Trowbridge, Wilts.

Chapter One

Appraisal

Introduction

The White Paper *Excellence in Schools* (DfEE 1997) reported that the appraisal arrangements currently in operation did not provide an adequate check on students' performance. The targets set often failed to focus on improving teacher effectiveness in the classroom and were not specific or measurable. OFSTED (Office for Standards in Education 1997) identified five main weaknesses in the appraisal systems operating in schools. They were lacking in rigour; there was poor evaluation of the impact on teaching quality and the pupils; there was unrealistic target setting; infrequent or ineffective classroom observation; and there was a failure to link appraisal to training. In effect, appraisal in the majority of settings had become a perfunctory exercise.

In the same year the National Union of Teachers (NUT 1997) reported that teachers feared that the results of appraisal would be used against them. This indicated a lack of trust between the appraisers and appraisees. The NUT insisted that appraisal must be linked to professional development and not to pay, promotion or capability procedures. Shades of the debate which had raged more than a decade earlier when formal appraisal was first introduced. In other words all the attributes which good appraisal schemes might be expected to offer had somehow been bypassed and appraisal had become a paper and pencil exercise in keeping with the worst predictions. The proposed solution was to return to a system of payment by results which had first been rejected in 1902 for its failure to achieve the desired effects.

Research by Wragg *et al.* (1996) in 400 schools found that only 28 per cent of teachers were observed teaching and this occurred only once instead of twice as in the appraisal regulations. In many cases the observation lasted for less than the 30 minutes minimum recommended span. There were also doubts over what was being appraised and it was largely left up to the teachers to decide the focus for the observation. The foci chosen were teaching methods in 28 per cent of cases, curriculum in 7 per cent; assessing children's work in 4 per cent of cases. Of those who had been appraised 60 per cent thought that it had improved their work performance. Whether or not it was more than a Hawthorn Effect or a 'feel good' factor was not tested.

Although appraisal schemes existed and were in policy documents in schools surveyed as part of the preparation for this book many of the schemes had to all intents and purposes lapsed. The clear exceptions were in relation to the appraisal of Newly Qualified Teachers and to Capability procedures. Appraisal had in the main become a perfunctory desk-based review infrequently entered into. Because of the renewed attention to appraisal most schemes were in the process of being revived and strengthened by classroom observation. The training of Senior Management Teams had begun, followed by training for Departmental Heads and the whole school staff in a supportive form of classroom observation linked to promoting school development. Where full appraisal schemes still operated staff generally chose the focus for the lesson observation with differentiation, equal opportunities, special educational needs, provision for the more able, classroom management, questioning techniques and curriculum being the most popular. The choice of focus tended to depend upon the areas of competency and interest of the observer and recent inservice training inputs, as well as the expertise of the person observed.

Currently the DfEE is conducting a review of the appraisal scheme as there will be a sharper focus on teacher performance (DfEE 1999). It will be based upon classroom observation linked to pupil results and the annual performance targets. Newly Qualified Teachers will be formally appraised and assessed on a Pass/Fail basis so that those found wanting can be excluded from the profession. Appraisal for all staff is to take place on an annual basis and will be 'marked' on a five point scale. Performance related pay will be given to those who score in the top bracket and who improve their SATs and public exam scores in line with the schools' targets. How this will be funded from the school budgets which are already overstretched has yet to be determined. There will be a system of fast tracking for 'able graduates' who become skilful teachers and a cadre of 'superteachers' can expect to be paid up to £40,000 a year to encourage them to stay in the classroom and not seek promotion and financial gain by going into management.

In this climate, books on appraisal which act as a support to good practice and help improvement where there is underperformance are essential. There is a danger that a system concerned primarily with targets and performance related pay can cause participants to overlook quality in education by emphasising 'schoolhousing' (Renzulli 1986) and to narrow the curriculum targets to those defined by the SATs (Feller 1994). It is important that teachers retain and build their professionalism in the face of this form of increasing bureaucratisation or 'civil service mode' of education. This conflict seen in education does not exist for other professions. They are not professions commanded by a bureaucracy such as the DfEE propelled by Government. The aims of educators and bureaucrats are inconsistent. With bureaucrats in control, education in the UK is being driven towards increasing levels and layers of paperwork. Teaching feels as though it has become a subsidiary activity to the pursuit of correct paperwork. In this atmosphere if there is not a written policy on every aspect of school life then it is not a 'good' school and OFSTED inspectors can fail its provision.

Experienced and expert teachers continually report being unsure of their competencies in appraising the classroom performance of others. They were clear about being able to recognise and deal with failing performance but less secure about how to retrieve it and to appraise with some exactitude the broad range of competencies which they might meet. Senior teachers were often concerned about their distance from the classroom, the role which they brought to any observation and the effect it might have upon pupils, and their lack of subject expertise except in their own domain. Devolving appraisal to subject leaders and heads of department equally did not fill them with confidence. Others who were involved in the appraisal of NQTs and in capability procedures often relished the negative powers that their new role brought and enjoyed the title of 'axeman or woman'. This can hardly contribute to the health and wellbeing of a school as a developing organism.

None of these concerns are new. It is in fact surprising that since appraisal began to be introduced into schools over twenty years ago, these issues have not been resolved. Is it that some of these problems have no resolution? Or indeed is it that the appraisal strategies which have been applied have been misguided, borrowed as many were from industry and commerce? Do we know what does work and is appropriate? A second look at the issues and a review of what we have learnt since they were first discussed may well prove helpful.

Appraisal: issues, nature and purposes

As early as 1972 Handy had already reviewed the three main systems of appraisal currently in operation, mainly in commerce and industry. The categories were: appraisal for financial *reward*; appraisal for *promotion* and appraisal for *performance enhancement*. He detailed the advantages and disadvantages of each and concluded that staff development was the best and most successful purpose. It was surprising that what followed paid no attention to this, indicating that a different agenda was to be pursued.

Appraisal systems can be *formative* or *summative* and some claim to be both. The formative approach is very much concerned with staff development and giving feedback on performance. In the latter the appraiser compares the performance with external criteria and judgments are made about pass or fail. Sometimes levels of attainment and rating scales are used as in an OFSTED inspection. It is difficult to make appraisals using only one type of procedure whether formative or summative.

According to Scriven (1986) the criteria for summative personnel evaluation should have either a logical or a legal connection to teacher performance and they must be necessary for good teaching. The popular focus, for example on questioning techniques, selected for a classroom observation may be neither necessary nor sufficient for good teaching to be taking place and therefore avoids the central concerns of teaching and teachers. The most common reason for declaring a teacher incompetent (Wise and Darling Hammond *et al.* 1984) was inability to control the class. This is still true today and evidenced in the annual reports issued by the DfEE on behalf of the Chief Inspector for schools. However, it is mostly in the classrooms of newly qualified teachers and those heading for capability procedures that classroom management is a major concern. It is also frequently addressed in capability procedures with little success.

In general many linked purposes of appraisal can be identified within the three main categories: accountability, payment and reward, performance related pay, promotion, assessment, quality and school development, personal development, career enhancement, communication, motivation, valuing and job satisfaction, motivation and warning, monitoring, references, inservice training, target setting, discipline and capability. There are also three major issues which arise within them whatever the process, these being *credibility*, *autonomy* and *roles* discussed later.

For example, it is important that the procedures selected are fair and are seen to be so. Inextricably linked to the notion of fairness is that of *credibility*. Lack of credibility can quickly undermine any system of appraisal. It is therefore necessary, before embarking on appraisal that these issues are fully explored. This exploration demonstrates the necessary commitment to the process by all concerned. It is vital that all the staff share an understanding of the criteria to be used and the processes to be experienced. It is thus better if they share in the development of the criteria and processes rather than have them imposed. This problem is implicit in any national scheme for it is important that there should always be some autonomy at the local level. If there is not, then people do not identify with the aims and purposes and do not feel that they have ownership of the system. It is then in serious danger of becoming a paper and pencil exercise.

Appraisal schemes tend to flourish only where there is a tradition of self-evaluation. Then it is seen as a natural development of a process already in operation. It is also important that any results from appraisal are linked to appropriate action such as training, development or career enhancement. If they are not then the procedure may be seen as an empty one soon to be discounted. However, there are also periods when consolidation is appropriate and a positive system of appraisal can be very motivating and satisfying, enhancing the communication between professionals.

Appraisers who cannot control their own classes, command subject knowledge and pass on teaching wisdom suffer from lack of credibility.

Accountability

The accountability movement began in 1872 when a system of 'Payment by results' was introduced. Over time it lapsed until the Education Act of 1902 discontinued it. It re-emerged with the Ruskin College speech of the then Prime Minister James Callaghan in 1976 and now again under a Labour Government (Christian Democrat style) in 1998. Callaghan launched the 'Great Debate on Education' arguing that a section of the economy which consumed such a large proportion of public money, £6 billion, should be more accountable to that public for the way the money was spent and the value which resulted. He wanted value for money. Accountability was linked not only to costs and value for money but to *standards* and the *questioning of autonomy* in the education system. Professional autonomy was no longer to be sacrosanct.

There had been a move from a selective tripartite system of education in 1970 to a mainly comprehensive style of education. This had raised concerns in many quarters about standards. It fuelled public concern about education and appraisal was seen as a method for ridding the profession of failing teachers. This of course made all teachers feel somewhat threatened as there were considerable differences of opinion about teaching methods, styles and contents (Bennett and Jordan 1975). This gave rise to a central concern about the credibility of the appraiser and the process in the pursuit of accountability. The issues related to roles are discussed in a later section.

At the time 'appraisal by walking about' was the most common method in operation. Few schools had instituted formal appraisal procedures although there were some notable exceptions. In many small primary schools heads and deputies joined in the classroom work with staff and so were able to claim that they had observed their staff teach. The same could not be said of secondary school heads and college principals however. In addition to this a wide range of teachers helped in the training and appraisal of students in their own classrooms contributing to the College assessments. This participation slowly increased until the present when mentors in school may be the prime teaching practice supervisors and assessors.

Formal appraisal of teachers' performance became an important issue only when the then Secretary of State for Education, Sir Keith Joseph (1983) proposed that as part of the process of accountability teachers themselves must be appraised. He later linked appraisal with remuneration, next enhancement and then career development (Joseph 1985a, b).

The appraisal movement: staff development, motivation, job satisfaction and communication

The movement for some system of appraisal had been gathering momentum during this period. Thus research on the *Evaluation and Enhancement of Teaching Performance*, Programme Four of the Learning Difficulties Research Project (LDRP, Montgomery 1984) began in the Spring of 1983. It involved shadowing pupils for a day at a time to find out what kind of curriculum they were being offered following systematic inservice education planned by the school. Nerys James, a deputy head of the secondary school in which the programme began wrote as follows:

> Diane Montgomery visited Heathside School in the Spring Term of 1983 to look at curricular developments in action in the classroom. What she saw and what we thought she would see there were not always one and the same thing...We had in many cases worked on the basis of what we thought was going on, and not on factual observation.

Our subsequent discussions turned to how teachers, some newly qualified and others who were finding some of their classes too challenging, might be helped. It was usually only these individuals who were being observed and given feedback on their performance. However, the checklists and methods of appraisal being used by the school were not found to be improving the teachers' performance. At this stage another secondary school close by with similar problems joined the project. They were already also using classroom observation and video feedback as part of their appraisal processes. Despite this they were not able to improve the performance of several teachers and were about to institute dismissal procedures as they were then known. They were also moving into pupil questionnaires to give feedback on teacher performance.

Samuels (1983) at Heathlands School and Trethowan (1987) at Warden Park already had well established appraisal systems emphasising performance review and target setting. These too emphasised appraisal for performance enhancement. As a result the systems also were found to enhance motivation of the staffs concerned and increased their job satisfaction. They also led to improved communication within the schools. There was, however, a dearth of evidence in quantitative and qualitative terms to show how performance could be and was enhanced.

Despite the considerable evidence which was being accumulated at ground level on workable systems acceptable by the staffs in the various schools and beginning to be adopted by others, the Department for Education and Science (DES) commissioned the Chief Education Officer of Suffolk Local Education Authority (Graham 1985), to research appraisal schemes. The research team consisted of three head teachers, one from the primary sector; the Chief Education Officer; a deputy CEO and the Senior General Advisor. The head teachers had some experience of running their own appraisal schemes under the LEAs' encouragement and were helping others develop their own schemes through advisory work.

The team's method of research review, however, did not include the range of terms or key words which would have given them the database for a comprehensive review of relevant research (Burgess 1990). He concluded that they used the wrong key words to do their computer based literature search. They used 'review', 'assessment', 'appraisal' and 'evaluation' but not 'methodology', 'qualitative research', 'ethnography', and 'observational techniques' (p.30). This resulted in most of their appraisal literature arising from industry and commerce. He stated that this created further problems. 'Many of the difficulties stem from importing the male-dominated hierarchical power structure that is currently in existence in schools into the system of teacher appraisal. In such situations, power relations become important to the context of appraisal' (p. 31).

At the same time Turner and Clift (1985) found in their review and register of appraisal that only a small proportion of schemes involved appraisal of teaching performance. In fact there seemed to be a general reluctance to do this and in our researches (Montgomery and Hadfield 1989, 1990) we found a lack of theoretical and practical knowledge about how to do it.

External agencies were pressurising the appraisal movement to adopt the systems in operation in the Civil Service and in industry, models which Handy (1972) had already found wanting. Nevertheless national conferences funded by the DES, the

Unions and so on included speeches from the Permanent Secretary for Education (Hancock 1985) and industrialists and trainers. Some of these such as Patterson (1985), an industrialist, insisted that there was no need at all for classroom observation in the appraisal of teachers. These assertions, the lack of time and extra funding and the lack of classroom observation expertise in the profession moved the process towards desk-based reviews with job descriptions, performance indicators and input and output factors, whilst teachers themselves consistently affirmed the need for observation of classroom performance as part of an appraisal scheme.

The fact that there were over one hundred Departments/Schools of Education across the country involved in the training of teachers and using various forms of performance observation techniques was ignored. Small scale studies had found that there was no coherent framework used by all of them (McCulloch 1979) and so they were left out of the survey. No attempt was made to identify college models which were working effectively and improving the quality of student teaching.

The Suffolk Report (Graham 1985) having failed to define effective teaching went on to discuss appraisal skills rather than what was to be appraised (Burgess 1990) and made a number of recommendations. Appraisal schemes should recognise and support effective practice; should identify areas for development and improvement; identify and develop potential of individual teachers. For schools, appraisal should work to improve the opportunities for all pupils; improve the management and support of the learning process and improve the 'tone' of the hidden curriculum. It was considered essential that the process should enhance the quality of learning of all the pupils; that teachers were supported in their efforts to increase their effectiveness and the process should include some reference to their career aspirations. Thus the main emphasis of the report, *Those carrying Torches*, was on the professional development of teachers. It strongly rejected the linking of merit payments to appraisal. Following it, Local Education Authorities (LEAs) had to publish local guidelines, scheme management, provision of documentation, skills training courses, resources and monitoring procedures.

As a result of the Teacher's Dispute ACAS (the Advisory Conciliation and Arbitration Service) set up an independent panel, The Appraisal and Training Working Group, which reported in June 1986. The group was made up of 2 CEOs including Duncan Graham of the Suffolk Report , 16 Teacher Union Representatives, 2 DES officials and no Teacher Educators or Appraisal Consultants.

The ACAS (1986) document outlined the structures and procedures so that appraisal should not be a series of perfunctory events. It should be a continuous and systematic process which was intended to help teachers in their professional development and career planning. The process was also intended to be a positive one that should improve quality in schools and enhance the job satisfaction of teachers. The agreed principles were that appraisal should feed into the planning of induction into teaching and assess fitness for transfer to Main Professional Grade; inform inservice training; assist professional development and career progression; identify teachers in difficulty and give them support; and inform staff appointment procedures and references.

ACAS identified the stages in the appraisal process as follows:

- self appraisal and preparation;
- initial review discussion centred on a prompt list;
- classroom observation;
- the appraisal interview;
- appeals;
- records.

Despite these recommendations Nisbet (1986) observed that appraisal would strengthen the mechanisms of power and control over teachers and Dadds (1987) commented that it was a process thrust uncritically upon an already overcrowded agenda. The model was also a 'top down' one with the classroom observation undertaken by an immediate superior.

A second volume by the Suffolk group *In the Light of Torches* (Graham 1987) considered the implications of appraisal in terms of time for negotiations, training, implementation and money. It discussed head teacher appraisal procedures; classroom observation; training in appraisal interviewing; resourcing an appraisal system; and the report of a study visit to California featuring in particular the San Diego Instrument. This was a set of check lists, rating scales and criterion referenced scales for appraisal of head teachers and teachers as a whole. This time 'effective teaching' was defined but the lack of a common set of guidelines was bemoaned. The characteristics of effective teaching were summarised in the report published by the Industrial Society (1987) as follows:

Effective teachers

- believe that *all pupils* can learn, and such teachers take responsibility by organising and assigning appropriate tasks and by other means to see that pupils *do* learn;
- keep pupils 'on task', use unambiguous cues and provide evaluative feedback that is clear and instructive;
- use a variety of teaching methods ranging from 'whole group' to 'individualised' teaching, from didactic teaching to discovery approaches. Skill level, subject matter and the aims of the lessons determine the method chosen;
- use direct teaching when basic skill acquisition is the aim;
- are good managers of the teaching/learning process and of people. They use a variety of good management practices including setting a classroom 'tone' or 'climate' conducive to learning, preventing disciplinary problems through planning, eliminating disruptions and delays; monitoring pupil attention, i.e. keeping all pupils involved, and establishing clear rules and expectations for each lesson and for the class;
- develop a leadership style which is essentially democratic yet authoritative (not authoritarian). They view their role as helping the development of potential and assume that a sense of responsibility is inherent in every pupil. (pp.22–23)

The report announced that good teachers are both born and made, but mostly made, and that effective teaching was both science and art. It went on to give the above summary list of the characteristics of the effective teacher who was 'characterised by some or all of the following' (p.23). There then followed a list under three headings: *Planning and Preparation*; *Classroom Management*; and *Evaluation*.

For the purposes of this book a closer look at the Classroom Management list will prove interesting if not helpful:

The teacher

- makes clear the rules, consequences and procedures on the first day and adheres to those rules consistently throughout the year;
- provides for a sustained rate of success by using a range of learning activities which are appropriate to each pupil's ability;
- keeps pupils on appropriate activities and promotes necessary content coverage;
- works to improve individual learning deficiencies with specific transferable skills;
- provides a role model for pupils by a businesslike approach to teaching;
- uses direct teaching with the whole class or small groups when teaching basic skill mastery;
- creates a supportive learning atmosphere by showing concern and respect for each pupil. (p.23).

From this list a later prompt list was derived which the authors stated was 'neither prescriptive nor exhaustive' (p.25).

Once again can be seen the lack of a coherent and shared theory and practice of education. These are descriptors which have been agreed. They describe the observable *outcomes* of what are perceived to be effective teaching characteristics. They do not deal with the *how* these outcomes are achieved and performance thereby improved. This is particularly well illustrated by item three. Precisely how does the teacher keep the pupils on task? What are appropriate activities and how shall they be defined? Similarly, on point five: some of the best teaching is not necessarily businesslike. On the final point: demonstrating concern and respect for each individual can be shown to be a necessary but not sufficient condition for establishing a supportive climate. We have to resolve these problems before an effective classroom observation appraisal system can be set up and be guaranteed to work. It needs to specify how successful teaching is to be achieved and be able to demonstrate it both quantitatively and qualitatively.

The section of 'More Torches' (Graham 1987), on classroom observation, provides a range of different types of checklist. These include prompt lists, profiles, rating scales, formative observation checklists, behaviourally anchored rating scales (BARS) and criterion referenced scales. Again the North American examples are much in evidence e.g.

Domain 3 – Instructional Organisation and Development

3.1 Efficient Use of Time:

a. Begin classwork promptly

b. Organise class to keep the lesson going

c. Shift systematically from one subject to another

d. Control interruptions

e. Organise efficient distribution and collection of materials

f. Provide structure for those students who finish classwork early.

Three different observers, principal, vice principal and a peer all rate the teacher as satisfactory (S) or needs improvement (I) based on their different observations. In this rather formal framework of a 'good lesson' what happens when the teacher does not and cannot control the interruptions? It is of little help to be told that this is what must be done for the lesson to be effective. The teacher probably already knows this but cannot find a way to do so and unless he or she does they are on their way towards a capability procedure. It is in this area that appraisal systems have failed. Teachers and principals do not know how to set these matters right. They can do it themselves but do not have the vocabulary and the constructs to describe what they do which makes them effective. Until this 'nut' is cracked appraisal of a genuinely valuable kind will not be developed in schools.

Administrators, bureaucrats and industrialists cannot help in this. The answers have to be sought within the field of teaching theory and practice itself by teachers. How do teachers learn to teach? They will mostly aver that 'they did it themselves'. Now we can only assume that this is mainly true or that they were trained by those best leaders whose followers always say 'we did it ourselves'. In the course of training there is no doubt that students learn examples of what to teach and are exposed in college and in schools to different examples and models of teaching. What they seem to have to do, however, is to construct their own theories and practices of teaching and learning from a somewhat inchoate programme. Some are better at this than others. The ten quick tips to teaching which someone invariably gives them is like water off a duck's back as they blunder through their early lessons repeating all the mistakes of generations of teachers before them. As long as they are not confined to one practice school for long and can recover or leave their mistakes behind them they can start afresh, hopefully one step on from before. The students and the teachers who do not learn from their mistakes on a continual basis and who keep repeating them will be the unsuccessful ones who finally leave the profession or finish up on capability procedures. How can they be helped to break this cycle of feedback blindness?

In my experience in the observation of over one thousand lessons there is a cycle of disconnections which can be healed in the majority of cases except where the person has a particular form of perseverative neurotic personality problem. The successful professional teacher has learned to become a reflective practitioner. In many instances these processes are implicit but where they have been made explicit they can lead to enhanced performance. However reflection on practice alone cannot necessarily lead to the identification of transferable skills underlying good teaching. Teachers may think this is so but they need the opportunity to research the skills in practice. Thus it is that Adelman (1990) estimates that a consortium of teachers working on this will take at least three years to come to a conclusion. Teacher reflection and research on practice must be an integral part of any professional appraisal system but it is also foolish for teachers to be asked to reinvent the wheel in every new decade.

None of the outcomes of the use of classroom observation schedules and scales thus far except the LDRP scheme (Chapters 2 and 3) have been evaluated in a research programme. This needs to be done in the appraisal context to see if they achieve any of their aims such as enhanced performance. Any system which a school adopts should have enhancement as a primary focus. The system must demonstrate that it can work with teachers in general and those on capability procedures in particular and the evidence should be public and verifiable.

The HMI Report on Appraisal (1989)

The DES next funded pilot studies of appraisal in six LEAs – Croydon, Cumbria, Newcastle on Tyne, Salford, Somerset and Suffolk. During the period 1987–9 HMI visited these six centrally funded pilot project LEAs as well as a much larger number of 'non-pilot authorities'. In the introduction to the report it is stated:

> We found that when it is sensitively planned and practised, appraisal has much value. It has contributed to the better identification of inservice training needs and subsequent provision. The management of staff and the curriculum has improved as a result of better communication and awareness. It has had a marked effect on the performance of individual teachers (p.1 para 2).

It would be interesting to speculate on what counted as evidence for these benign effects since this is never stated. There were no pre- and post-test examples of experimental data collection exercises which could warrant such assertions. Presumably it is the 'feel good' factor in operation again as well as the Hawthorne effect whereby merely being observed improves performance.

HMI noted that LEAs had not fully articulated the purposes of appraisal and that a national system would need to have a large measure of common understanding throughout the profession about aims. Introduction of the national scheme would not be cheap if it was to be effective. At the time of the survey teachers were more concerned about the implementation of the Education Reform Act (1988) and the National Curriculum (1989). HMI estimated that the cost of appraisal would be the full time equivalent of 1800 additional teachers (£35m) and they raised concerns about the time scale. The Government had proposed introducing legislation in 1989 to give effect to the national agreed framework. Their other concerns were over recruitment to shortage subjects and turnover problems in certain areas of the country. Further and Higher Education would also be included in the legislation.

They found that there were three main categories of aims. These were the professional development of individual teachers; those relating to the management of a school or college, and those concerned with improving the quality of teaching and learning. One third mentioned identifying inservice training needs and other aims identified were: raising morale, motivation and job satisfaction, identifying staff strengths and weaknesses and providing support.

All the pilot LEAs included formal classroom observation whereas only six of the 63 non-pilot authorities did so. Only one fifth of the institutions had guidelines for lesson observation. Some had detailed schedules and one used rating scales. On the whole LEAs and institutions were opposed to applying numerical categories. The most common length of time for the observation was 45–60 minutes. In primary schools it was usually the heads who did the appraisal and in secondary schools other senior staff took part.

> The pilot LEAs have adopted a cautious approach to observation; in one the criteria are a matter for negotiation between observer and appraisee. In another, the arrangements are thorough but the emphasis is on description rather than judgment and evaluation. In one urban pilot LEA one or two objectives are set before the observation, and in another specific focuses are expected, such as questioning techniques... In general, the relationship of classroom observation to the overall purposes of appraisal has yet to be developed and so have the criteria for observation.' (p.17, para 44)

The six pilot LEAs had devoted a great deal of attention to the main or review interview which focused mainly on staff development. The structure of the interview was usually left to the participants and any guidance provided centred upon topics which might be discussed.

Virtually all the schemes included a written record but there was no consensus on ownership and access, lifetime or even use of the record.

The Education (No 2) Act of 1986 made appraisal a legal requirement in schools, this being used as the backing for the LEA pilot projects. In 1991 the Education (School Teacher Appraisal) Regulations were passed under the direction of Kenneth Clarke, the then Secretary of State for Education. It was his view that regular appraisal would help develop the professionalism of teachers and so improve the education of their pupils.

Large numbers of teachers began to leave the profession early, some because they did not wish to work on the National Curriculum, others on the grounds of ill health and stress. There threatened to be a shortage of teachers and moves were made to get women who had left to have children to return to teaching. In *An Effective Return to Secondary Teaching* and its companion volume on primary teaching (Buzzing 1992) stated that after a seven year interval a new Government had taken up the pursuit of ineffective and failing teachers and appraisal has been placed squarely on the front burner.

It was the next Secretary of State, John McGregor in 1993, who agreed that appraisal should then be placed on the 'back burner' as there was so much with which schools were having to cope in relation to the National Curriculum. Schools and LEAs were encouraged over the next few years to continue with the development of local schemes.

Appraisal remained on the statute books and was later made an integral part of the OFSTED framework and thus once more it was placed on the agenda of schools. This time however, by writing it into inspection, the issue of funding had been avoided. Once the full impact of the process is felt then no doubt this issue must be dealt with as the costs inherent in a fully developed system cannot simply be absorbed. Perhaps a different answer to additional funding will have to be found such as extending the teacher's day and/or developing pupil autonomy in learning and resource based learning?

Appraisal 1999

In February 1999 the DfEE issued a consultation document *Teachers, Meeting the Challenge of Change*. It focused upon pay and performance management. The document proposed annual appraisal to recognise teachers' achievements in a systematic way, to provide an account of how well they were doing and to link their performance to the school objectives. It aimed to recognise and reward teachers for successful performance in relation to targets. The new system will include:

- the setting of objectives which are clear and measurable so that appraisers and appraisees know what the priorities are and can assess how far objectives have been met;
- the inclusion of targets related to pupil performance;
- the assessment of teachers' performance against their objectives in the context of national professional standards and teachers' observed strengths and weaknesses;
- the use of appraisal outcomes to influence pay decisions as well as to inform teachers' further professional development;
- training and support to ensure those involved know their responsibilities and are able to conduct appraisal fairly.

(DfEE 1999 pp.8–9)

The new procedures will be set out in statutory regulations in Sept 1999. The new links between pay and appraisal outcomes will be introduced in 2000.

Classroom teachers will be appraised on the basis of their job description and at least three objectives agreed at the start of the appraisal cycle in the context of the school's development plan and national teaching standards. The appraisal will 'draw' on classroom information and other information gathered in the appraisal process. Each cycle will conclude annually with an appraisal interview with a senior manager to assess performance and to set new targets for the following year.

From May 1999 teachers achieving Qualified Teacher Status (QTS) will have to complete a statutory induction year. They will teach a reduced timetable of 90 per cent during this period. They will receive induction training and support based on needs identified in the 'Career entry profile'. After a series of formal reviews heads will make a a recommendation to the appropriate body (unspecified) as to whether or not the teacher has met the induction standards

Teachers who hold nine spine points for qualifications and experience will be eligible to submit a portfolio for assessment to determine whether or not they should pass the threshold and proceed along the salary scale. They may then be subject to a further round of performance appraisal. This will be conducted by the head teacher and an external assessor drawn from a pool of 'nationally trained experts' (p.12).

Here we have it. Despite the demotivation of performance related pay, annual assessments and gradings, teachers are to be subject to them. More carrot and a lot of stick. Here there is no appeal to professionalism and the satisfaction of a job well done. Instead there is an interminable round of grasping and clawing for money, scoring and bullying and wearing down of senior managers. Getting people to do the smallest little extra for experience or the good of the children and the school in general will be supplanted by unwillingness to do anything seen as extra, leaving it to those who 'enjoy the favours'.

However fair a system is intended to be, it is impossible for it to work in this hugely complex area without upsetting large numbers of good quality teachers. In situations where there is favour and preference, and this is human nature, it will lead to a cadre who do nothing except for personal gain and the rest who do the minimum possible. In Higher Education where this system has already been introduced tutors regard it as spurious. A truly professional person always does their best and works their hardest in the interests of their pupils or students. No amount of extra money can buy more. Nor is there enough money to reward all of those who really deserve it and the criteria can always be weighted on the basis of multiple factors to reflect the sums of money available rather than the worth of the teachers' contributions.

This is not the best way to treat teachers and improve their professional skills and standing. Teaching is not a system of factory workers and piece rates nor an insurance company, or sales and marketing where input-output levers need to be pressed. We do not 'lever up' education standards, it is not a valid concept of the process of change. Nor do we achieve it by extrinsic pressures such as threat and bribery. Just as in 1988 a major error was made in the sweeping away of the literacy and numeracy hours in primary schools to introduce the National Curriculum based upon the Secondary School organisational model so in 1999 another is about to be made in relation to appraisal.

Daily hours of literacy and numeracy teaching have had to be reintroduced into the primary school but where are the culprits who damaged a decade of our childrens' education? They of course have moved on and no doubt upwards.

Similarly we see a decade of change in teacher education introduced by CATE in 1983 and taking effect from 1989 creating a cadre of teachers who have no theoretical basis upon which to develop or change their teaching. They are subject specialists but have not been trained adequately to teach children to learn (Chapter 5). The appraisal and induction programmes are seeking to identify such weaknesses but who will be left to help them learn what to do? The training has been devolved to training schools separating theory even further from practice when they need to be married.

Many thousands of responses were made to the consultation document and it is currently under review.

Appraisal: some further issues

Monitoring

Monitoring is an, informal essentially private troubleshooting process. It identifies the problems but then the monitors fail to deal with them successfully (Eraut 1990, p.21). Monitoring he considered unnecessary for the identification of poor performance. In a sense it identifies itself by the raging noise from the classroom and the poor results when the pupils' progress is assessed and compared with peers. SATs results for parallel classes are already used by schools in their monitoring processes.

However, lazy or marginally effective teachers can boost their classes' performance by selective revision of internally set examinations and tests and by going sick at critical intervals so that concerned heads of department take over the classes and boost the results. Monitoring must include such records.

Eraut's other criticisms of annual appraisal were that it was so frequent that it would lapse into tokenism and was unlikely to address issues needed to be raised in the OFSTED review cycle. It would also be unlikely to be intimately related to curriculum evaluation. All these problems would make it lacking in cost effectiveness. The process was expensive and would divert money away from staff development.

Capability

It is most important that when a monitoring system has picked up that a teacher has a problem, frequently one of class control but not always so, the appraisal, including classroom observation, first concentrates on staff development. There need to be several classroom observations and feedback interviews. After each one, targets for change and improvement should be identified and after a period for practice another observation can take place. This should identify any progress which has been made and set new targets and strategies for further development.

After a cycle of such appraisals conclusions can be drawn about whether the person is capable of development or improvement. It is extremely difficult for a failing teacher to retrieve the failure with older classes. It may be necessary for there to be time for a new intake and a change of classes to take place to get the necessary degree of improvement. When this does not occur then capability procedures need to be entered into and this point should be very carefully marked and made quite clear to the teacher. The first verbal warning can then be followed by a new appraisal cycle which starts the capability procedure. Thus it is important to act very quickly once monitoring procedures identify a problem, otherwise the process can become too prolonged to the detriment of the pupils and the school as a whole.

Not all failing teachers fall into this category: a very small minority exhibit quite a different problem. They can maintain discipline albeit in the quieter backwaters of a disciplined school, perhaps a girls' school. There they rest, making very little effort of any kind in terms of preparation and marking. On inspection days they can always pull out the stops and put on a creditable performance. However, compare the results achieved by their classes with those of the rest of the school and the problem is revealed. Head teachers in the past have often been unwilling to enter into capability procedures over such cases for a variety of personal and other reasons. Not least of these is the vilification to which they themselves or the school may become subject. They choose to carry such an individual as the evidence of the incompetence can be buried. In some subjects hard data in comparative terms is not readily available.

Credibility issues

Appraisal of teaching without classroom observation is problematic since teachers widely share the view that for most of them it is a central activity in their professional life. There is thus a credibility gap in schemes which operate without it. This is not the only problem of credibility which our researches uncovered (Montgomery and Hadfield 1989, 1990). The main one was the credibility of the appraiser and secondary to this the credibility of the process. Teachers in their college experiences had seldom found that their performance in the classroom was properly observed and evaluated with them by their various supervisors and teacher mentors. There were, of course, notable exceptions. What was needed were the research resources to identify these successful appraisers and to study their systems with them. Instead, the lack of universal instruments for classroom observation and the emotions generated by unhappy experiences were made reasons for inventing entirely new and untried systems by those not intimately involved with teaching. We also found, in a survey of 100 probationary teachers on an inservice training course, that in their college courses they had not been given training in teaching methods. Most had received a generalised talk on classroom management giving some quick tips. There had been no systematic attempt to train them in classroom management techniques and their rationale.

All our initial and inservice training courses had included substantial studies of teaching and learning and classroom management but our experienced teachers reported that this was the first time they had been exposed to any such experience. Thus it would appear that a large proportion of the senior teachers had no substantial background knowledge to support their practice and although most held theories about teaching, these were implicit. This in part accounts for the rise in the

Reflective Practitioner movement (Pollard and Tann 1994). Teachers reflect upon their practices with a facilitator-cum-researcher and formulate their grounded theories of teaching and learning (Adelman 1990). There are some shortcomings with this technique for theory construction in that what teachers regularly do may or may not be what they should be doing. It tends to confirm existing practice rather than point to what teachers should be doing.

A system of appraisal (and initial teacher training) which depends for its validity and credibility upon an untrained cadre of peers is unlikely to achieve its most desired results. It is also not surprising that senior teachers engaged in appraisal are concerned about their lack of skills and feel vulnerable. The purpose of this text is to try to ease some of these concerns by identifying key professional issues and practices in which teachers engage, showing that certain of them can be justified in terms of theory and research. It is hoped to show the direction in which teaching should be moving and give practical examples and systems which work and do produce enhanced professional performance. By showing the validity of certain strategies and their positive effects on professional development it should be possible to improve the credibility of appraisers. The critical test of such procedures will be to work with teachers diagnosed by schools as in difficulties and to show that they can be brought back to a satisfactory level of performance in the majority of cases. Such a system to be effective has to be transferable. Others have to be able to learn how to use it and to get similar results.

Such evaluation studies have rarely been done on industrial and commercial appraisal practice, according to Eraut (1990). He pointed out that there were dangers in drawing analogies with such practice for the comparisons are based on two ill-founded assumptions. These are that evidence about performance is readily available and that the appraiser's judgment of that performance is accepted. In teaching most performance takes place behind closed doors. He argues that student learning is not an entirely reliable indicator of teaching quality. This is because individual students' capabilities vary and also because of the number and diversity of the learning outcomes. We might suggest that the teaching strategy should encompass the wide range of learner capabilities. However his second point is most important. In any lesson there will be a substantial number of different learning outcomes. These aspects will be exemplified in the later chapters on teaching and learning. If teaching a class was similar to assembling a can of beans or running an office then industrial and commercial systems of appraisal might have been helpful – but it is not. Such systems operate merely as a managerial tool at best massaging the egos of the personnel and creating the 'feel good factor'.

Eraut suggested that the credibility of the appraisers was questioned because they did not know the subject. As the appraiser in most schemes was a more senior member of staff this also created a credibility gap because promotion to senior rank was perceived as based upon other qualities and qualifications than good teaching (p.22). He concluded that the cost of appraisal of teaching was higher than for other jobs because of its complexity and that annual appraisal was too infrequent for monitoring which he distinguished from appraisal.

Role issues

The appraiser thus far in formal schemes has been the head teacher, a deputy or one of the senior management team. Additionally, heads of department have also been involved in appraisal in some secondary schools. It is thus essentially a 'top down' process such as envisaged in the DES/DfEE documents. What is found is that the higher up the school hierarchy the appraiser is then the more difficult it is for them to leave this role at the classroom door. When the head is there for example, the pupils usually behave much better. If they do not then the head is put in a difficult position and may 'take a hand'. Often the observer sits at the front or perches on a desk to be informal but then stands out like a beacon. If at the back the pupils can 'feel' the eyes boring into their backs and behave differently from usual.

Of course, in small primary schools these problems are not so apparent as the head is often teaching and working with the teachers as one of a team.

The role problems can be diminished if the observer is in the room in advance, is seated at the back out of sight of most pupils, maybe at one of their tables, makes no eye contact with any of them, keeps a very low profile and just writes and writes. This is the 'fly on the wall' method and after a few minutes the pupils forget about the visitor and start to behave in their normal way. If this gets no overt response then they will continue as usual. The same result is achieved when they are being video taped: within a few minutes they ignore it.

A critical issue is that the appraiser is collecting and analysing a large amount of qualitative data derived from the techniques of classroom observation and interviewing. The appraisers are therefore thrust into a key role. The theories and ideologies held by these persons and the sophistication in their research skills will direct the way in which they collect, manipulate, interpret and present the data they collect.

In the many appraisal training sessions which have been run in the LDRP a practice video extract and feedback session starts the course. It enables the way in which would-be 'appraisers' mangle and remould the data to fit their favourite themes to be made explicit. It can call forth some horrendous statements and assertions and the whole frequently presents a very negative picture of failure in a session which is not bad but could be better. Even when teachers are aware of this they find it almost impossible to couch a critical point in other than negative terms.

In addition to this, other role problems are carried into the sessions. The head or senior teacher carries with them role authority and pupils may well not behave in their usual ways and so biased data is collected. Similarly in the feedback session the authority of the role may cause what is said to be accepted and acted upon when in fact the advice is not of good value and works only with the backing of the role status. Evidence from teacher job interviews by these same senior personnel would, according to Morgan *et al.* (1983), lead us to have little confidence in their interviewing skills because they appear to be far from skilled when using evidence to evaluate teachers. Add to this the range of personnel now at these interviews in the form of school Governors and it makes the interview a very unreliable device for employing or redeploying staff – about 25 per cent reliable. It is therefore essential that the recruitment of teachers should include seeing them teach even if only for a shortened session.

Video observation?

All methods have been tried, such as video and audio recording, sitting in the prep room, cupboard or next room with the door open. But the 'fly on the wall' method has been shown to be the best for gathering all the data. A video can never filter out the ambient noise nor see the changing focus of disruptive events. It cannot follow critical multiple interactions and still catch others at the periphery of vision. A video or audio record can be useful for the teachers to see themselves as others see them. Some can learn from the experience of watching themselves, others need tutoring with the video. This was the method selected by Marilyn Hunter reported in the Suffolk Report (Graham 1985). She used a behavioural approach taking a small video extract and analysing it in detail with the teacher. This method has also been used successfully by Norma Hadfield (1999) following our research programme. She reports it is particularly effective where teachers select their own section of video to discuss.

Hunter, interviewed for the Suffolk Report (Graham 1985) said it was an effective method but the evidence for effectiveness was never clarified. After such an event it is very likely that a teacher will have learned something but can this be converted into improved performance in the classroom? How is this improvement quantified or assessed and is it externally validated?

Appraisal criteria

According to Borich in 1977 there was no agreement on a definition of the criteria that could be used to assess teaching performance or to establish competency. Elliott (1990) found that the LEAs whose advisers and inspectors had for many years been appraising teaching performance of school staff on a regular basis emphasised different aspects of teaching in their checklists so that a core understanding of the process either did not exist for them or was not shared by them. This is not surprising since advisers and inspectors were most often experienced senior teachers seeking a particular kind of power and responsibility that inspecting gives. It is a career route for those who wish to leave the classroom but do not wish to become heads or deputies. If there was no coherent theory of teaching in 1983 according to Wragg then it is not surprising that these senior ex-teachers were not in agreement, trained as they were in earlier decades. If there is still lack of definition of criteria then that certainly poses a problem for appraisers.

The Suffolk Report announced that effective teaching was at the heart of teacher appraisal but at no point did it define what was meant by 'effective' or 'good' teaching. It also referred to 'below par' performance without describing what was meant by it. This attitude belongs to the school of 'we all know what we mean by good teaching' and 'when I see it I know it' or 'it's just intuition'. Such appraisers can judge as good teaching a range of performance from indifferent to downright bad. Teacher educators will recognise these viewpoints put forward in the defence of students on teaching practice from both teacher mentors and college staff.

The 1983 DES document on *Teaching Quality* welcomed the recent moves towards self-assessment by schools and teachers and thought that these should help to improve school standards and curricula. It went on to state:

> But employers can manage their teacher force effectively only if they have accurate knowledge of each teacher's performance. The Government believe that for this purpose formal assessment of teacher performance is necessary and should be based on classroom visiting by the teacher's head or head of department, and an appraisal of both pupils' work and of the teacher's contribution to the life of the school (p.27).

Clearly the managerial model is in mind but the content and purposes of the appraisal are missing. It was not surprising that the media adopted the stance that it was Sir Keith Joseph's intention to use it to get rid of failing teachers.

In *Better Schools* (DES 1985) there was little about the process of appraisal except to say that it involved the collection of information that is 'reliable' and 'up to date through systematic performance appraisal' (p.55). *Quality in Schools* (DES 1985) gave the following definition:

> appraisal emphasises the forming of qualitative judgments about an activity, a person or an organisation'... 'it may start as self appraisal'... it will normally involve judgments by other persons responsible for that teacher's work – a Head of Department or Year, the Head Teacher or a member of the senior management team or an officer of the LEA (p.7).

As can be seen it considers who but not how to get reliable and valid data nor what constitutes such data.

The CIPFA (Chartered Institute of Public Finance and Accountancy) Indicators of good schools were published for discussion in 1986. These were an industrialist's inventory of items which could be added up to give an index of teaching quality per school. It included the following:

- Client satisfaction – the number of appeals per 1000 transfers (mainly Secondary schools), percentage pupil attendances; surveys of opinions of parents, employers and pupils.
- Career paths of secondary school pupils.
- Examination (and now SATs) results – ranking of schools would be made possible by these results.
- Quality of teaching – percentage of graduate teachers; pupil-teacher ratios; average class size; class contact hours; percentage on secondment (shades of a bygone era);

percentage of teachers with subject qualifications, or three years experience in specialist subjects; LEA appraisal and performance review policies.

- Costs per pupil – gross costs supported by costs for teaching staff, books, supplies and services; home/school transport.
- Use of premises – pupil numbers as a percentage of places. Costs of pupils on planned or unplanned maintenance.
- Social and economic context – factors which will be used to weight the results e.g. children born outside the UK or from ethnic minority groups; from semi-skilled or unskilled manual worker households; households lacking standard amenities or with high density; families of more than four children.

This list represents the attempts by accountants to treat schools as production units using the input-output model. The economic performance of a school is an important analysis to make for ensuring cost effectiveness and financial stability. However, the teaching quality indicators are somewhat misconceived. A school with 50 per cent of the staff with PhDs and 90 per cent of pupils gaining at least two A levels would thus score high on these performance indicators of 'teaching quality'. There may, however, be very little going on of any quality. The pupils may even be being taught badly. An example is the A level Botany teacher who dictated from his degree notes to his students. They played noughts and crosses in the mock exams to pass the time as they could recall so little and gained very low scores. They decided to take matters into their own hands and set about learning to learn for themselves in the lead up to the finals. They all passed and some gained merits and distinctions.

Having a first class honours degree in a subject seldom equips a person for teaching. It can even be a barrier to pupils' learning as the content of degrees seldom matches the National Curriculum subject. The degree work has often been so easily absorbed by the graduate that there can be a failure to understand the needs of ordinary learners and the difficulties many have in learning by verbal instruction.

According to Burgess (1990) no national or local appraisal initiated by administrators has been based on criteria from systematic teacher's research into their own practice. He states: 'Instead adaptations of researchers' observation schedules and items from findings of experiments on learning are preferred by administrators. They then claim objectivity and fairness' (p.37). The observation schedules were devised for research not teacher appraisal. To then make an amalgam from various checklists as schools do without researching them is equally unacceptable

He makes the important point that research reviews of the past 60 years of process-product studies of teaching have shown meagre returns.

'teaching that attends to the set task, giving students the opportunity to learn what is later tested, is weakly correlated with learning achievements' (Rosenshine 1979).
'Learning has but a contingent and not a causal relationship to teaching' (Borich 1977).

'The extent of teachers' knowledge of the topic being taught is not correlated to learning outcomes' (Borich 1977)

On teacher effectiveness. 'So far no powerful concepts have emerged out of the data. All we have are some low level empirical claims such as direct instruction or academic learning time, which are masquerading as conceptual models.' (Tom 1984)

'In competency based teacher education there is doubt whether skills practised and then tested transfer to the real classroom' (Burgess 1990; McIntyre 1980; Elliott and Labett 1974).

Adelman (1990) proposed that consortia of teachers from mixed backgrounds should research their own teaching. After three years minimum, peer judgments of consortia markers might be made. Admitting one's own shortcomings is of a different order from responding to someone else's decision that one's performance is in some respects wanting. If the details of the process do not allay the sense of threat, teachers will respond to appraisal with anxiety and resentment, cynicism and anger according to Winter (1990).

Since the Secretary of State required agreement to national appraisal of teachers in 1986 before the negotiation of salaries and salary structure with the teacher unions it is now part of the conditions of employment in England and Wales. This somewhat preempted the Cambridge Institute of Education's (CIE 1987) brief to evaluate the findings of the six pilot appraisal schemes. The researchers had resolved to ask six questions based on the ACAS proposals:

- In what ways has the appraisal improved the quality of induction of Entry grade teachers? Has it made assessing their performance easier and more reliable?
- Has appraisal changed the way in which teachers participate in INSET?
- Has appraisal led directly to new or modified roles for teachers and how have those involved perceived the process?
- Has appraisal successfully identified potential for career development? Has the related support been made available?
- Has appraisal helped those teachers who are experiencing performance difficulties? What relationship with disciplinary procedures has emerged? How is this difficult area perceived by those involved?
- What relationship, if any, has emerged between the records of appraisal and appointment procedures and references?

There were a number of methodological problems with the analysis, which the researchers had little chance of overcoming. For example, it would be expected that the results would necessarily contain the 'Hawthorne Effect'. This famous study in the Ford factory in 1929 found that people just by being observed improved their performance and this was maintained after the observations ceased. The pilot studies also were based in LEAs already interested in appraisal and dealt with volunteers who are a special sort of sample and likely to 'show' improvements. In addition, when someone takes an interest in you and your work this inevitably engenders the 'feel good factor' especially when the interest is a positive and supportive one. It could only be concluded that appraisal of whatever sort the LEAs employed with their volunteers would be seen to be 'a good thing'.

Some of the real benefits would be more accurate records, references and reports, and the ACAS scheme would be duly endorsed and was.

Scriven (1986) proposed four dimensions of merit for summative teacher evaluation, these were:

- quality of content taught (not the quality of content known);
- success in imparting or inspiring learning;
- mastery of professional skills e.g class control;
- ethics seen in the avoidance of racism, sexism, classism and so on.

He found that good lesson plans were not critically related to these dimensions but they were often in evidence and that poor teachers could not make up in subject knowledge for their inability to control a class.

McIntyre's (1990) summary of the situation was: '... there are no general theories of teacher competency which could provide a basis for summarising accounts, and it is not plausible to expect any such theories will be developed' (p.71).

I do not happen to agree with this and would suggest with Snow (1973) that research undertaken is defined by the theories held and the experiences which reinforce them. As with the Suffolk group the literature research will be defined by the key words entered and by the literature with which the researcher is familiar. It is only when we look across the vast domains within education that new theories and research to support them can be found. Coherent theories of teaching and learning do exist but often do not appear in mainstream educational literature. They arise in Instructional Psychology, Gifted Education, Moral and Philosophical Critiques, Cognitive Psychology, Special Education and so on.

Processes and models

Target output model

In the target output model a set of objectives is agreed with the teacher then the teacher's work is compared with them (ACAS 1986, p.4). The objectives may arise from the job description or attainment targets for learners. An attempt is then made to measure how far the targets have been achieved. It is a productivity contract, a quota fulfilment model. There is no necessary analysis of how the objectives might be achieved. Because teacher objectives are frequently vague, e.g.

- offers a well-balanced curriculum;
- makes provision for different levels of ability;
- shows evidence of good classroom organisation;
- shows evidence of enthusiasm for the subject,

it is very much a matter of opinion rather than fact as to whether the objectives have been achieved. Putting a scale of numbers on these and recording three out of five is wholly arbitrary and scientifically illiterate. Now that pupil attainments are to be the target this could prove to be even more threatening and as arbitrary. Already teachers are being accused of focusing on A,B and C graders at GCSE so that the school's rating is increased. This has produced a wider gulf between the higher and the lower achievers with more of the latter failing (GCSE results August 1998). Another interpretation of the same data could be that the methods of teaching promulgated by the Chief Inspector for Schools (Woodhead 1998) known as 'interactive teaching' is disadvantaging the less able, focused as it is upon verbal learning and memory techniques.

Performance criteria model

This teaching model is skill based and the performance is analysed into a list of competencies represented by indicators. However the DES (1985) writing on appraisal of teaching performance in *Better Schools* state that 'Research has not unearthed any simple or comprehensive indicator of effective teaching' (p. 70). Nevertheless they then proceed to give examples of performance indictors which could be used e.g:

Communication with learners:

Indicator 4: Gives directions and explanations related to lesson content.

Indicator 6: Uses responses and questions from learners in teaching.

Indicator 7: Provides feedback to learners throughout lesson.

Indicator 8: Uses acceptable written and oral expression with learners.

(DES 1986 p.75)

If these criteria were applied to work I recently observed in two classrooms by teachers on capability procedures the honest response would be that they performed each of these activities satisfactorily. However the classes were out of control. Boring and mundane lessons might also pass on these indicators as well as very good ones. There is redundancy in such items. It is of note when they are not present perhaps but even so I have observed some very good lessons in the absence of items 4, 6, and 7. Performance criteria such as this can pose problems for they can impose a set of procedures on lessons and a teaching process which assumes interactivity and teacher dominance when it may not always be appropriate.

Performance criteria such as these usually require another set of criteria before they can be used. These would specify such notions as – acceptable, related, satisfactory, feedback and so on. The use of checklists incorporating such items is therefore equally problematic: they merely lend a spurious air of scientific exactitude to a bad procedure. It does not matter how many staff put their heads together to produce such a list.

The diagnostic model

The ACAS (1986) document linked appraisal to the diagnosis of potential as an agreed principle. The process of classroom observation should be used to identify training needs and career potential. In practice the problem is that the appraiser may not have the necessary skills or knowledge to do this whether head of department, coordinator of special needs or head teacher.

The appraiser and appraisee may have different ideologies each of which may be successfully used by the individual. If the appraiser diagnoses a need for change and development it may not be relevant. It may be the appraiser who needs the development. The career advice and development plan resulting would in the circumstances be most unwelcome. In addition, needs might be identified which the school does not have the budget to fund.

It is also possible to fail to identify important needs and perhaps even more problematic, to find a lack of development and career potential in an ambitious individual.

The bureaucratic model

The bureaucrat draws on authority from superiors and carries out procedures to the letter. There therefore has to be a considerable detailed attention to the paperwork and its various specifications. This model is concerned with products and procedures in which information travels up the system and decisions travel down. The information collected has to be at a simple level preferably convertible to number values and statistics. It can then be used by any official for a variety of purposes usually to do with resources and expenditure. No doubt the interest currently expressed by the DfEE linked to pupil attainments and school development (targets) will result in a national scheme in which the teacher's performance can be measured.

The process model

In this model the professional possesses a personal licence to practice (Winter 1990). Here there is a special responsibility and relationship to the client, the patient or pupil. Thus the allegiance is downwards and reference is to an internally specified set of professional theories, practices and criteria.

'Client cases . . . cannot be decided upon by the application of general rules (given from above) but only by the discretionary interpretation of specialist knowledge . . . This means that professional workers are continually learning (increasing knowledge and enhancing their skills) through the actual practice of their profession. (Winter 1990, p.50).

Winter goes on to explain that in the process model of appraisal the value is in the process itself. It is this process which will result in professional development or the effective learning by the teacher. Thus the contradiction is revealed of a bureaucracy presiding over a profession, a situation which does not exist in medicine or the law.

Maier in 1976 made an interesting analysis of the systems which appraisers used to structure the appraisal interview and these can still be found today. These are described in the following three sections.

Tell and sell method

In the telling part of the session the appraiser tells the appraisee how he or she is getting on. Here immediately we might question the authority and credibility of the teller. Having given an opinion on the performance, selected aspects of that performance might be described to illustrate the points made. If a check list is part of the procedure the appraiser may simply go through the list and even indicate a score if rating scales are attached. Other appraisers compile a list of seven or eight problem points to tell the appraisee. Sometimes it can be difficult to find some problem points and areas for improvement and then the appraiser may focus on trivia or raise issues not present in the session as omissions merely to have something to discuss. All this can have a highly demotivating effect on the recipient. The 'selling' part is where the appraiser has to persuade the teacher to accept the evaluation and feedback as valid and then to implement the proposed remediation.

Experienced teachers may simply not accept the evaluation or the procedure as valid and see the source as lacking credibility. NQTs and teachers in difficulty may have to accept what was handed down and implement it until the pressure is off. Easy-going staff may uncritically accept the authoritarian leadership which this method embodies and it can lead to docility and conservatism rather than development.

In this system of 'top down' appraisal the implicit assumption is that the appraisal will be fair, accurate and acceptable to the appraisee who will want to carry out the improvement plan. However, 'this approach relies on the interviewer having the skills and knowledge necessary to persuade and motivate the appraisee to change in the prescribed manner, and to gain acceptance of the evaluation, without appearing to dominate the interview or "preach".' (Montgomery and Hadfield 1989, p.20). According to Maier (1976) there are two possible outcomes in using this method. One is that the evaluation is rejected and the other that it is accepted with little enthusiasm. In either case the results offer a poor prognosis on the health of the organisation.

Tell and listen

In this style of interview the appraiser presents the evaluation in full to the appraisee without interruption. In the second half he or she sits back and listens to the appraisee's response acting as a non-directive counsellor to enable the teacher to express feelings and opinions openly. The idea behind this is that if people are allowed to express their feelings and frustrations the defensive mechanisms will be removed or diminished and and there will be an opening up to change.

The appraiser in this situation does not always expect the appraisee's agreement and needs some very good counselling skills in accepting and understanding the often aversive responses. In a successful interview misunderstandings can be clarified and communication and feelings of support and understanding enhanced.

Despite this apparently more open system it is still in the 'top down' mode and mishandled can cause just as much strife as the 'tell and sell' technique. It can also lead to the appraiser feeling much abused by aggressive and personal critical responses. Because of the non-directive nature of the 'listen' section it can cause the appraisee to regard the appraiser as knowing nothing helpful to pass on. This can lead over time to lack of credibility in the appraiser and the process.

The problem solving system

This is a form of negotiated appraisal in which over a period of time appraiser and appraisee discuss problems and issues in performance and ways in which these might be tackled. The purpose is to come to a shared view of the way forward in a mentoring relationship and also to increase motivation and job satisfaction. It enables the teacher to analyse the performance constructively rather than defensively and so own the process and the outcomes. In Maier's view this system can have far reaching and beneficial effects. It is a positive system of staff appraisal. However, the skills required for this individualised form of appraisal are not widely available and require extensive training and experience to achieve. In the hands of such a person any system of appraisal can be expected to work.

Difficulties can arise if neither of the participants have any ideas on ways to resolve a problem identified or if the needs of the individual do not match those of the institution.

Summary and conclusions

Appraisal of teachers' performance has always gone on whether by pupils or colleagues. In recent times serious attempts have been made to develop systems of teacher appraisal which will enhance performance and offer job satisfaction without the tangible rewards of performance related pay. These have on the whole been beneficial and successful but have tended to lapse because of the extensive demands upon teachers' time. Full appraisal which includes classroom observation is much rarer and most schools engaging in appraisal operate a system of desk-based retrospective review. After twenty years of research and development, appraisal for professional development is still seen as the most important purpose to which appraisal may be put. Other aspects are secondary to this although apparently not according to the current Government perspective.

A full appraisal operating on a three year cycle for main professional grade teachers is a realistic goal in terms of the investment costs. New teachers in schools and others experiencing difficulties need a personally tailored programme which takes account of their needs and works on a much faster three to six month cycle. Both need additional funding if they are to be made to work properly and HMI have already costed this. The new proposals (DfEE 1999) are that all teachers should be annually appraised.

Although performance related pay schemes have already been tried there is not enough additional money available to fund a system-wide scheme which can recognise the achievements of teachers. It is thus better to put this money into inservice development and training which can give broader coverage and satisfaction. The DfEE proposals are that fast tracking teachers and superteachers should receive extra payments and that there should be a bar at scale point 9 which can only be passed if appraisal results permit.

The issues of accountability and credibility can be resolved if teachers themselves have some professional autonomy in the development of the appraisal schemes which their schools are to use. The extent of this autonomy or lack of it will be seen after the consultation process is over – as you read this.

Analysis of teaching performance and its enhancement are not simple issues to be resolved by checking a few boxes and completing tick lists. Appraisal must therefore include professional development guided by thoughtful and reflective practitioners. The deskilling which teachers feel from the poverty of the new training and the prescription of the National Curriculum is not the best preparation for this. Teacher Education and Inservice Teacher Training need to be revisited.

In reviewing the appraisal schemes in operation across the country we might even have to say that we would not want to start from there. What is may not be what ought to be in operation. The failure to specify in the latest DfEE documents what constitutes threshold standards of teaching instils very little optimism. The consultation responses and no doubt another round of focus groups will provide specifications which are wish lists, unrelated to factors which create teacher success in classrooms.

An example of this would be the Category One teachers described in *The New Teacher in School* (HMI 1982):

Many showed exceptional confidence and natural talent... enthusiasm, perceptiveness, energy, hard work, common sense, intelligence, firmness, adaptability, tenacity, intuitiveness, sensitivity and friendliness... a high degree of competence in classroom planning and organisation, excellent relations with pupils, good lesson preparation, skilful questioning, good pacing, sound subject knowledge, imaginative teaching approaches (para 3.3).

This list is mainly of personal qualities relying heavily upon the perception of the observer. It is not criterion referenced and neither valid nor reliable. It resembles those suggested in the pre-professional era of the 1920s.

Chapter Two

Classroom Observation

Introduction

A survey for the Council for National Academic Awards (CNAA) was made by McCulloch (1979) of the methods of evaluation of final teaching practice of students in initial teacher education. It failed to find an agreed assessment instrument. Training for the role of the assessor seemed to be inconsistent or significant by its absence. Where it did operate it amounted to 'sitting by Nellie' and introducing the new tutor to a few schools. Later there was much more training but far less supervision for much of it had been transferred to schools along with some funding by some institutions.

Some institutions had well-developed and extensive checklists which were almost impossibly complex to use at one extreme and at the other were perfunctory. Other institutions and individual tutors operated the intuitive 'system'. In these instances supervisors would 'just know' when they had seen a good lesson. A series of such 'good' lessons over a practice would rate a pass. In some institutions distinctions were awarded as long as the school, the supervisor and the moderator agreed. Over time most institutions became more systematic in their assessment procedures. They established teaching practice committees to look into and develop their methods of practice assessment.

Traditionally for classroom observation many college supervisors had used a system of sitting in a lesson and compiling a list of corrective points where improvement was needed. Occasionally some might also note some of the good points. They would leave this list behind for the student and some would go through it with the student after the lesson in a debriefing session. It is not surprising that teachers who have come through this system would use something similar when they also were going to appraise a classroom performance. They now tend to link this to the checklist that the school has adopted or developed.

The ILEA (1977) booklet *Keeping the School Under Review* influenced many Local Authority Education services in the preparation of their own appraisal schemes. However the significant feature of these proposals according to Clift (1982) was the total lack of any reference to the evaluation of the professional qualities of the teacher. The reason for this, he suggested, was that in the preparation of the schemes teachers had been subordinate partners. Pupils, parents and employees had no representation at all. His research led him to conclude that these schemes and instruments were incapable of raising the quality of education, and that self-evaluation was probably a necessary but not sufficient condition for professional and institutional improvement.

LEAs involved in appraisal established committees for developing their own appraisal systems and so did some schools. A committee sitting down to develop a method of appraisal of classroom performance must perforce come up with a list of teacherly behaviours associated with good performance. They may then assign rating scales, make check lists or criterion referenced scales in response to these agreed lists. As a result the widespread use of questionnaires and checklists has developed. The 'appraisal instrument' has arrived and then is tested out on NQTs or students in college, refined and clarified and is thereby 'validated' in use. It can easily be seen that it has face value – the items are associated with performance perceived as good teaching. It must not be assumed from this that these instruments are thereby legitimate and valid in raising performance. Most often the checklist of what constitutes good teaching and the criterion referenced scales can be used with more or less accuracy to rate the relative effectiveness of a lesson, that is, they are summative forms of assessment. They can be reasonably validated and tested for reliability in distinguishing very good from satisfactory from poor performance. If they are at the same time used as a formative assessment they can show areas where there are strengths and weaknesses. What they cannot seem to do is be used to enhance performance in a diagnostic-prescriptive fashion. However this is often how they *are* used – for all three purposes at once.

The critical tests of reliability and validity are seldom if ever made. These would be to use them with a failing teacher and after one or two sessions convert the teacher into a success. Instead the instruments are used with these teachers and on numerous occasions they fail to improve their performance. Strangely enough this is never taken as invalidating the instrument for that purpose. Instead the teacher is failed and capability procedures entered into. Can this be fair?

Scriven (1986) said that the criteria must have a logical or legal connection to teacher performance and must be necessary for good teaching. If the feedback on the performance showing the strengths and weaknesses does not result in change even when the appraisee accepts the verity of the information can the items be necessary?

After the publication of the Suffolk Reports (Graham 1985, 1987), including the San Diego instrument, the checklist and behavioural rating scale were embraced by all concerned. After all the method was now in print and this enhanced its credibility.

The Further Education Unit (FEU) commissioned a review by Tuxworth (1982) of competency in teaching. The report described and discussed performance based (PBTE) and competency based teacher education (CBTE). P/CBTE is consistent with a reductionist view of teaching. It serves to break it down into a series of discrete parts, the teacher performances or competencies. Once these are established it is then assumed that if teachers are trained on these parts this builds towards the whole and results in effective teaching. This behaviourist view of teaching can be criticised for its lack of cognitive organising principles in an essentially cognitive and interactive activity.

The FEU report also criticised it from the point of view that it had a very weak research base to support it. It had not been widely demonstrated that the approach improved the pupils' learning or the performance of the teachers who had been trained in C/PBTE. It discussed an example from the USA in which 30 training modules were drawn from 100 possibilities covering 83 teaching skills and put together to make a teacher training course. At the cost of two million dollars the scheme was put into operation with a cohort of teachers. What was discovered was that although a teacher might gain a 'good' pass on all the 30 modules and have received training on all 83 skills it was no guarantee that any of them could successfully teach a class of pupils.

It was ever thus! It is only surprising that such a project could attract funding. Research on skill development has shown for decades that training on the separate parts does not lead automatically to competent performance. For this the learner has to practice putting the whole lot together. During this period the feedback on performance of the 'coach' can significantly contribute to high levels of performance. The better the coach the higher the levels that can be achieved even by the less skilled. Experience from a misspent youth as a spring board diver and later as a coach confirms this.

It is therefore surprising that CATE (1991) drew up a list of competencies for students in ITT and the DfEE, encouraged by subsequent Governments, are still pursuing these approaches. A curriculum for ITT is to be laid down as a result of their deliberations. Since few of them have ever trained teachers with total responsibility for their success or failure over several years and have not engaged in appraisal research on effectiveness it is unlikely that what will be produced will work. Undertaking short series of inservice courses on appraisal and staff development hardly counts since the inservice trainer seldom has to pick up the pieces or 'see their chickens come home to roost'. As it will take ten years to find out that the methods proposed do not have the desired effect the proposers will all have retired or moved on.

Methods of classroom observation

Naturalistic observation and ethnography

Observation in its specialised sense is not a set of comments or thoughts of a person looking at a lesson. Observation is the act or practice of noting and recording facts and events as they happen. Psychology has borrowed the term 'naturalistic observation' from comparative studies in which biologists observed animals in their natural habitats to learn about their habits and behaviours. In sociology the term used is 'ethnography' derived from social anthropological studies.

Naturalistic observation has played a significant role in child development studies but psychology in general until recently has favoured the experimental procedure of testing hypotheses by comparing experimental and control groups. The criticism of these is that because of the overemphasis on the experimental paradigm it has never truly been established by systematic observation what is usual in human terms.

A number of different techniques of observation have been developed because even in the simple case of observing one individual child there can be far too many behaviours to record. For this reason video or audio records are frequently made to enable an observer to go over the events many times to collect all the available data. The problem is that even a video recording of a class lesson spanning the whole room cannot 'see' all the events which happen. An alert and experienced observer, however, can see most of what goes on. The problem is of course that it cannot all be recorded. It is for this reason that there has to be a careful selection of methods.

Gazing about

The observer usually sits with the pupils and looks at the teacher teaching the lesson. When the pupils are settled down to a particular task the observer may get up and walk around looking at what the pupils are doing and perhaps give some help and raise questions to find out if the pupils understand what they are doing.

After the lesson the observer and teacher retire to a quiet area and the observer shares thoughts on what was seen using 'tell and sell', for example, or any of the methods already outlined. At the end of this session the observer may write a summary report of the main views on what was seen, not always modified by the discussion which took place afterwards.

There are a number of problems with this technique. One of the main ones is that there is no factual data afterwards to discuss. Anything written is *ex post facto* observation or historical recall which may in the process have been changed or manipulated. The whole procedure may be very idiosyncratic and unreliable and it cannot be 'proved'. It is very often used by observers to conceal a lack of knowledge and inexperience about what to do and say.

Participant observation

In this system the observer records at intervals whenever feasible and at other times is engaged with the pupils or the teacher as a participant in the lesson. Team teaching can give rise to this form of mixed data. The observer may also actually sit with the pupils as a participant in their discussions or may engage in individual or small group teaching following up the teachers' work.

In each instance it is difficult to participate and record at the same time and so the data is somewhat limited. Standing back from the situation and looking at overall patterns is not really possible in this method. As a participant the observer is also responsible for creating and changing some of the data and is thus responsible for the success or failure of the lesson with the teacher.

To help ITT students it is often necessary for the mentor or observer to sit with a difficult group and help control them in order to enable the student to have the experience of teaching the rest of the class without too much interruption. It can also provide small lessons in behaviour management afterwards for the student to try later. Taking over a class even when it dissolves into chaos is not a good strategy. The students never appreciate it because the control however tenuous has passed from them. The next time they will find it even harder to maintain discipline. Taking over control from a colleague in difficulties is also not recommended for the same reasons. This is often difficult for the observers as they can feel that they are condoning the misbehaviour. They then often engage in nonverbal and covert strategies to stop the bad behaviours. This is in effect assuming control and changing the data.

Diary description

It is often recommended that the observer makes a running log of all that is seen. As can be imagined it is impossible to do this on a continuous basis for a whole lesson or for that matter record all of what was seen in any case. Too much is going on. Having once started recording, the observer can still be writing about one event while others follow in rapid succession until there is a lag of five or ten minutes in the record.

Observers are also idiosyncratic in what they record. They are obliged to be selective in these circumstances and they tend to target their preferred items. They may often have decided what the teacher's problem might be before they enter the room and are looking for the signs to write down which will support this.

Many simply begin recording the pupil entering behaviours and start of the lesson strategy. 'Beginnings' are considered crucial to getting a good start to the lesson. Thus they branch out into classroom management procedures and this can colour the whole record. Their own preferred strategies may also be in evidence.

Time and event sampling

Sampling is frequently used in formal observational studies and has been tried in classroom observation studies. However it gives a somewhat fragmented record because recordings are made for example from 30 second observations – looking – and then three minutes of recording. In the recording period events happen which invariably the observer would like to record. Sometimes the record is 'fudged' to include these critical incidents.

It is probably best used as a research tool when observing many lessons to educe general patterns rather than as a technique in appraisal.

Problem points lists

This used to be a favoured technique used by college supervisors with students in initial teacher education. Thus all teachers will have experienced some version of this. They may indeed adopt it as their own favoured method.

It involves the minimum of effort on the part of the observer. Observation is still conducted by gazing about and in this method when points for improvement are identified these are noted down. Examples might be:

1. Try to get your class in more quickly.
2. Why not let two monitors give out the exercise books?
3. Don't let Trevor M. shout out answers.
4. The revision of last lessons' points went on too long.
5. There were several pupils at the back playing about when you were doing the explanation of the task.
6. Quite a number still did not know what they had to do although you explained twice.
7. Some of the homework had not been marked correctly.
8. Don't let them take over the ending of the lesson and rush off.

They usually used to seem to try to find seven or eight points. Occasionally a positive statement might be inserted by some tutors. As can be imagined, such lists can be demoralising and demotivating, especially as they were usually left in the file and the tutor disappeared without comment. In addition, what is not always appreciated is the anger and frustration such a strategy can engender. It is also extremely difficult to learn from a negative. The person knows what not to do but not necessarily how to put it right.

Teaching is such a complex interactive and dynamic activity that whilst attending to one aspect the novice invariably misses out on several others that were originally going well.

Checklists

Check lists are in a sense a proposed sampling frame. However, the categories or titles under which the observer records are usually established on the basis of experience in classrooms and discussion rather than naturalistic observation and analysis narrowing down on patterns and categories.

It is not surprising that there has been a general move in the appraisal of teaching to focus upon the checklist as an answer to the criticisms. It is usual for the school to collect a number of examples of such lists and then to produce a composite one which represents what can be considered to be their committee's view of items related to good teaching. To these they may attach the rating scales, behavioural outcomes or criterion references. They then try this instrument out on a few NQTs and perhaps in some peer appraisal sessions. After minor changes it becomes part of the agreed policy of the school to use it as the appraisal instrument. As already indicated it is a summative instrument not useful to the promotion of staff and school development.

Because the checklist has been agreed with the staff there is a general acceptance of its use. In practice as long as the results are presented in a supportive atmosphere and there is opportunity for a dialogue on the contents it is likely that targets for the following year can be agreed. However, these may bear little relationship to what was observed in the lesson(s) but concern wider school and role issues. The targets according to OFSTED (1997) are also on the whole too general to be of much value.

It thus becomes a procedure to be lived through and the data are shelved rather than used as a tool for staff and school improvement. As already noted it is only when the checklist is used on a teacher in serious difficulty that it is seen to fail. The appraiser is not enabled to use it in a way that can retrieve the situation. At this point capability procedures are discussed and entered into. Until recently capability procedures have taken two or even three years to complete. The costs involved are mainly hidden but high. There are also a range of strategies which desperate staff may use to avoid them or hold them off for as long as possible as they see their livelihood slipping away.

Much of this can be avoided and most capability procedures can become unnecessary for on most occasions failing behaviours can be remedied if the appropriate methods are used. Most teachers in difficulty can be helped to succeed and this can save the huge costs involved in dismissing a trained person and improve the attainments of the pupils. It can also save the costs involved in terms of the extra time that other staff have to give in order to pursue capability procedures. This can be therapeutic for such procedures can result in damage to the reputation of all of those concerned not just the appraisee. The stresses and strains created by all the many emotions that are generated can affect the whole of the staff in different but adverse ways. Even the short span of six months now envisaged for capability procedures will not circumvent these problems of negative effect. What is also questionable is using the same instruments and procedures for appraisal and capability.

Sampling frames

The instrument which was devised for classroom observation to promote teacher development was a sampling frame. A sampling frame is really only a set of categories under which the observer records. It is however based upon research and usually begins with diary description and time sampling to evoke patterns and clusters in the data.

The records in the frame or table may be simple tallies and ticks. An early example of this was a table for recording levels of play observed in young children e.g. solitary; looking on; parallel, and cooperative play. There was no such frame available for looking at classroom behaviours but over time one was evolved.

The development of the appraisal sampling frame

There is a wealth of qualitative data thrown up by classroom observation however it is collected. The following framework to be described for classroom observation is based upon the formal observation of over one thousand lessons. It began with the search for helpful methods of observation of teacher education students on their various teaching practices. More or less every technique just described was tried out. Because the students were talked through the observations and invited to give their own thoughts on the process it was possible to begin to identify what worked and what did not. At the time there were few guidelines to help in this process. It was research grounded in classrooms. At the same time these studies were set in the psychological research context. Here data from the USA was beginning to suggest that positive approaches to discipline at least with individuals (Becker *et al.* 1967; Scott MacDonald 1971; Blackham and Silberman 1971) was working, at least temporarily. These studies in Behaviour Modification became very popular in education training courses (Harrop 1984; Wheldall and Merrett 1984) but lacked the wider application to general classroom management. They mainly targeted the challenging behaviours of individual pupils.

Over time it was possible to begin to form a set of strategies which could be taught to students based on lesson observations which would enable them to improve their performance on classroom management as well as lesson planning and implementation.

The key problem identified in failing teachers is their poor classroom control and behaviour management of pupils. Any appraisal and staff development procedure must thus first take account of this. It is of course a major problem for ITT students who are always told that until they get class control they will not be able to teach anything. It was quite clear that the research in psychology could be used to suggest indicants and cues which might be relevant to this problem of classroom management. However, in developing a theory about what were key behaviours to bring about change and improvement, successful class management techniques would need to be identified and defined.

Over time in hundreds of lessons a hierarchy of steps in which the qualitative data has been brought into some kind of order can be identified as follows:

1. Counting: words, items, occurrences, indicants, cues – frequency counts.
2. Patterning: observing and noting certain recurring patterns in the data in successful and failing lessons.
3. Clustering: groups or categories of activities, settings and so on with similar characteristics are brought together e.g. behaviour management strategies, questioning techniques, cognitive challenge and motivation.
4. Factoring: cluster groups are reduced to a number of factors with some explanatory power – this process resulted in the identification of the three clusters represented by CBG, 3Ms and PCI.
5. New relationships – may be sought between factors. These factors were used to help students in training become more effective in classroom management in addition to subject tuition and management. Tactical lesson planning was outlined to help structure the time span of the lesson in relation to the learning needs of learners posited in theories of learning.
6. Causal networks: The above may aid in building causal networks particularly if findings relate to already established general and theoretical frameworks. A

developing teaching skills model developed in this process may also be used as a model for retrieving poor performance.

This process over a period of about five years resulted in what is called a 'sampling frame'. This enabled the observer to attend to and record a limited range of potent items in the observation period. As Scriven (1986) has pointed out, these items must be intimately related and relevant to improving the teacher's performance. Once the sampling frame was established it was possible to use it as a formative hypothesis and test out whether it was indeed capable of improving performance. During the development period for the instrument a range of techniques for using it were also tried. It can be used as a checklist itself, a frame in which counts are recorded and so on. None of these produced the supportive atmosphere and the factual record which the appraisee would find beneficial.

Recording

The technique which evolved with the sampling frame over time was the '*continuous running record*'. By this is meant that the observer simply wrote continuously everything that could possibly be recorded in relation to the three variables of the sampling frame. Times were noted at intervals down the side of the page. Everything written had to be a factual statement or record of what was seen. This did not preclude asides and comments and questions as the record ran on but this needed to be made clear either on the record or afterwards in the debriefing. In addition when wrong things were seen the way of dealing with them was to try to restate them in a neutral or even a positive way e.g. 'Did you notice that when you lowered your voice they became quieter too?' instead of, 'Don't shout'. The one essential was very rapid writing often whilst looking at ongoing events.

Until 1983 the technique had only been used with students in initial teacher education by the originator. However, the student feedback showed that it did work and that they could go on developing after the supervision period was over by referring back to it and using the strategies they had learned. They had language and conceptual framework for referring to complex teaching events and a metacognitive framework for reflecting on their teaching and their thinking about their thinking.

The classroom management sampling frame

Changing the learning climate and changing the behaviour using CBG

The initials stand for 'Catch (them) Being Good'. There is a considerable amount of research which has shown that teachers spend most of their time attending to pupils when they are off target, not working and being disruptive (Kounin 1970; Scott MacDonald 1971; Wheldall and Merrett 1986). When they are working and being constructive they receive little positive support and encouragement, the teacher accepting their good behaviour without question.

Pupils who receive little attention, support and approval at home will tend to seek it at school from teachers or failing them, from peers. If they cannot gain this attention and recognition that they crave through their work they will find other means to satisfy their needs.

The strategy CBG is one which every teacher thinks they use but when they are recorded the number of desist and negative unsupportive behaviours and comments outweigh the positive and supportive ones. The less successful the teacher, the fewer the positive responses and failing teachers gave none (Scott MacDonald 1971).

The CBG strategy requires that:

- The teacher positively reinforces any pupil's correct social and on-task responses with nods, smiles, and by paraphrasing correct responses and statements and supporting their on-task academic responses with such phrases as, 'Yes, good', 'Well done'. Incorrect responses should not be negated but the pupil should be encouraged to have another try, or the response should be, 'Yes, nearly' and 'Yes, and what else...', 'Good so far, can anyone help him or her out?' and so on.

- It is very important to remember to CBG behaviour as well as answers to questions. It needs to be done more discreetly. It consists of going to children when they are on-task and working, and making quiet supportive statements and comments. They may not choose to respond immediately but over time they will be found to increase their time on task even if they laugh off any praise.

- When pupils are working and it is not a good idea to interrupt them at that moment, simply standing near them and looking at their work and smiling is very supportive. Detailed looking at work as they are doing it and moving on shows them you are interested in it and them. They know or feel you will intervene if there is a problem even if you yourself are just looking and murmuring 'Good'.

- It makes them feel that you are actively involved with them and the work they are doing for you and that you consider it to be important enough to give it and them your attention. If a teacher sits at the front and marks the books of another class it demonstrates an 'us versus them' attitude with tasks handed down to the lower orders without them having any intrinsic worth. Even if the teacher is marking that class's work and is calling individuals up it is far better to be out and around the room doing the marking.

- At its simplest, CBG is one form of Behaviour Modification technique in which the teacher positively reinforces desirable behaviours emitted by the pupil, gradually *shaping* them towards desirable ends determined by the teacher, without the child being aware of the goal towards which they are directed. In this technique there is no cognitive input.

- When supportive discussion about the work and the behaviour takes place this moves it into the cognitive sphere and the behaviour changes; CBG comes under cognitive regulation and is more likely to be sustained. This places it in the constructivist or schema realm of theory and research.

In the original researches (Becker *et al*. 1967) the teachers were told to ignore any undesirable behaviour and only support those directed towards the target ones. This of course had deleterious effects on the other children who saw the target child getting away with misbehaviour and so the behaviour of the whole class could deteriorate. To avoid this situation it may be necessary to tell the pupil to stop talking, sit down, open the book and start reading but then *immediately* he or she does, give attention, support and encouragement for the on-task behaviour.

Children learn vicariously how to behave in classrooms as much from what happens to other children as from what happens to them and thus it is important to stop unwanted behaviours at their outset and when they are in their earliest stage. This may be compared with the strategy of 'nipping things in the bud' described by Lawrence *et al*. (1984). Where a child is very disturbed it is possible within these parameters to ignore a significant proportion of the unwanted behaviour for the other children identify him or her as a special case. In some circumstances it may be necessary to seek the support of the rest of the children in helping an individual gain mastery over unwanted behaviour.

3Ms – Management, Monitoring and Maintenance

3Ms represents a series of tactics which effective teachers used to gain and maintain pupil's attention whatever teaching method or style they subsequently used. When teachers with classroom management disciplining problems were taught to use these strategies in observation and feedback sessions they became effective teachers (Montgomery 1984,1989).

Management – phase one

The teacher makes an *attention gaining noise* such as 'Right!', 'O.K class 3', 'Good morning, everybody', 'Uhummm!' or bangs the door or desk, or claps hands. Some teachers simply wait quietly until the noise subsides as the pupils notice s/he is present. Next the teacher gives a *short verbal instruction* such as: 'Everybody sit down', 'Get out your English folders', 'Come and sit on the mat', 'Sit down and listen carefully' and so on. At this point twenty of the pupils will do as requested and ten will not. The effective teacher pauses, looks round, spots those who are not doing as requested, quietly *names* these pupils and individually instructs them to stop what they are doing and to listen. This is usually quite sufficient if a *check back* look is given to bring the whole class to attention.

The mistake that the ineffective teachers make is to begin to shout 'Be quiet' and 'Sit down', as a general instruction to all pupils. The raising of the teacher's voice and the general command to those who are already behaving as requested begins to engender hostility in them. Some who were attending now begin to chat causing the instruction to be repeated louder still, thus contributing to the general level of classroom noise and seems to transmit the information that the teacher is not quite in control and can surreptitiously be disobeyed by an even larger group. Thus in a short period of time the class has become out of control. The teacher at this point usually becomes very exasperated and red in the face and shouts the class into submission. These 'shock tactics' become less and less effective the more they are used and it takes a considerable amount of time and effort to reconstruct this teacher's behaviour to make it effective, allowing the opportunity actually to teach something (Montgomery and Hadfield 1989, 1990). Many give up the struggle and 'teach' over the noise so that the level of attention and achievement of all pupils is low.

The effective teacher, having gained the pupils' attention and silence will immediately launch into the introduction to the session or begin reading the story. During the teacher talk or story it is necessary for a range of attention gaining and maintaining tactics to be employed, for example:

- pausing in exposition to look at pupil talking until s/he stops;
- walking to pupil and gently removing tapping pencil or note;
- asking the talking or inattentive pupil a question;
- repeating the phrase just given;
- inserting 'and Goldilocks said to the three bears!' in the middle of the story, looking hard at the miscreant;
- using hand signal or finger on lips cue to quieten;
- using 'stink look'

The main point about this phase of the lesson is that if there is a need to use a lot of controlling techniques then the material and the mode of delivery should be reconsidered and wound up as soon as possible.

Monitoring – phase two

As soon as there is an activity change from pupils listening to getting out books and writing or going back to places to work this is when disruption can and does arise. The monitoring strategy needs to be brief, perhaps lasting no more than 30 seconds. As soon as the pupils are at their places the teacher should move round the room to each group or table, very quickly and quietly, settling them down to work. It is essential not to linger to give detailed explanations at this point but to say that you will come back shortly to help, going to the noisiest group first but making sure that all are visited. If there is not a lot of space to move round then a vantage point should be selected and the monitoring directed from there by calming gestures and quiet naming.

In addition to activity change, monitoring should be used when pupils are engaged with tasks and the noise level and attention seems to be slipping. This can be noted at any time by the well attuned ear and usually only requires that the teacher looks up and round the room to the talker. A pointed look may well be all that is required or very quiet naming. The important thing is not to nag and be noisy about criticism and having told a pupil to be quiet for the teacher to look up and check back on the pupil within 3–5 seconds.

Maintenance – phase three

Once the pupils have been settled to the task by the monitoring techniques, it is then advisable for the teacher to move round the class to each individual to find out how the work is progressing. In the maintenance period all the requests and queries of individuals can be dealt with. During a lesson period or period of study within a curriculum area each pupil should expect to receive some form of individual constructive and developmental comment on the work – PCI. This has been called *Positive Cognitive Intervention* (Montgomery 1984, 1994, 1996). In this steady move round the room the teacher should look at the work with the pupil and offer *developmental* advice which makes a positive statement about progress thus far and then offers ideas and suggestions for extension or through constructive questioning helps the pupils see how to make the work better or achieve the goals they have set themselves, for example:

- 'Jason, I enjoyed your story very much. The beginning section was good, it set the murky scene very well. I think you should look at some of Roald Dahl's quirky characters – your style at the moment reminds me of some of his better books. You might have a gift for story like him. If you look up one or two I will show you what I mean.'
- 'Chrissy, the contrast colours and the texture you give them in your picture are good, next time I want you to explore the effect when you use a palette of three.'

At intervals during the maintenancing period the noise will fluctuate. As soon as the level goes above 'interested work' or an individual's voice is clearly audible and does not stop after a few moments then a quick monitoring session should ensue. This may only need to be the raising of the teacher's head to look in the direction of the noise to cue the pupil to silence or it may again involve 'stink look' and quiet naming. If this does not suffice then it may be necessary to go over and settle the problem. A noisy pupil who continually causes the teacher to go and attend to him or her needs further consideration for this is an attentional problem which is gaining illegitimate satisfaction which will in itself maintain the unwanted behaviour. At this point it may become necessary to institute some behavioural modification procedures to cause the pupil to spend more time on task in seat. There may well be a learning difficulty which underlies this behaviour which needs direct and individual teaching to overcome. In addition the lesson/session plan and pedagogy needs to be reviewed to assess whether these can contribute to restoring general good classroom behaviour.

PCI Positive Cognitive Intervention

In PCI the teacher should discuss the work with the pupil and offer *developmental* advice. This is a positive statement about progress thus far and offers ideas and suggestions for extension as already noted. The constructive questioning, helps the pupils see how to make the work better or achieve the goals they have set themselves. This is also the cognitive aspect of the approach. When the work has been completed again there should be written or spoken comments as appropriate and further ideas.

In addition to this form of *developmental PCI* there is also the need to design lessons which do offer some cognitive challenge. Although open questioning is a favoured method this is not sufficient. In addition there needs to be a system of differentiation and the use of *cognitive process teaching methods* if all pupils are to be more motivated and challenged. These latter will be explored in a later chapter on teaching methods.

Some individual behaviour management strategies

Building the causal network and the EBD policy

Just a few pupils are serious problems and disruptive with most staff. They are of course at their worst with teachers in difficulties. The following outline strategies are those which schools may have to adopt to help such pupils retrieve their problem behaviour. It may just have gone too far with the problem teacher and so it may be helpful to have these strategies in mind and written into the EBD policy to support all teachers.

Shaping. Behaviour modification strategies are most frequently advised upon by the School Psychological Services and they may also offer training courses to help the management of particularly difficult, often disruptive pupils. BATPACK courses (Wheldall and Merrett 1984, 1985) and their books on Positive Approaches to Teaching are all based on the principles of reinforcement established by Skinner (1958) in his studies of Operant Conditioning and most books on classroom management and managing difficult behaviour include this (Cheeseman and Watts 1985; Chisholm *et al.* 1986; Luton *et al.* 1991) The pupil emits unwanted responses which the teacher learns to ignore but reinforces the closest opposite and desirable response. By a process of continuous positive reinforcement the behaviour is gradually 'shaped' towards more 'desirable' ends.

Elements of all of this have been described in the foregoing as well as some of the problems which can result if it is not used well. The difference in the case of a disruptive pupil is that close observation and identification of the target behaviour is needed together with the drawing up of a reinforcement schedule and school behaviour management plan. Even so it is impossible to reinforce each occurrence of the desirable behaviours and it may be better to put the pupil in a much smaller class – a group of 8–12 with a specially trained teacher whilst the main part of the programme is being implemented. Rogers (1994a) suggested withdrawing disruptives for regular 20 minute sessions to give social skills and behaviour management training from trained teachers.

Other colleagues, including playground and canteen helpers need to be made aware of the main elements of the 'therapy' if all the work in the classroom is not to be undone. Many of the studies in the USA used positive reinforcements which not only included giving merit points for good behaviour but also enabled them to be saved up to spend time on hobbies, games or to buy candy, paints and even make-up. As a rule it is not surprisingly found that when the novelty has worn off the pupil decides not to work for more credits. This is supported by the work of Deci and Ryan (1983) and Ryan *et al.* (1985) who found that extrinsic rewards such as these actually cause a decline in motivation over time whereas intrinsic motivation is raised by a *positive supportive learning* environment. It is thus the teacher who is the real source of motivation and it is the teacher's smile and genuine support and praise which is the all-pervading and prime motivator. Younger pupils like to earn stars and merit points but it is mainly because they are the tangible expression of the teacher's appreciation that they are so effective.

Modelling. is another strategy the teacher may use (Blackham and Silberman 1971). At its simplest level it involves the teacher saying such things as 'Very well done, the Green table is ready', 'Show me who is ready', 'Michael was really listening so he is doing it well', 'Sharon has a good idea, watch how she does it', 'I like the way Gary helped him' and so on. Other children vicariously learn by watching the reinforced model (Bandura and Walters 1963). In more sophisticated versions the model is reinforced and then the pupil watching is reinforced for any approximation towards the good behaviour of the model. A range of different models need to be selected so that one child does not become a 'star' for the others to dislike and even bully.

Time out. (from reinforcement Blackham and Silberman 1971) is another recommended strategy. Where pupils have become overexcited or distressed, are upset or having a tantrum 'time out' with head down on arms on desk, eyes closed, can be very useful. Pupils can give themselves 30 seconds peace and quiet to recover or they can be sent to a quiet area of the room (if possible) knowing no other pupil must look at them or speak to them until they look up or it is agreed that they can come out now they are calm. It is not advisable to send them out of the classroom for they may run away and be involved in an incident outside. If the pupil is unmanageable it is wisest to send another responsible pupil to the head or deputy to summon help.

Behaviour control. Disruption on this scale is serious and of course the parents would need to be consulted about underlying difficulties and join in efforts to help the child. For a period of time it may be essential to draw up a *'Behaviour Contract'* with the pupil and parents stating attainable goals (Rogers 1994a) and the ways in which the pupil will behave and this will be signed by all the parties. The class teacher and any specialist teachers will sign the record at the end of each session or write a comment on the pupil's conduct. At the end of the day the record is inspected by the head or deputy and commented upon. This should only need to be kept up for two or three weeks and then the pupil should be officially signed off for good behaviour and the record filed. Such periods can give an opportunity for attitude change and a review of the child's needs in more detail and may be enough to deal with the problem. The contract may have to be redrawn at a later stage as some new factor arises. It is so often found that the counselling relationship which is established between the pupil and the person to whom the daily report is made can develop strongly enough to make the pupil want to work for the good opinion of that person. The pupil will then seriously try to iron out what before may have seemed to be insuperable difficulties.

Coping with confrontations and disruption

These are most often explosive episodes involving an individual pupil and teacher or pairs of pupils in a fight. There may be little done to have provoked the outburst or it may be the end of an episode of noisy disruption ending in verbal abuse which the teacher in desperation seeks to stem and which causes the final outburst. The teacher may already have tried calming strategies and may have asked the pupil to stop the tirade or to sit still and get on with his or her work. The pupil has thrown down the gauntlet and challenged the teacher verbally or physically. The teacher has a range of options to select from – summon help if necessary; offer choices (Rogers 1994 a,b); recover the situation (Montgomery 1989) by:

Deflecting (the confrontation) – putting it on *hold* (give time for things to cool down and for brains to be engaged) – *normalising* (continue with the lesson as though nothing had happened and support the work effort) – keep pupil behind at the end of the lesson and then *counsel*. Deflecting the confrontation includes saying 'I'll deal with you later' and writing a title or question on the board for all to copy (hold).

Assertive Discipline (AD)

AD was developed by Lee and Marlene Cantor in the USA in 1976. It is a method of disciplining based on behaviour modification. It consists of a highly structured and administered system of rewards and punishments. Rewards may be stars, merit marks, play time, and even tangible rewards such as prizes and gifts earned by the collection of tokens or merit points. Gifts are less popular in this country than in the USA. The punishments or consequences are at no more than five levels of increasing severity; i.e. having one's name put on the board; keeping in for five minutes at playtime; isolation for a short period; reporting to the head; informing parents. At the first infringement a warning is given. Having the name put on the board five times leads inevitably to the next stage of punishment and the penalties are non-negotiable. It can ensure a quiet, calming discipline. Cantor insists that no child's name should be put on the board or the list until two others have been praised. The system is graded according to individual school's policies and the staff team must agree to implement it systematically. Teachers learn to establish no more than five clear rules, for example: follow instructions the first time they are given; put your hands up to answer questions, keep noise level low; keep your hands; feet and objects to yourself; do not talk whilst the teacher or other pupils are talking.

Behaviour Management Products Ltd was set up in the UK in 1991 to carry out the AD training and claimed that over 2,000 schools were using the system. Makins (1991) reported that schools adopting the system were able to see the difference within a day.

Tactical lesson planning

In the work with students in ITT it was usual for the supervisors to meet with their individual students to go through their Teaching Practice plans in the week before the practice. This included the general curriculum to be followed in each subject or topic area to give a broad and balanced curriculum. It had to follow on or develop from where the class or subject teacher had left off and in consideration of what they wanted the pupils to do next. The students had TP notes issued by the college that insisted that they must write up schemes of work and prepare their first weeks lesson plans on the model: Title; Objectives; Content; Method; Materials.

It quickly became apparent in observing lessons that the model was not in fact a Lesson Plan. It was a way of helping the students organise their thoughts about the lessons they were to teach. It resulted in a general title and sometimes some relevant objectives, often repetitive, two or three pages of teaching content and one or two lines on the method, followed by a list of materials sometimes including 'toolbox' items such as pens, pencils, rulers etc. to fill up the space.

It was quite clear that when the students were in the classroom many of them were focused on the content. Much of it might have been new to them, for instance the English specialist with history subsid. was grappling with the geography in environmental studies and the Secondary Physics student with the biology of the fish from studies long past. Now they are having to learn the intricacies of the National Curriculum before having to teach it. Learning it and teaching it are two very different activities. It became clear that for the teaching side of things a different sort of plan was helpful.

It began with a concern for what the pupils were going to do in any situation. The students' plans really focused on their own learning not their teaching. Given that the content was determined the lesson plan should show clearly what the pupils would be doing in relation to it at any point. Thus content and method need to be more closely linked. When this was done with the focus on pupil learning the pupils were found to be much more absorbed with the content. From this the notion of a Tactical Lesson Plan evolved. It was found to be particularly successful for helping students experiencing difficulties with their teaching. Those who were successful were in fact phasing their teaching on a tactical basis and so these observations reinforced the plan.

It proved difficult to get students to change their habitual ways of writing up their lesson plans until they experienced the effects of doing so with tutorial help. The institution's staff would not readily change a system that had been in use for 30 years and which had just been formalised. The tutors themselves had probably been asked to write it that way.

The Tactical Lesson Plan has the following pattern:

Central objective Formulate the central objective as a single statement about what the pupils are to learn. This is the main point of the lesson or series. It can form the title of the lesson or the title can be a separate item which indicates the subject content.

Introduction (3–5 mins) This occupies the first few minutes of the lesson when the teacher:

– outlines the main purpose, states the objective of the lesson;

– and/or revises previous related work;
– and/or revises by questioning the pupils.

Phase one (About 10 mins depending on age and concentration span of the pupils) Presentation of the first part of the lesson content including where possible any visual/auditory stimulus or concrete examples. Probably mainly teacher talk pupils *listening*. If things are going well a dialogue can be extended to 25 minutes, then it must be realised that slower pupils will need more help and structure for the follow up.

Phase two (About 5 mins depending on task requirements) This must present an activity change for the pupils so that from listening in phase one they can turn to writing, drawing, practical work or to discussion. Making a legitimate opportunity for pupil talk at this point e.g. pairs discuss…can be a very useful tension release for them. Otherwise they talk through the next activity to compensate. Pupils *talking*.

Phase three (About 10–20 mins) This should present another activity change for the pupils so that they now settle down to something such as writing or recording. This will quieten them down.

Phase four (About 5 mins) At intervals as pupils become restive this phase can be introduced where perhaps some of the pupils read out what they have done or there is some more Question and Answer. The teacher may offer some additional advice or input. Pupils *talking and listening*.

Finishing activities In short lessons the finishing activities might be those described in Phase Four. The whole class are brought together for a brief summing up or concluding activity before being dismissed.

In double lessons or long sessions the number of phases can be increased. The additions might be *practical work* including role play. Even in art and design lessons there should be opportunities to bring the group together to rest briefly from the individual concentrated effort to think and listen and perhaps discuss points and techniques.

Very often the cue to the need for an activity change is increasing restlessness amongst the pupils and an inability to settle for long when asked. This restlessness is frequent where the content is unstimulating or difficult. This should easily be picked up during the maintenancing periods when pupils are getting on with written work for example.

Too long a period on written work can in itself lead to fatigue and pain for some so introducing legitimate periods of relaxation by giving an activity change such as hearing some pupils read aloud what they have written; by introducing additional material; by going over the main structure; by discussing some further ideas, or by revising material already presented etc.

In lessons where there is extended practical work it is advisable to set methods and tables for recording data so that practical work and recording on task take place in the same period. At any point it is then possible if the class is becoming noisy and inattentive to settle them down to check the data collected so far and reorganise the work to its conclusion.

Tactical Planning involves activity change based on the attention span of the class from e.g. listening to reading to writing to practical work to speaking to writing and so on. In many subjects group problem solving would replace practical work. In tactical planning it is important to realise that *it is the activity which changes but the content remains the same.*

The validation of the sampling frame as an appraisal instrument

In February 1983 after 'shadowing' a pupil in Heathside school in Surrey whom the school were concerned about the project in appraisal began. The day had been spent observing the pupil's experience. The feedback illustrated the kind of experience to which the pupil had been subjected. As he had a mild language difficulty it was of concern that for the whole eight lessons no teacher had spoken directly to him and he had not answered one question or spoken more than once or twice to ask another pupil for a rubber. The language development, study skills and learning strategies about which we had jointly planned and shared training days might not have been. This was despite the positive feedback received by the trainer after two linked training days and a series of curriculum development follow up meetings by the school.

Today this might seem to be a glimpse of the thunderingly obvious. However, training days, cascade models and suchlike are still in operation in schools. Seldom are they evaluated six months later in practice observations.

After the feedback session discussions ranged over a wider area with the two deputies and the headteacher. They had several teachers whose classroom discipline they were concerned about, as were the teachers themselves. The school had already spent considerable time and effort trying to help them. It was found that when a deputy went into the classroom the role appeared to modify the situation and prevented them seeing as much as they might. Even so the strategies they suggested, the counselling and video review sessions, were not working in these specific cases to bring the teacher up to satisfactory performance.

It was at this point that the gauntlet was thrown down. It was basically, 'You are a teacher trainer, you are supposed to know how to train a teacher, sort this one out.' This was regardless of the fact that these were experienced teachers trained in other institutions and that the school had been supporting them often for more than six months.

Nevertheless the challenge was an interesting one and was picked up. The method the tutor used had never been written down in a formal way. Now this had to be done as part of the project if other people were to be enabled to learn how to use it. At the preliminary stage the deputies were invited to accompany the tutor to experience the method with some postgraduate students in training from a variety of colleges in the area whilst the procedure was formalised. Before this programme began another secondary school close by also jointed the project. This school was involved in developing its own appraisal scheme and having some problems in helping one or two teachers.

The notes for the sampling frame given above remain substantially unchanged from their first publication in the pilot project (Montgomery 1984). They are in continual use in consultancy appraisals and the most recent revalidation was in 1998 and 1999.

Appraisal: the ten point plan

From the original studies in the two pilot schools an appraisal plan was drawn up. This was then tested out and applied in the next stage. In 1985 a research assistant, Norma Hadfield, was recruited to join the project for three years. Her role was to test the system out in a wider range of schools and do a comparative evaluation of it against other methods. Thus a number of other schools in the area, both primary and secondary, joined the project. The method had been developed and used in the full range of schools from nursery classes to sixth form colleges. It was therefore transferable to each of these situations and could also be used across all curriculum subjects. Thus the user did not have to be a subject expert to appraise the lesson. Where there were content concerns these could be discussed later with heads of department. In the case of students in training this was more often necessary than with teachers who were already trained.

The appraiser should follow this protocol:

1. The teacher should voluntarily agree to be observed.
2. The appraisee selects a time and lesson which will show a typical performance unless otherwise agreed.
3. Observer and teacher must agree the focus, terms and nature of what is to be observed, in this case classroom management.
4. A complete lesson must be observed as though by the 'fly on the wall'.
5. The observer makes a continuous timed, running record based on the agreed sampling frame.
6. Every record must begin with a positive statement and all 'negatives' should be couched in positive terms.
7. Immediately after the session both should retire to a quiet room for the feed-back in a comfortable, relaxing setting.
8. The observer first asks the teacher how the session went. This permits tension release and to put right all the imagined wrongs.
9. The observer does not enter into discussion but next reads aloud the running record. Stopping at intervals to give and receive comments, clarifications, develop suggestions and ideas.
10. At the end of this, two or three targets should be developed and agreed. These should be noted down and a copy of the whole document given to the teacher.

Both should experience satisfaction and a feeling that it has been a worthwhile and in-depth encounter. At intervals news of developments can be exchanged in the more informal setting of the staffroom until the next observation. A review interview might be the appropriate follow-up in the next round.

NQTs and teachers experiencing difficulties will benefit from a second observation and feedback session. This should not occur before three weeks have elapsed for the consolidation of skills to take place but should be within six weeks so that improvements can be reinforced and consolidated. After this the teacher can be expected to go on developing the techniques. Opportunities to start again with a new class are also important so that the newly learned techniques can become part of the automatic response repertoire.

If there is no improvement at all then a third observation session can be entered into. In this case it will probably be necessary for the observer to step out of role into that of trainer during the lesson. This means that at critical points the teacher is drawn to one side so that whispered suggestions on monitoring and maintenance strategies can be made. On a few occasions it has been necessary to move round the class demonstrating the PCI strategy to show how it can calm and motivate the students.

The debriefing interview

It really is important for the debriefing interview to take place immediately after the observation session. Lessons, lunches, and days should not be allowed to intervene. The reason for this is that the appraisee is in a most anxiety inducing position which is not helpful especially if improvement in performance is wanted. It is also important to make the feedback immediate if the nuances of performance are not to be lost.

The setting

The setting for the debriefing should be a small comfortable room with coffee or tea available and an opportunity to eat sandwiches if necessary. Corridors, classrooms, and staffroom are definitely unacceptable – we have tried them all. The setting needs to contribute to the relaxed and comfortable atmosphere rather than destroy it.

There should be two armchairs with a space and an angle of about 30–45 degrees between them for the participants to relax into. A small coffee table should be placed in front. It should be possible to reach the cups on the table and for the appraiser to read the sheaf of notes forming the observation to the appraisee. The appraisee should also be able to see the notes and if necessary at points to read it as well.

Beginnings

It is crucial at the outset that the appraiser's first words should be to ask the teacher how he or she felt about the lesson. The reason for this is that during the lesson there may have been a series of things which concerned the teacher and this is the opportunity to get them off his/her chest.

Whilst it does not worry some teachers, the more anxious may have a stream of concerns which they must pour out and things they feel they must put right first. Until they have done this they cannot really hear anything that is said to them.

It is then helpful for the appraiser to establish how typical the session was. As soon as this is done it is useful to simply state what is going to happen next e.g. 'I am simply going to read the record that I made to you and will stop at intervals so we can discuss or clarify points.'

Middles

This is then what happens. The running record is read to the appraisee. It is helpful if times have been noted down the side at intervals so that time spans of sections of the lesson can be looked at in the summing up stages if relevant or in relation to the tactical lesson plan which is illustrated in chapter three.

Every record should start with a positive statement because this sets the emotional tone of what follows and because people can learn to grow better from their strengths. The record should be descriptive and specific. It should refer where necessary to things that can be changed. This can be in the form of asides, suggestions and questions either written into the record if possible and if not raised in the debriefing.

If suggestions are offered the appraisee should have options to try where possible rather than just one thing that must be done. This gives more autonomy in selecting the courses of actions to apply.

During the reading of the record it is possible to stop and discuss points, broadening the ideas and explanations. It is also possible to check the record, to delete anything which is incorrect or not well articulated. Some events may be seen differently and such things can be negotiated and ideas shared as well as any suggestions made for intervention. The teacher may well know individuals much better than the appraiser.

At suitable intervals in the record the main points established should be summarised. The record can then be resumed. It should seek to affirm the strengths of the teacher and the interview may do more of this if it is too short in the record. At the same time there can be counselling and guidance as in any helping interview.

Endings

When the final section of the record has been read then the two or three main targets need to be discussed. With teachers in difficulty the main targets will be CBG and the management and monitoring in the 3 Ms. With successful teachers tactical planning and the higher ranges of PCI may be discussed. The teacher may have more ideas to improve the performance here than the appraiser.

Because teacher educators not only contribute to students' planning but also see such a wide range of lessons and classrooms they usually have a rich repertoire of suggestions. Teachers who have only worked in a few schools and seen very few lessons especially those of other departments may be hard pressed to come up with ideas. It is in this respect that SENCOs are building up a wider repertoire as they do support teaching across the curriculum.

At the end of the interview it is a good idea to summarise the main points again and to identify several areas and aspects which can be singled out for genuine praise for all appraisees. Those who find it hard to praise anyone should not be engaged for this work.

Feedback can say as much about the appraiser as the appraisee and it is helpful for the question to be raised – 'How did you feel the appraisal went?' From this, even if the teacher is in difficulty there should be very positive and satisfied feelings about the appraisal itself. The teacher should feel helped and motivated, willing to try to gain mastery of the techniques and the situation.

Administration

When the interview is concluded the running record can be photocopied and the appraisee given a copy. The original should be kept for reference by the appraiser and should not be shared without the explicit agreement of the appraisee. The targets once negotiated and agreed need be the only paper item which is kept for the record.

In this way massive files do not need to be stored. In the second observation session it is possible to record which targets have been met and which need further work. The time span for this can then be indicated.

When capability procedures have to be entered into it is then possible to use an entirely different instrument which has a summative scale attached. An example of different observation records and the use of summative scales may be found in the next chapter.

Summary and conclusions

This chapter has considered the nature of types of classroom observation which can be undertaken with some of the problems which are involved. The technique which it was found had most to recommend it for professional development was the diagnostic – intervention method based upon a particular sampling frame. For summative and some aspects of formative feedback the standard checklists and rating scales developed by schools would serve the purpose as long as their inter-observer reliability and 'fitness for purpose' is established.

The sampling frame method was based on research in hundreds of classrooms. It is a naturalistic record involving rapid writing of factual events as they occur.

In order to cut down the amount which needed to be written a sampling frame of three key types of classroom behaviours was identified. These were subsequently referred to as CBG, 3 Ms, and PCI. Details were given of each. It had been found that it was these which had the potency to improve ITT students' performance.

When used with experienced teachers in difficulties they were also able to benefit and failing performance was retrieved. Satisfactory and good teachers also had their performance enhanced whilst very good teachers' performance was consolidated. The teachers were introduced to a theory and practice of teaching which underpinned the method in the process of the appraisal. This gave them an opportunity to reframe the ways in which they reflected upon their own teaching and also provided them with a vocabulary to communicate complex constructs about teaching and learning.

Other wider frames of theory and research were referred to in support of this sampling frame, in particular behaviour management and others were touched upon. These will be explored in chapters 4 and 5 in more detail and concern effective learning and teaching.

Chapter Three

Case Studies in Appraisal

Introduction

In the pilot study (Montgomery 1984) which represented the first use of the sampling frame and the observational method with qualified teachers, one of the first quantitative studies of performance enhancement was undertaken as well as qualitative appraisal based upon the sampling frame. The procedure was that after the first and second feedback sessions a summative criterion referenced rating system or check list was also completed.

There were eight categories: Personal and Professional Qualities; Verbal and Non-verbal Skills; Planning and Preparation; Relationships with Pupils including Class Control and Organisation; Presentation of Material; Achievement by Pupils (differentiation); Recording and Evaluation; Pupils' Learning. These were based upon the Kingston Polytechnic Criteria for School Experience designed by the School Experience Committee circa 1980 and trialled and validated over a number of years. Each category had four levels (0, 1, 2 and 3) assigned to it and was illustrated with several criterion references for each level. A 'Pupil's Learning' criterion had been added because the category 'Achievement by Pupils' actually referred to differentiation provided by the teacher. An example of level definition would be:

Level 0: Does not provide sufficient material. Presents material which is unsuited to the attainment of the pupils. Uses material unselectively.
Level 1: Prescribes tasks which are generally appropriate for the rate of progression of the class. Allows sufficient time for them.
Level 2: Prescribes tasks which are adjusted to the range of performance among pupils in the class. Provides for feedback.
Level 3: Meets the needs of a mixed ability class.

When the teacher's level of performance was compared with the scale a level of functioning could be identified. It was therefore possible to obtain a summative score and a profile of a teachers' performance before and after the intervention based on this checklist. The total score which a good teacher could achieve was thus 24 points. Because a deputy head from the other school was also in the lesson there was the opportunity to look at inter-observer reliability in the use of the check list.

There was no training given on the use of the checklist although its concepts and use were discussed in some detail. The mean performance of the group was 7.55 before intervention and 13.05 afterwards as assessed by both observers.

In addition to this form of quantitative analysis it was also possible to quantify item improvements in relation to the sampling frame recorded in the pre and post records. This enables the summative scale to be used as a formative instrument to give feedback on performance. Of course, what it could not do was improve that performance.

The observers and the teachers also recorded their impressions of the pre and post intervention lessons. The impression evaluation was that before the intervention one teacher was in serious difficulties across the board, the other three were having problems particularly with discipline. After the intervention it was recorded that each teacher was seen to have made a significant amount of improvement. All their performances had improved to a basic satisfactory level. Several years later all were functioning satisfactorily. The NQT had passed the probationary year comfortably and the one with the most serious difficulties had become the school's 'star' teacher.

The inter-observer reliability was very high in the use of the check list: 98.4 per cent in the Before condition and 95 per cent in the After condition. The teachers in each case rated themselves considerably higher than the observers. This is not untypical and their misperceptions are contributing factors to their problems.

In the next phase of the research (Montgomery and Hadfield 1989, 1990) a range of primary and secondary schools were recruited to take part in the three year research programme. It had already been shown that other appraisers could be trained to use the system and that this was most effectively done with at least one practice demonstration. The new researcher went through a similar training programme and also had supervised practice.

The programme was set up to produce public verifiable evidence of the improvements in performance which can be achieved by the system through videotaping of lessons and pre- and post-feedback interviews. The feedback was frequently given without the video as this was not found necessary to the method. The tapes were also made so that data mining could be undertaken as well as to use them in training sessions. In this research programme a range of local schools were invited to participate and although the schools through the heads were volunteers most of the subjects had not volunteered. The input was used as additional support to the schools' system of appraisal and this time dealt mainly with successful teachers.

In one series of evaluations experienced teachers on inservice training courses were shown unedited extracts of the before and after lessons and were asked to judge in which extract the teacher had been more effective. The order of presentation was varied. In 99.5 per cent of cases they were correctly able to identify which was the more successful lesson and this correlated precisely with the second lesson after the appraisal feedback (Montgomery and Hadfield 1989).

In a separate study Hadfield also looked at the relative effectiveness of the sampling frame method compared with the use of checklists and personal construct strategies as feedback in obtaining improvement. Controls in this field work were difficult to achieve. It was not as in the perfect laboratory design.

However, it was shown that the sampling frame method was significantly more effective than the other two methods in producing positive improvements in teaching performance. In relation to the other two there was also a general 'feel good factor' in operation as they were both positive methods in their approach, but there was no detectable change or improvement in teaching performance.

It became clear that as in all consultancy there needs to be an element of teaching (Dare 1982) if change for the better in performance is to be achieved. The extent to which a consultant has the necessary developmental teaching skills therefore becomes crucial. This is no doubt why many teachers engaged in appraisal have difficulty in carrying it through as they do not have mastery of the disciplines which contribute to and underpin teaching and learning nor the breadth of experience in classrooms. Specific curriculum subject knowledge is necessary for being a subject advisor but is not sufficient for the role of appraiser. In this particular method there is a significant amount of 'coaching' involved.

One of the deputy heads (James 1989) in the pilot study went on to become an advisory teacher with responsibility for probationers in the LEA secondary schools. The work involved disseminating information and setting up training groups for deputy heads who were in most cases the probationers' mentors. She decided to compare the probationers' feelings about the methods of appraisal which they had experienced. There were two types: the appraisal and feedback given by the LEA inspectors, and the appraisal and feedback given by the researcher trained in the method discussed here, using the sampling frame. There were considerable differences between the two experiences not all of which could be ascribed to fear and anxiety induced by the title of inspector.

In the sampling frame method the probationers valued being made to feel relaxed and at ease; the classroom observation was felt to be supportive and unobtrusive; there was a general feeling that the experience was positive and helpful; they welcomed the detailed observation and time given to offering specific feedback.

In relation to the appraisal visits of the inspectorate the probationers felt nervous, uneasy, on edge, apprehensive and uncomfortable about being observed by the inspector. Some probationers had found it difficult to manage an inspector's visit particularly when the inspector interrupted or wanted to take over the lesson, arrived unannounced, or after 10–15 minutes wanted to discuss the lesson there and then. Some were disappointed with the negative feedback or in other cases, no feedback at all.

When the probationers were asked what they had learned from these experiences of classroom observation it was found that from the researcher/advisor they had an awareness that they were doing well and of the skills they were using; they learnt of the importance of developing positive relationships with pupils; and an understanding of the importance of positively reinforcing pupils' work and behaviour. They also had a greater awareness of classroom management strategies.

In relation to the visits of the inspectorate 50 of the 78 probationers felt they had not learned anything as little or no feedback was given. Those who had learned something now displayed more pupils' work; tried to be more effective in the use of the voice and had developed some classroom management strategies.

Inspectors were obviously on a tight schedule and unable to give time to this work among other priorities. In the event it may well have been sensible to have relinquished this work to several trained specialist advisors. The inspectors had themselves been the recipients of a three day LEA training course on appraisal.

Difficult cases

There is a tiny minority of cases in which a teacher is in serious difficulties and finds it extraordinarily difficult to change habitual behaviours. Most teachers, of course, will have relapses. But in these particular cases where they have been given the feedback on the first and then the second lesson with the three week interval or more in between, only a tiny amount of progress is seen. It is episodic as suddenly they remember to CBG or use the quiet naming and monitoring techniques. One male teacher was actually persuaded to stay out of the Art room cupboard for the whole lesson.

With the agreement of the teacher a further stage of intervention can be engaged in, based on the system. At no point must the observer take over the lesson but instead at appropriate points can draw the teacher to one side and murmur strategies in the ear so that the teacher can move off and implement and then come back and discuss (be CBG'd).

To this procedure can be added a further exercise in modelling and reinforcement. The observer accompanied by the teacher moves round and does small demonstrations of CBG, Monitoring or PCI and then follows as the teacher goes off and does likewise. Each time the teacher successfully uses the technique the coach is there to murmur praise. The pupils must not become aware of any of this except that there are two teachers working in the room.

Once the habit barrier has been broken and the pupils start responding well they give the teachers the feedback needed to encourage them to keep going and keep working on their technique. Monitoring progress should then be enough to keep them going until the next classroom observation cycle.

Two examples of postgraduate appraisal records

The reason for including these will show the difference in the records that sometimes have to be made for students in training. There is a far greater element of teaching that needs to go on especially in relation to the subject content. This is, of course, not entirely surprising although these are graduates who have completed a degree programme. There is always a mismatch between the degree coverage and the pupils' needs in the school curriculum.

Mrs G.   **A Secondary School**
CSE Biology with 4th Year/Year 10 (Mixed Class of 23 pupils)

Topic: The structure and function of the kidney

1.30 Good, when we arrived you had a nice working atmosphere and reasonable noise level.

Large room always poses problems for projection of voice especially science laboratories.

Notes on board – did you consider and reject giving them the first word cues for them to write the rest in their own words? Might have been useful to use as a check immediately afterwards to confirm they had grasped the essentials. Of course they do like to copy, it's comforting to have the correct answers straight away, but it lacks the cognitive thrust (i.e. Piaget's accommodation is not likely to occur).

Good, nice clear instructions but when you give them make sure that you have the attention of *all* the group e.g. the table at front were quietly chatting still, with backs to you. Need to take account of this as a slight undermining of authority in insidious ways. Probably not important here – but it did mean you had to go back to two of them and get them to join the rest.

Some good phasing of the lesson, e.g.

Introduction: Q/Ans, Recap.

Stage 1   Some copying (writing)

Stage 2   Practical work.

I wonder whether you might have been advised to give your instructions for the dissection for them to list first so that they could try to follow these. (Following written instructions quite difficult task). As it is you are dissecting the kidney, issuing the instructions, and trying to control them – three things.

'Will you be quiet when I am talking!' This was issued loud and strong but in some desperation. It shows in your voice that you are somewhat under threat, they can sense it. I suggest that you think about saying things in a series, e.g.:

1. 'Listen when I am talking' (Not 'will you' because it is a question, rather than an instruction). Say it firmly but not pleadingly, then pause and say:

2. 'Listen Joanne'

3. 'Turn round Allison' Pause

4. 'Good, now... I want you to ...'

When they moved the desks around that was an opportunity to create a row – try saying:

a) 'Move the desks quietly.' Drop your voice to give them the cue. Then you can say e.g. b) 'John, I said quietly.'

Consider whether

a) It is worthwhile not putting all the desks together but have them gathering in groups round the tins with their written instructions which you can move round and monitor.

b) You might put the desks together for the lesson before they come in.

In this instance a) might have been the better bet as the dissection session was so short – 2 or 3 minutes.

Good – encouraging attention, now saying 'Come on'.

Good, you are ensuring that all are quiet and listening. I think that you could use some names – not, 'You three on the side', but, 'X turn round please for a minute'. Good try – useful effect.

When you say, 'I want you all to listen' you introduce a pleading note as though you are not absolutely convinced that you will succeed; e.g. you say 'List – ern' try 'List'n' all on one note.

One or two nice bits about 'kidneys and your tea', *nice smile*. Try to move round now that they are drawing and say something to each group, if possible each individual, but in particular find something *positive* to say e.g. *Catch* them *Being Good*. A lot of your contribution whilst going round is *control statement* and *information* plus the odd *nag*.

e.g.'If you can't see the board move closer' – tone of voice is nag/control. It seems as though you are really implying – 'You ought to be able to see it, if not you must do something you possibly do not want to do, move closer'.

To go back to the practical:

Are you a scientist?! How do scientists study, discover, investigate?

Don't they do dissections, experiments etc. and then very closely and in detail observe what they dissect? Is this not how discoveries are made? Part of teaching biology is teaching about scientific method as well, so this is best done by getting them to draw *what they have dissected*. Don't allow them access to the books to copy yet. Make it an exciting voyage of discovery. When they have drawn what they see *then* let them check with the book – even let them score points for the observations correct, marking their own.

'*Will you* listen, you won't be able to answer the questions otherwise!'

'*Will you* list ern!' 'Yes' (pupil). You are back to this habit.

3 Ms

Whilst you are going round *maintenancing* – i.e. working with individuals – and *this is good*, it is keeping these more difficult girls at the back going, but the three boys in the middle have been switched off for 5 minutes or so.

2.25. Most of the class now sitting back relaxing because so much of your time is being devoted to the girls at the back. Move round faster. Boy with missing pencil, always have a spare, try not to get into a confrontation over something so small however irritating.

'Miss, I've done it!' 'Good, hold on'. Nice response. They like the attention you are giving them but again try to intersperse some smiles, some 'goods', some positive comment.

End of lesson, you are getting tired, don't weaken and talk over them. The one or two little bits of baiting from the girls at the back you handled quite well i.e. you did not get angry; you could also smile and say 'concentrate' quite pleasantly.

Some general points (Whilst you are clearing up)

1. Positive support, smiles – non-verbal control, CBG.

2. 3 Ms Management, *monitoring* and maintenance; do more monitoring.

3. Cognitive aspects – e.g. observation can contain cognitive challenge – in the exploration of the tubule bit, you may ask them to listen to your explanation and then get them to try to pick up the story of a molecule of urine round the class. You could also introduce a few bits about when things go wrong in kidneys and what is happening to them, e.g. Why do people need transplants? Morbid facts do tend to absorb them and help them remember even e.g. Why do some people persistently have to go to the loo? When should this be used as an indication of illness other than nerves, when should they check with the doctor? Types of urine test, diabetes insipidus, indications of liver and/or kidney failure in their pets etc. You could even get them to collect newspaper and magazine cuttings to stick in their exercise books. Such things will gain their interest and help them remember the more formal aspects of the lesson.

1. I think you have some good potential which it will take a little while for you to realise. If you could gain some more practice in easier control of your voice this would be very helpful under stressful conditions. It could involve simple things such as perhaps practising singing in the bath or round the house and then inventing and singing control statements such as you might use in the classroom. Practice in reading aloud will help phrasing and breath control. Also try sitting in front of a mirror and shouting at yourself practising vocal control techniques. If you have a friend who will help, sit opposite each other and speak crossly at each other in random numbers e.g.

$$43, 52, 61, 98!$$

$$1, 3, 7, 21, 9!$$

$$32, 54, 9, 68, 31, 2, 49, 64, 68, 38!$$

2. Concentrate more on trying to put cognitive challenge into the lesson as indicated and giving more time to structured practical work. You were particularly successful when you did this.

Plan your lesson like a military strategy and do not talk too long. Q/A e.g. Introduction to lesson . . . revision Q/A. Then

Listening	Stage 1	Teacher information giving, story telling
Writing from head	Stage 2	Pupils writing main points
Talking	Stage 3	Check facts by pupils telling part of this round class
Writing from dictation	Stage 4	Dissection instruction, dictated
Practical	Stage 5	Practical work
Drawing	Stage 6	Pupils drawing dissection
Checking	Stage 7	Checking and marking drawing from text books or board
Listening Q/A	Conclusion	Revision of the main points, homework.

(The left hand column represents activity changes for the pupil phased throughout the lesson whilst the content remains the same. be careful not to spend 25–35 minutes just in teacher talk at the beginning).

3. Keep on moving around the class as much as you can to help and support individuals. Good effects when you do this.

Mr W. PGCE Student   A Secondary School
2nd year/Year 8 History (Class of 30 mixed pupils)

Castles – Scottish History

11.00 Good, you lined them up outside insisting that they went in quietly. Good use of the pause and waiting for silence at the beginning. Good, you altered the strong voice and once it was quiet you dropped the pitch and spoke very quietly. Very effective use of contrasts. Well done.

After giving out the books which was done well, the 'listen then please', *'Look this way without talking'* very good effect. But if not entirely effective after two general statements use the names of one or two individuals. One boy two desks in front of me at the window was still 'refusing' to attend i.e. by body attitude had shouted to you. Watch out for this – make eye contact and gesture him to turn round.

Good, nice smile, nice use of questioning.

Good, lots of reinforcement – e.g. you say 'Yes' and smile after their answers or you paraphrase them. Good techniques.

Nice use of voice and good tone making it interesting. Good during introduction on Scotland used opportunities well to ask questions relating this to previous knowledge.

These pupils appear very well behaved, any little misdemeanours are quite subtle, e.g. flicking over pages of another's book, quiet asides, gazing out of windows.

Good use of the gurgles about the 'Wallace', nice smile, gentle humour, made pupil feel significant, and not put down, the others were being a bit derisory (e.g. his surname was Wallace too). I think that you could not always expect such a quiet and attentive audience i.e. you have been story telling for ten minutes without interruptions from barracking, distractions, comment or question. Unusual these days. It used to be typical of the old Grammar school settings 20 years ago. I expect you realise this.

By the way, did you know that the girl Michelle whom you asked to read it was able to do so reasonably or was prepared to? Such a request can send some pupils into paroxysms of fear and make a slight difficulty in reading become magnified so that others deride and ridicule.

There is now perfect silence and all the pupils are concentrating in some good measure. Not entirely due to intrinsic interest in content or your control I think. Our presence, the school and environmental ethos. Do you know which? How far is this typical of them and other classes.

Good, whilst Michelle was reading you were looking up and watching out for any potential difficulties; it is at these points with difficult classes that you need to use the eye contact and gesture to exert class control. So keep this up. Not always necessary to say anything in these circumstances, if absolutely necessary use pupil's name without interrupting the child reading.

Good, you handled the question about the stone very well and admitted you did not know, maybe you could go a step further and say 'But I/we shall try to find out'.

11.25 *Cognitive Challenge and Relevance*

I should like you to consider the notion of cognitive challenge and the principle of Accommodation (Piaget) You are achieving this in some degree by asking questions which require inference, e.g. 'What is the meaning of the "Hammer of the Scots" and use of past knowledge in the current context. But so far by 11.25 the course of the lesson is:

Introduction and setting 5 mins Q/Ans

Stage 1	10 mins Story telling some Q/Ans i.e. information feeding.
Stage 2	10 mins, Story reading – some of same information being told plus a few Q/Ans.
Stage 3	Drawing of map/tracing of map i.e. visual information, telling reinforced through drawing and writing.
Stage 4	Completion of work sheets with questions about foregoing so that what has been done is reinforced.

What I think you might at first find unpalatable is that this could be seen as a memory training/rote learning activity. At least consider this for if it is so then if you apply this technique to another class when you are in a different school, in perhaps a less moti-vated setting, you may find the pupils see no relevance in this task – i.e. Why should this knowledge about old men in Scotland be of use or interest to them? Why should they bother to read about it when it is more interesting to talk about last night's aggro or create some by poking the pupils in front? Even more so, why on earth should they write it all down when it is already neatly written in the book?

11.32 After several minutes at the front with one boy you went back to the same boy twice. Good, now you are beginning to move around.

Your remonstrance at front for them all to be quiet, 'Noise level too high!' was effec-tive, they are back again on the right level. There are other ways which you should consider to achieve the same effect when this does not work e.g.

Consider during each lesson – try to move round and have a few words with every individual child about his/her work, try to be supportive as you can and find things in *every pupils' work to praise*. For some children a whole day can go by without anyone saying a word to them except in anger or correction. The more difficult the pupils the more *absolutely essential*, this is. It helps enhance self-esteem and increases moti-vation on these tasks which pupils may perceive as not really relevant.

11.40 40 minutes into the lesson; they are getting a little tired. Good, you have stopped and given them a bit of a rest, i.e. an activity change – 'Stop, put pencils down' and very nicely made sure that they all did, this small detail is crucial and is contributing to your success with this group for even they would begin to misbehave a little if you did not quietly insist. *Very good technique.*

11.45 Some of them are getting quietly restless. Your tennis quip gave a few more the idea to watch too. From where they were sitting I don't think those boys could see the tennis through the curtain. In another class this could have caused an uproar of accusations and denials. Try to be accurate and very fair.

Going back to cognitive challenge:

A 1. The Scotland bit and the death of Alexander. Given the setting that they know about, you have choices.

	a) to tell them what happened
Cognitive challenge:	b) to get them first to hypothesise what might happen in this situation. Then tell them what did.

2. Maid of Norway bit:

	a) to tell them about her and what happened
Cognitive challenge:	b) to tell them about her and let them hypothesise what happened then tell them the story.

3. Relevance: Are there comparable references you can make to similar situations today – parallels drawn etc?

B The map work

11.46 Children like to copy and colour in maps; it makes them think they are learning something, it looks nice and it allows chat. But consider what they have really learned.

Cognitive challenge: Could they, before they look at the map, rough out what they think Scotland looks like and where they think these things happened? Fascinating results when they draw the original they will have the incentive to observe in more detail the proximities and contours.

On the subject of contours and distance this kind of map drawing from the text book gives very little concept of space and place. Why were there places where they were, the battles fought there and not here? etc.

When you try to *make them hypothesise* and predict you are helping them bring their own prior knowledge and experience to the learning and then when they observe differences between their own knowledge and the information presented they will be able to adapt to this new information more readily and extend their knowledge hierarchies or schemata.

12.05 Good revision session at end.

12.10 The settling at end precarious indicating that some of the above will be - applicable.

Summary

This was a good lesson, well-structured, prepared and presented.

You have a nice style, firm but kindly. You explained that you made efforts earlier in the term to make quite sure that they listened as a class even if initially you spent more time on this than on teaching. This proves to have been worthwhile and successful. Now you need to concentrate upon motivating them so that they want to learn because it is interesting and challenging. Consider for the future when you are not in such a sheltered environment:

1) Relevance perceived and felt – motivation to learn.
2) Cognitive challenge.
3) More use of non verbal control techniques will be needed.
4) More use of smiling and personal positive comment will be needed e.g. CBG, Catch them Being Good.

DANGER AREA. About 50–50 control and information questions used, only some positively praised or supported.

Summary from the two PGCE records

From these two early demonstration records it can be seen that the technique is still evolving. There is a large element of teaching in both in relation to PCI. In the first record the class is an older one and has within it a number of difficult pupils who would stretch most teachers' management skills. The student here has a particular disadvantage in that her voice even under mild duress becomes high pitched. She has great difficulty in controlling it. This is the first time we had met her but it was apparent instantly and the pupils tended to play on the fact. It was important to help her with voice control as in the notes at the end but without continually referring to it in the record.

The second lesson was to some extent a model lesson. Control skills were good. However when the situation was probed below the superficial level not enough was being learnt by the students in such a well controlled environment. The CBG levels were not high enough to ensure a positive classroom ethos and there was a lack of PCI. There was thus the danger that this student could be given a good pass in this situation only to find that in the next there were serious difficulties.

As each were training observations for the deputy heads it was important to raise all these questions in the one session. It was in the first session that the other observer developed 'role conflict' and wanted to sort out those difficult and cheeky girls instead of behaving as the 'fly on the wall'.

Two example primary school records

Miss M. **Nursery Class in Infant school**

(2 years experience) (Approx 30 children)

2 nursery helpers, several parents

Good, the activities taking place were nicely varied:

1) 3 children drawing with crayons – one a house, one a 'lickel girl', one writes name and letters preparatory to drawing.

2) Jigsaw table large wooden pieces, 6 upwards, range of inserts for increasing sized cats, teddy, bus. Good, increasing in difficulty and different concepts. Nursery Assistant also engaged in questioning.

3) Matching cards to template – 6 pieces, four sets.

4) Number table – numbers in series 1 – 5; Nursery Assistant and 1 child – matching. 3 X shapes sets of jigsaws. 1 – 5 shapes. Could be helpful to reinforce number 'names' as placed on prongs rather than just shape words e.g. N.A. may need guidance here.

5 Sticklebrick table – 3 boys doing construction work. Lorries and carts.

6) Simple 2 piece jigsaws – mixed number, 1 cow, 2 cats 3 kangaroos.

7) Pastry table.

8) Paint table.

9) Floor/carpet wooden trucks and cars

Story: Rosie the Hen

This was read by the new nursery Assistant (her first day). She did well, good questioning, good use of voice and gesture. Children engrossed. Accepts their comments very well and uses them to keep their interest. Reinforces number work – how many... Reinforces the naming very well, encourages joining in. Is going to read another short story – children very pleased.

The children demonstrate well a number of interesting features about your teaching. They are socially skilled for their age, they do not shout each other or the adult down. They are sitting quietly and not interfering with each other in spiteful or disruptive ways. They have obviously already learnt the classroom rules and roles ready for their move up into the reception class next term.

During the part of the session before the story the room was well laid out and there was a very busy working atmosphere. All the children were engaged in constructive activity except perhaps there was one with a tendency to wander although I did not have time to check this out.

A useful range of play apparatus outside. All well in use. I think I might have one more large box out for them to sit inside and perhaps occasionally a very low narrow balance apparatus. All the apparatus was being well used by both boys and girls except the trolleys, trikes/ scooters – I think I should keep an eye on this for possible sex role reinforcement and positively encourage the girls to use them. It may just, on the other hand be a feature of this particular session.

One little girl in pink still on the rocket.

Do you sometimes engage in structured play over and around the apparatus or use the opportunity to engage in developmental work in relation to individual needs in terms of spatial/body concepts? Have you any children who are developmentally clumsy? It could be helpful if you keep records on this aspect e.g. balance on one foot then other (for 5 sec). Climbing up steps alternating feet (central apparatus). Descending steps one by one (the wooden steps here). Height – some often seen to jump from heights with ease and good balance; balance on low rail.

10.28 One girl has now taken over a scooter and a boy is on the rocket giving it what for. Another girl has to hand over a trike. Interesting pattern – boys first, girls later when boys are fed up with these items. Another girl has taken over a scooter and another boy the rocket. At the slide you are now keeping an eye on them and making sure they go feet first and don't crowd on the steps. The slide always needs watching – well done. Good, you are engaging in a little bit of language work here and at the centre of the apparatus.

Very little imaginative play going on around the apparatus – some in/on the box near the door – plus a territorial disagreement. You might encourage the imaginative play by suggesting one or two ideas when the occasion arises or join in if appropriate. Very good, you found the girl in pink on a trike and were very encouraging, she did seem to find it a bit tricky to get started but she is going very well now.

10.40 Out here the children are very talkative to each other. Some interesting imaginative play about being on the bus, over by the wooden steps and boxes. In the classroom they seem to be less so . . .

Good, you are doing some language work on the seat with the small group.

They seem quite shy of a strange adult, less talkative than one might expect. Is this typical of what you find and is it related to the area and home training?

What would you say was the emphasis of your college training? Good little bit of language work with the three boys at the water table. You have a nice manner with them, a pleasing style.

Although you felt very distressed by the difficulties and pressures of having new children, potential runaways etc. none of this was apparent in the calm of the lesson and the way in which the children behaved. They were a credit to you all.

Mrs D (30 years experience)   Infant School

Class of 6-7 year olds (Year 1) (26 children)

1.40 Good, when we arrived there was a very nice steady working atmosphere.

1) A table flow painting

2) A number card table doing addition with a range of different levels of card

e.g. 3 and ____ = 8   1 + 1 =

3) A weighing table with a large work card on an easel

4) A writing table

5) A flash card game on butterflies which you were winning.

1.52 Several of the groups – especially number and weighing are becoming a bit noisy. You notice the change in noise level and speak to two different children by name across the room. As you pack up the flash card game 7 or 8 children come over to you for special help.

Prior to this a nice little teach-in with a girl, J on 4 + 0 (sweets in hands). Good, changed to counters from the abstract to the concrete – immediately she was able to do it. Might be a strategy for her to use for a little while (i.e. separate hands) I worked through the first sum with her e.g. Collect 4 add 1 to them and count them all up. She could only do it whilst I 'programmed ' her behaviour. As soon as I stopped she 'forgot' and came to you.

1.55 Quick threat to L. – 'Do you want to be moved!' Another threat to a boy across room. You help with the weighing and get them going again.

2.00 Offer help to boy with writing. 'Oh Lisa, that's not a very long story. I am sure you can write a much longer one, a big girl like you.'

2.02 'Simon are you doing your work?' Helping boy in grey write his sentence prompting. Now positively reinforce one pupil with 'Good'. V is having a bit of difficulty with the words he is copying. L sent round the corner to be quiet. 'Excuse me young man, I thought I told you to take your work...I am tired of you running around!' Helping weighing table children again. Good you are moving round. You say 'Ssssh, don't shout!' But this itself was rather loud.

2.05 'Boys! What are you doing? Will you get on please!'...Several just standing by the 4 girls with the sticklebricks. You are now sitting at a table helping with number work and look across, *monitoring*, to another table and say 'Ssssh' quietly. Well done, this was much more effective than previously.

Good, two positive comments in quick succession to two different pupils who have come to you. (Children now around you needing help.)

On the carpet beside you one of the boys has done a brilliantly imaginative construction (Barry). The Tate Gallery would pay money for something like that! I wonder what he has in mind – it's not buildings, it is abstract form. I think he is not too talkative. J who kicked it may have done so on purpose(?) Maybe because I commented on it to B in a positive way? I thought you handled the little scenario very well, making him apologise and assuming it was not a quick 'nasty'. Very good strategy.

Wall display. This is interesting and well mounted and very well set out. Not crowded. Do you put up their writing and number work too? e.g. Writing when they first started or at the beginning of the term and then now (their latest best)? Can do this for a few at a time.

Now writing a whole word in a pupil's spelling book for writing story. Do you sometimes ask them to guess the first sound to start?

Nice little bit of questioning over the tulip and what was missed at the centre. Another bit of praise to child. Good the effect of this ripples out over others. Very nice handling of L. Instead of a quick nag you helped him find the crayon and settle down again. Good with Daniel, 'You weren't being silly were you? I liked your polite manner. 'Excuse me A' 'I am sorry I am in your way darling.'

You are working very hard. Good now questioning Helen about what she has made – her blue construction. Good bit of imaginative play with Tracy e.g. sandwiches and tea without sugar.

Lisa – a lovely little session when you read her writing back to her. You have a lovely smile. You should use it more often, the children respond so well. You are just beginning to relax? Pleased with another child's work, keep working on the positives – CBG.

Nice session of imaginative play going on in the home corner with the telephones. They are a lively class, very forthcoming. Pleasant open manner with visitors.

2.30 Tidying up. getting under way very slowly. L and J made to stand with noses to wall for being silly – but they have thereby avoided having to do any tidying up. L is addressing you in a very loud voice. You don't want to speak to him. You might try saying you will speak with him when he stops 'shouting' at you. Tidying up still going on, other children milling about. The sand timer is out, the five minute gong goes. You are still working hard. You very loudly say, 'Are we all quiet?'!

Nursery rhymes on the mat. Good idea just to hold the hand of Daniel to calm him down, 'You've been a silly boy. You can go and say you are sorry.'

'Are you ready? Is everyone lining up?' Again you don't sound as relaxed as you might be. You are still looking very worried. You could try the, 'Show me who's ready' routine.

Summary

Thank you for letting us observe this session. It was a very busy one, lots of different levels of cognitive activity were catered for as well as individual children's needs in other ways e.g. emotional and supportive. You did well to provide for and teach on all these different fronts. I think that it was setting a high standard for yourself e.g.six cognitive challenges to maintain is at the limit of our human span of attention. Be a little kinder to yourself and settle for four or five!

I felt throughout the session as I said that you were under strain and having to assert control more strongly than I would expect in voice and manner. After talking with you I can see why this was. You had your class back after a term in which they had someone else who was inexperienced and not used to English primary method. They seemed (the class) as though this was your first week with them under your regime and I was puzzled that your control cues and calls were not well responded to but had to be demanded or emphasised. But of course it was, in effect, your first week with them. I should like to come again as we discussed and see them as you would have them. I am sorry that you were also feeling unwell with a headache this obviously added to the pressure and made you look worried and sad some of the time.

When you *'caught them being good'* and when you smiled and praised and cheered them on even the naughty ones began to behave. So it was all there.

You have a lively class and a few awkward characters but I enjoyed the session and all the children seemed to learn something and progress in the tasks set.

I will try to find some materials for you that relate to the handwriting learning difficulties we also discussed in relation to the childrens' written work. I suggested that cursive writing might be looked at as a development in school policy to overcome a wide range of such needs.

Summary of the two primary reports

These two reports were compiled in the initial phases of the funded research project whilst the researcher was being trained in the sampling frame method. It also took place during the period of 'Teacher Action' by agreement of the school staff.

Both reports were part of a series in which the whole staff had agreed to participate in the project as part of in service and school development planning. They have been selected here because the records illustrate that there are aspects of the teaching which can be developed in the presence of satisfactory classroom control.

For example in the first record there were two related issues. These were that there appeared to be a need for more development work and training to be done with the Nursery assistants. Perhaps a more assertive role in leadership of the team from the teacher needed to be developed.

The question about the teacher's initial training was to flag a need for information gathering on the style of this. There was a clear policy in operation in the classroom on language development arising from the activities on which the children were engaged. There were some directed activities such as story, number and literacy in which all children were encouraged to participate but there seemed to be a need to do more exploration of cognitive challenge across the full range of the curriculum and perhaps a more systematic approach to encouraging imaginative and fantasy play. This did not seem to come naturally to the children and perhaps reflected wider issues typical of the local area and parents attitudes and experience.

In the second example we can see a highly experienced teacher finding herself under some duress, possibly unnecessarily, and perhaps an over strong response to this. The emphasis was therefore on describing the terms of the interactions and illustrating the positive effects on the pupils, even the 'awkward' ones of much lower key interventions. Sometimes teachers are completely unaware of the very strong and positive effects of a smile and a mild word or two of praise. In this case the differences of the effects on the children were very marked indeed.

Two examples of pre- and post-intervention records

Mrs D. Newly Qualified Teacher from Secondary School

Longman's French (3rd year/Year 9) (Mixed class 30 pupils)

First Visit   **November**

(The CBG, 3 Ms and PCI notes had been sent in advance of the visit).

Good, you worked hard at the beginning to get them to concentrate and listen. Good, you've just got them completely quiet and switched on.

Well done, you achieved this by calling individuals by name. 3Ms strategy.

Extract on tape

Followed by questions. I liked the way when the girl gave her answer you said, 'Good, you have got the meaning.'

I wonder whether it would be a good idea to play the tape twice to really help them clue in before asking too many questions. I do not think they were well orientated. I had problems first thing on Monday getting into the French pronunciation. Good asides e.g. 'Louise your scarf'.

'Karen are you ready?'

'Anthony...'

Nice smile at 'Superman outfit' and you said 'I don't think so'.

'Just be quiet please', followed by naming , 'Louise' good technique.'Will you *put you hand up* . Do not say this unless you mean to observe the rule yourself. When a pupil puts his/her hand up you did respond but then you accepted called out answers.

'Look at your text again now please ... Simon'. 'Good'

They have settled down to the written work and you are working very well moving round helping and involving them.

3 Ms needed (Monitoring phase).

11.10. Good, by your detailed help you have managed to get them all to do some work. Keep your eyes lifting to monitor and settle those who are not. Settle them by gaze or gesture before you go to help them. Two boys to my right not doing anything.

11.13 Very good, they are nearly all except these two quite settled. Good, you have arrived at them and now they have started – within 5 seconds of you turning your back they are not working again. Watch them more carefully – they respond to control by eye contact.

Good, you are working very well on an individual basis. I think I might intersperse the lesson with a little more contrast such as:

e.g. Tactical planning

some listening/oral work

some writing

some more oral; work or Q/A

some more writing.

Some reflections – I hope not against policy!

I do not think I should be so quick to translate the French into English. When they are misbehaving or talking ask them a question about the work in hand. If they cannot answer move on and ask someone else.

You are working very hard but over their basic mumble noise. Our presence is probably preventing you from relaxing and taking some of this more slowly.

I do not feel you have explored the tape as much as you might have done. You might have found it more advantageous to read it yourself more slowly. I found it a bit quick – probably because I was writing at the same time as listening.

Might they have taken the parts of Yves, M.Lagard or Danielle (p. 30 Longmans Stage A 3 Audio Visual French) – or is that for later?

In Summary

Despite all this you could at any time you really exerted your will obtain their attention. They were obliging and obviously were not resentful or alienated showing you are capable of developing a good working relationship with them and it showed at intervals throughout.

I think the key factors were:

a) getting the best tactical phasing of the lesson with activity change for them

1. listening

2. writing

3. checking Q/A

4. oral work

5. writing

6. reading out etc

Then 'tuning' to extend sections that are going well, and b) concentrating more on the monitoring phase of 3 Ms and making sure to use the 5 second check back to make eye contact or gesture to maintain the on-target behaviour.

You have a nice way with this group, just emphasise your own good points and with practice I think you will do very well.

Mrs D.   **French**
                              (4th Year/Year 10)

Second Visit   **February**

9.30 Good, nice working atmosphere when we came in. Tape playing – good you stopped the tape to quietly tell several of them to put pens down and listen whilst following the pictures:

The questions, e.g. 'What are they doing first of all?'

               'Shaving first of all?'

               'Brushing their teeth?'

Good:

1. You ask questions and repeat their answers briefly.

2. You ask questions and say 'Right' when they give the correct answers.

3. Now also try to nod 'Yes' and smile when you accept an answer.

4. Try to say 'Good' more often – you do it just occasionally. It plus the smiles will enhance your interaction and the quality of it for the pupil.

9.40 Some good questioning. Have you tried using this as a control device? e.g. Asking a pupil who is day-dreaming or not responding. There are a number sitting at the back.

Tape section lasted 10 minutes.

Good, you have introduced a different activity over 'mine and yours'. I think I might have acted the sequence and then got them to try to construct the response rather than telling them at the outset.

(Is it useful sometimes when talking about a word used e.g.'secours' to compare it with an English word which perhaps (?) come from the same root? e.g. Succour. It helps me remember such a word. It is an especially important word to remember we may all need it.)

Good, you spent just about the right time on the practice of 'mine and yours' – should it have been written down on the board, there seemed to be about 50 per cent mishearings e.g. 'bien'.

9.45 *Activity change*, good. They now have to write the grammar in their books.

Good, very clear board work, very well written and laid out.

9.50 Continuation with writing now to do an exercise.

Did you notice the disruption which can ensue at the activity change border? You handled it very well. I think if you used the 3 Ms strategy it would go even more smoothly, e.g. 1) General remonstrance. then 2) Individuals by name.

When you do use a pupil's name e.g. Andrea and she says 'Ay?' don't let her get away with this, she did it deliberately, rudely or provocatively. You could say something like – 'No, Andrea not 'Ay', in French you say 'eh', and smile at her. You can add 'Or even better you could say 'Pardon'. Just judge how far you can push this to make your point.

10.00 '*Alan*, will you settle down please?' Good use of hard sound of name to draw attention and then quiet question.

Very good work now whilst you are going round helping. I think you need to go to those three boys at the back especially as they are talking loudly and for the second time you have had to call to Alan. Good, you are there now and already the noise has dropped. The others use their noise (that group) as a kind of barometer.

10.02 Good general finishing noise now and you have stopped them very well insisting quite quietly that they sit, pens down and listen. Very well done. This was excellent.

You did this again excellently after the Routiere dispute conversation. You surprise me by talking quite a lot in English and using the English version of their names. The odd 'Ecoutez' would help begin to build their vocabulary until perhaps a fair amount of instruction could be in French.

10.07 Quick outline of what is going on in the cartoon. Could any of them be persuaded to read the bits aloud?

10.08 Very good use of 3 Ms e.g.   'Er!' Attention gaining noise.

'Alan'. Quiet naming.

'Who is talking about . . . in the picture?'

'Who is talking about . . . in the picture?'

Very good strategy you deflected his attention to the exercise by asking a question about the work after getting his attention – and all the others became quiet. *Very well done.*

I think I might have followed this up by going to the back where they are and settling them down to write something. They are now sitting back again and yarning quietly about something else. You need to try to cut down their off-target activity – they have got into bad habits. They need to build up an expectancy that after any instruction to write etc. you will follow it up and check.

10.12 Good, you are there now doing this, try to close the gap between the *setting and the checking* with this group. Two of them have continued working, it is the boy in the middle who continuously distracts them, viz Alan.

I wonder if, since there was a dispute in France over the lorries etc., you should spend a few minutes with each class you meet on the news? A few pictures of lorries, vans and scenes from the newspapers and Sunday supplements might provoke some discussions in French at the level of their vocabulary/grammar. It might encourage a few to keep a folder of what goes on. Enrichment activity?

Much more confident approach to all the work. Class control strategies are developing well. Good preparation evident. Now concentrate on smiling as non-verbal feedback and they will become more responsive and relaxed about their attempts.

I might,   a) put the key words on the board and get them to guess/hypothesise the meaning

b) establish general concept of what the tape is about

Good, you are waiting for quiet – got it again.

Do you think some or all of your simple questions should be in French? Is there a policy on language and/ or comprehension?

10.17 'Read through quietly please'.

About 50 per cent of the pupils were not reading it through.

10.20 Writing vocabulary in vocabulary books. They are very responsive to you when you say, 'Listen please', they do – it takes a little time. You can afford to be more confident.

You have a very nice manner with them, one which does not put their backs up.

Work away at this.

Good use of long 'gaze' i.e. use of eye contact to gain attention.

Vocabulary work. I think I might put the French on the board and get them to guess? analyse the meaning? (PCI)

e.g. de bonne heure; douche; raser; -ment.

10.25 Good – you have dealt well with Jason e.g.

1. 'Jason!' – he ignores you.

2. 'Jason!' – he looks at you.

3. 'Jason turn round' – he moves round and looks at book.

Now whilst you dealt effectively with him you did not spend /waste time on him so the rest knew that your eye was upon them.

Good – use of gesture with Joanne, and then, 'Joanne turn *right* round' Must follow with the second look to check to see if she has.

I think I should get them to list the verbs for themselves first then check (PCI). Good, – 'Some people are being very rude and talking at the same time' – 'Shaun'. Long pause for looking round and ensuring they are quiet. Good. *Very well done.*

You lose it again on the questioning allowing the loudest to win.

Good, you ignored the loud cough (bark) noise – Anthony? Now he is attention seeking and banging the desk and turning round. He is very attention seeking, seems to have some personal problems. You could ask him a question and use it as a control device at times – gives him the attention he requires in the way *you* desire.

As the girl said, 'I can't be bothered to write the details'. They need to feel more motivated by being required to respond at a more adult level. It is a difficult balance to achieve but you are obviously making progress. We need to discuss this aspect further.

10.35 A little ragged in the activity change from finishing writing to sitting ready to go. Keep working at this.

Well done.

In Summary

3 Ms: You have made great strides in your ability to control the class and so you now have a good opportunity to teach them something.

Tactical Planning: This was good you phased the lesson well with activity changes just at the right moment. You timed this well.

CBG You engaged in a good amount of this and it helped motivate and interest them.

PCI I think that this is the aspect which you can now afford to concentrate on.

1. Your questioning reflects this well with both closed and open questions in appropriate amounts on introduction to the lesson but,

2. I think you could work to get more from them arising from the practical work both in verbal and written form. You could expect much more from them in this respect.

3. Begin to extend your work, for mixed ability teaching the more able need greater intellectual stimulation as we discussed.

First comments recorded by Mrs D after the first French lesson (November)

I was given a copy of the notes a day or two before this lesson. I thought they looked helpful and I tried them out next day on my 4th year. I did CBG I went round each one and if they had only scribbled half a sentence I took an interest in the idea and said something good about it. They were a bit surprised and looked at me strangely but they really did work hard. Their attitude was completely different. It was a really good lesson. I really enjoyed it. I was using CBG again today when I was going round individually, it really does work. By the time I got round they were all quiet and working except those last two. I shall practice monitoring and check back next time as well.

Mrs D's comments and reflections after the second visit (March)

In my first year of teaching it was with relief, but some trepidation that I accepted the challenge of being observed in a lesson; relief because I had reached the point where I was grateful for anyone who could point me in the right direction, and trepidation, because someone would actually see how difficult I was finding it to control and teach a class of often hostile adolescents.

A couple of days before the observation I saw some notes which explained about the 3Ms – so much of this was immediately applicable, and in the light of recent experience made a lot of sense.

The debriefing was painful in many ways – having one's weaknesses exposed always is – but it was also a welcome experience because I understood many things that I had not previously realised, or that I had realised but had not been able to express coherently or identify.

The fact that the various aspects of the lesson were talked about and discussed in such a constructive and professional way made me feel much more objective, not just about that lesson, but also all the lessons subsequent to it. I started to practise the various techniques suggested, and made a conscious effort to be less 'apologetic' in the classroom, in my instructions to the pupils, and in my general manner and bearing. The comments made about the lesson were always made in such a way that one could only be encouraged by them.

Time had passed between the first session and the second, and had inevitably made my task somewhat easier – the pupils knew me, and I them, I was no longer an unknown quantity, and therefore a threat to them. The second observation was easier than the first; I knew what to expect and was eager to learn more about how to teach effectively. I was not disappointed, the debriefing session revealed parts of my teaching, my manner and reactions to the pupils, that had improved, and, as before, identified those areas which I could greatly improve upon.

Again, the comments made were either about things which I had not realised at all, or about things that I had not completely sorted out for myself, e.g. how to react in different situations that arise in the classroom. There were also the valuable professional and personal aspects to the observation, not only ideas about how to improve the content and method of my teaching but also how to make all of that more effective e.g. by smiling or nodding at appropriate times, and generally how to relate better to the pupils.

The observations and debriefing sessions were not simply beneficial because of what happened on those days and the constructive and immensely practical nature of what was discussed, but also because they have put me in a frame of mind that is more objective and analytical – now I feel more able and better equipped, to stand back from a lesson and see just how much I am achieving through it, how much the pupils are actually learning and by what means or methods, and lastly how I can improve upon that.

Observation of the first debriefing session with Mrs D by the head of department

I was not, myself, present during the lesson, I was only able to attend the discussion session following.

It was apparent from the comments made that there were many positive indications of excellent preparation for the lesson done by Mrs D.

She had many of the natural attributes needed by a good classroom teacher and was learning rapidly to structure her lesson in such a way that allowed her to deal with a difficult class in an effective manner. A 'teacher's eye' was becoming evident.

Points to be careful about included:

1. Teaching over children's talking, mumbling and chatter must not happen.
2. 'Calling out' by children in response to questions must be dealt with effectively, immediately and consistently.
3. Getting quiet in a classroom must not involve the teacher 'pleading' it must be a direct request.
4. Worksheets provided a useful change of activity but careful monitoring is needed to ensure full use, by all the class, is made of them.
5. Getting a class to 'listen' *again* is very difficult – but was handled competently.

Apart from a general inclination to do too much work herself and not get the pupils to do it for themselves, the signs were very encouraging. Mrs D herself said she was beginning to gain confidence.

Comment: This was an unsolicited report of the feedback session and illustrates in several ways why Mrs D needed to be included in the project. She was certainly having difficulties but the feedback she was getting was of the 'points to correct' variety and so she did not know what to do to turn things round and was progressively sinking into despair and further difficulties.

Even so there is some attempt by the writer to begin with some positives before the list perhaps owing to the nature of the project.

One of the major difficulties in this form of classroom observation is to produce a running record which is positive but which does describe the problem areas. The second major problem is to read the running record and to put in the suggestions and critical points in a positive and acceptable way.

In a recent training session for appraiser heads of department it was difficult for many to find a positive or neutral way of expressing problem points and for a few to insert question and analysis because they simply praised everything somewhat indiscriminately.

Mr C.   **Science**

(3rd Year/Year 9) (12 pupils)

First Visit   **November**

Good, nice working attitude. Good use of quiet voice, it is keeping their noise down. One or two pupils on your right hand side seem to be getting more than their fair share of attention.

Good, you are looking at the two girls opposite for a response. One of them gives it to you but you have looked away. I think you could try distributing more of your questions to specific pupils – used as a means of control it is also effective.

The three girls opposite and the four boys are not joining in enough. Could try specifically asking them by name if you think they can respond and then work at getting the others to have the kindness to be quiet and listen whilst each of the others is talking – setting them slightly against each other to help you. They are tending to talk over you and each other, especially the boy with the loud voice to your right – the blonde one in particular.

They need to learn to have respect for each other's viewpoints and contributions – if they all talk at once only the loudest one has any chance of being heard. The boy opposite is responding quite well occasionally – you could support his responses more with a nod or smile or just saying 'good'.

Good. You have just done that and got a slight 'ripple' effect i.e. the boy next to him also responded well the next time round and the one the other side began to concentrate.

I think that one of the things which is most interesting is that when you change the pitch of your voice occasionally or when you harden the tone, you gain their attention. Your continued use of soft voice tends to lose their concentration. Practice variation.

The blonde haired girl has given up and is obviously dozing – seeking your attention. She tried several times earlier in the lesson to give you answers and suggestions. On the whole you accepted answers from other pupils and she gave up. Try to be more responsive in a small way by listening to her responses and saying 'Yes' and 'Good' or 'What do you think?' Initially the attention needs to be quite subtle otherwise she will react against and perhaps be silly, but she definitely is trying to work for you.

Tactics

For this particular group who seem to have such poor self images from their comments at the beginning i.e. 'We don't know any science.' 'we're no good at it' 'It's no use listening to us' etc., specific tactics can help them become more confident and less disorganised . . . (See lesson plan tactics – no time to note them.)

Their responses are disorganised, and immature, and if you are not selective in relation to those you are listening to you encourage more unwanted responses. i.e. you tend to respond to those who shout loudest first. You also give a reply or comment to every statement whether it is relevant to the task or not. Ignore some of the irrelevant asides and concentrate on the central issues.

Good, you hardened your voice and for a while they all concentrated. Thus it is still possible for you to bring them together to listen and work.

'If people will listen!' 'Julie!' 'You are the ones who said you wanted to go through it...' A pleading sound. This was not so effective in gaining attention, they responded better when you said: 'Listen! Look at Q 6, Julia.' Thus it is better and more effective to deliver a short reprimand or reminder than long ones pleading or nagging.

'David, can you just try and be quiet for a minute?... round your head...' Could not hear all this but constituted another desist response which was lengthy and negotiational, whereas short sharp instructions worked better. The 'round your head' bit seemed like an attempt to joke, best not to mix them.

Your relaxed style is good but it is acting against you – you pick up and respond to their asides when most often you should ignore them. I think you are also working too hard and doing *too much of the talking*. You seem to be doing almost all the talking and all the continuity lines as well. Your technique seems to be to catch them off target as well as CBG. Giving so much attention to their off target behaviours is making them engage in more and more off target attention seeking behaviour.

They need some help to learn to be less babyish. They are like 5 year olds with all their pointing and giggling and calling out. I think it would help them if you could decrease this. You seem by the way you respond to be not exactly encouraging it but at least maintaining the level. The effect in the end of all this is to inculcate them with the law of the jungle 'might is right' and he who shouts loudest gets all the attention and interest.

To go back to tactics

I think your plan to go over the paper for the first 10 minutes was a good one but in practice what happened was that it took 20 minutes till 12.15 pm.

I think that it might have increased the pace of this part of the lesson if you had allowed them to read out their answer or say what the correct one was, gradually working round the group, so that every pupil had a chance to respond. Whilst this is happening the other 'loud mouths' need to be told quite curtly to be quiet and listen to other people.

12.27 pm. 12 minutes looking at the pictures of the foetus, skin etc. and discussing them with considerable effort. I think you could have stood with the visual aids and ranged the pupils around a table with the table between you and them, they would have got a better view and you would be able to respond more formally to them. Sitting shoulder to shoulder with you encouraged their tendency to be over familiar... rather than just friendly and sociable. Their sexual innuendoes and blatant comments would then not so readily have reached you.

It is interesting that Vicki and the blonde haired boy both want to sit beside you. They actually want your support and approval but it might help you if you distance yourself from him in particular and from the group a little.

There have been some good patches but I do not think that you should have to fight against their noise all the time. It is very wearing for you and not helpful for them.

Tactical Planning

Your tactics:

11.55 – 12.15 Pupils listening, looking and answering about exam paper.

12.15 – 12.27 Pupils listening, looking and answering questions about picture.

12.27 – 12.35 Return to places and write something – maintaining their bodies.

e.g. *30 minutes mainly Q/A, 7 mins writing*

1. Could have speeded up the exam question section 11.55 – 12.05

   (Good – very good use of voice, clear instructions, '3 minutes to write about Body Maintenance' – Then you said . . . 'You are not helping, X' – negative aside led you into difficulty. Again negotiated rather more than you needed. Glad you kept firm and insisted he moved. All would be lost if you made a threat you did not carry out.)

2. Discussion of the pictures interested them, seating needed to be different as indicated. Discussion and pictures seemed to be less integrated with the task which followed.

3. Writing activity. This was a good idea and went quite well, I think the clues you gave them could have been points which you worked out with them on the board then they would have a structure to write to.

You are reverting to Q/A mode again, where you are doing all the work and taking all the flak.

Lesson balance could have been:

1. 11.55 – 12.05 Examination Q/A.

2. 12.05 – 12.15 Pictures + board work for structure Q/A.

3. 12.15 – 12.30 Personal report writing with you going round and helping.

4. 12.30 – 12.35 Read out own work.

(When they shout out at you, get them to repeat it quietly and don't let others talk over them. This is probably the key and needs to be slowly achieved.)

Good, now you are standing, not responding to any of their calling out and it is diminishing. I don't think they know what you mean or how to 'Look through the book'. They also need to know why they should look through it. They see it as a pointless exercise which is undemanding.

'Do you think I can have your attention now?' less effective than, 'Chris, I want your attention now.'

Immediately you have a pause get in and give them some short verbal explanations to get them interested, e.g. 'Look at page _ ' etc.

PCI

You could get them to survey the book and make a list of topics/units to be covered. They need more structure to help them do things, and opportunities for responding in legitimate ways.

e.g. 'looking through book' a little too open ended for them and seemed trivial. Try: 'Look through and list the main units'.

'This is a survey skill which is useful for getting a quick structure and overall knowledge'.

They need you to explain these things and show them HOW to do it first. Again it would give them a structure for learning and orientate their thoughts. It also offers them more obvious cognitive challenge.

In Summary

1. Try to discriminate more carefully among their responses and use CBG. Use it more evenly to all pupils.

2. Try to give them more structure for their responding and enable them to perceive the cognitive challenge.

3. Work on tactical lesson planning in relation to the pupil's task at each stage.

Mr C.   **Science (Making paper)**

(4th year/Year 10 pupils)

Second visit

11.50 Good, you settled them down well at the outsets – very well done. You moved David quietly and with no 'aggro'.

Good, you had an outline on the board to remind them of last time's work. Very good questioning going on now about this on short and long fibre. Good use of names quietly to control. Very good use of non-verbal gestures to control individuals. very good e.g. 'Let us go back to David's point'. Makes them feel confident and that they have something significant to contribute.

Good use of smiles in response to some of their responses, nice especially when you did not put down the girl who had written 'white paper'.

Good also when you accepted 'grass' mishearing when the boy said 'rice' – I thought that was an excellent sequence. They just began to take advantage after that because they had enjoyed that and you very cleverly immediately asked them to write it down.

I like immensely the courtesy with which you treat them. e.g. 'Shall we write that down, Sir?' 'Yes please, David'.

Whilst they are writing the outline from the board there is little noise, just the odd comment. Very good barometer of control. You are giving out the copy work sheets and so all are organised for the next bit.

Very good work all the way up to this point. In fact *excellent*. Good, now you are going round settling them as individuals are writing and commenting on their progress.

12.00 Very good sequence in this first 10 minutes, you have also kept a good distance from them when teaching the class group. This has given you more power and influence.

12.02 Now they are beginning to become a bit restless. Try to shorten the irrelevant bits of explanation e.g. about the different books. They now want an activity change and are all set up to start the experiment.

I think I would have let them get straight on, e.g. This would have tested their ability to follow instructions or recipes. This accounts for their restlessness. I think I would have wanted the challenge if I had been them – the scientific investigator approach. I might have resented being babied or read to at this point. I know some will proba-bly have problems in reading but their partner can help them out. I think that two learning styles might emerge:-

1. Those who will follow/check the instructions rigorously.

2. Those who will try to remember what you said and glance at the picture to remind them.

Very good idea to make notes on their scientific approach. This was obviously highly motivating. You could add, 'The task at the end is to see which pair can make the best paper to write on'.

I think that when one group is calling to another I might just turn and make eye contact to quieten them.

12.15 Nice busy working atmosphere. You could stand back a bit and look on now, let them get to it.

Good bit of positive verbal reinforcement to Chris(?). You could distribute a few more 'Goods' and 'yeses' around when questioning them, e.g. stand back as you did and nod, say 'yes' or 'good' very briefly as you direct the questioning. Good, you made eye contact with one of the pupils who raised his voice – it immediately stopped him. *Very Good*, try to do more of this to keep the working noise at a gentle level.

(I found it amusing when you said earlier 'squash the pulp first' that at least 3 boys immediately responded by banging the table like five year olds in Piaget's preoperational stage might).

Again a boy was loudly calling 'Graham', this time you ignored it and the noise level began to increase. Just try to remember the 3 Ms, *monitoring*.

12.20 Most of the groups have finished. What indeed are we going to do now? I think that I would now take away all the work sheets and ask them to write or draw their recipe with exact instructions. Then read out some to see if the stages have been missed or if their work is better than in the book. Good, you have set them to answer questions 5 and 6 and put away the apparatus. Are they going to stick the instructions in their books? If so my suggestion is unnecessary unless you want them to remember structure and sequence for later. Maybe a good idea sometimes as an alternative.

12.28 Most of them have settled down to writing. Two or three still pounding their cotton wool.

12.32 Answering qs 5 and 6 did seem a bit small a task for 12 minutes, most wrote one line on each.

I think that your decision to go over these answers resulted in the fact that some waited for this and wrote down what you said, the others did not seem to find this significantly challenging. I think I would have invented 3 more questions and given them 3 marks for each and gone round and marked them after setting the next exercise. Then I could have called in the marks at the end or taken them down later which would have concentrated their minds more on their own performance and accuracy levels.

I think you are doing well with the 3 Ms now.

You have structured the lesson tactically to obtain activity changes at the right moments.

The practical work is an interesting and useful activity. The only thing which I now have some reservations about is the cognitive challenge. You seem to be responding to them as though they were a younger class, expecting less from them than you might be able to get.

Extract from Mr C's reflections on the classroom observations

After the lessons – in the discussions after the lessons it emerged that these points needed a good deal of attention on my part:

i) Organisation   – planning use of board/books/apparatus

                  – time spent on each part of the lesson

                  – where I put myself

                  – where I put the kids

                  – class dynamics

                  – what the kids were doing and with whom.

ii) Control   – setting careful limits on kids behaviour

                  – not getting too familiar

                  – keeping interest up

                  – using question/answer sessions effectively

                  – different ways of getting kids to do what they need to do

                  – the use of goals to maintain steady work from the kids

iii) Behaviour modification

                  – the effect of ignoring behaviour

                  – the effect of positive reinforcement

                  – setting realistic goals

                  – using different methods of changing behaviour

Since the first discussion with D and A, when it was painfully obvious that these points needed attention, I have been doing just that, not only in lessons with the observed class, but others too. I think that these visits and discussions have been beneficial to me...

Evaluation of the 'Process Strategy' (Pre and post lesson observation) from Miss A, Design and Technology teacher. (Year 10 and Year 9)

My first visit from D.M. was in the summer term. The class to be visited had caused me some considerable problems with difficult noisy class disturbance, requiring a great deal of effort and struggle for control in all lessons. I agreed to the experiment, as I felt it would give me guidance, but more important the experience would help me sort out my teaching pattern and analyse the difficulties I was having.

Although nervous at the prospect of being monitored, as a Probationary teacher the days of tutors at the back of the class, rapidly scratching pen on paper, with raised eyebrows and knowing looks, had not been all that long ago so the situation would not be that unknown.

However what a different story it was, Diane appeared to blend into the background, although I was conscious of visitors, there was no atmosphere of tension and being watched, it was just a lesson as normal. Of course there was a slight feeling of nervousness, but mine was more due to the fact that I felt this was a difficult class. My result? I was strained, lacking in confidence and asking the impossible! My class as aforementioned were highly strung and noise had been the main problem. What I had failed to realise was it was noise related to work! Due to these problems, I stood at the front of the class, never smiling, unrelaxed and blasting rather frequently with an overpowering voice.

At the end of the lesson the debriefing was constructive and helpful. The lesson was written in depth and discussed in detail to each moment. It was amazing how you yourself can see where your high and low notes are and what can be done: 1) Concentrate on 3 Ms. 2) Learn to relax. 3) Try not to shout or rather control noise level. The second visit was in November, and by this time I had acquired a little more self confidence. I knew the pupils' names, etc. but was still a little unsure of how my teaching management would be.

The group was a third year Art class, I was going to attempt a lesson on face construction, a topic I had never attempted to teach before, and in fact had never drawn before, but I thought it would be a good topic to cover.

The group was of mixed ability as before, with some keen and enthusiastic pupils and a sprinkling of the highly strung. This time I was not at all nervous, but interested in the outcome. I had not consciously made any effort in changing my teaching, so what would be the outcome? The lesson went well, although the demonstration was rather long. The debriefing was interesting. I was slightly perturbed at my sense of humour brought into the class situation and probably curbed it more than usual. However I discovered that this can be accepted and a useful tool in the right situation. The analysis still showed the need to concentrate on the monitoring and maintenancing of the pupils, which I am still working on improving.

On the whole, I found the experience valuable. I found the information interesting and useful, and it helped me a great deal during the period of the first meeting and to the present time. Of course I still slip and 'screech' occasionally during lessons, or fail to respond to the 3/Ms but the experience has taught me to analyse these lessons and to recognise where these weaknesses lie.

The final comments on Miss A's lesson observation notes were

In Summary

A good lesson. Objectives well achieved. Good PCI, good CBG, some maintenancing.

Concentrate on: 1. Activity change *monitoring*

2. Maintenancing – individual support.

It was such a vast advance upon the first session you must have felt it too. Congratulations and keep up the good work.

Mrs N.   **An Example of a Pre- and Post-Intervention from a Primary School**

(7 year olds/Year 2) (Mixed class, 19 pupils)

This classroom observation was the result of a special request for help and advice from a teacher who knew of the work of the project. The first visit took place in the last week of November and could not be followed by another after a three week interval because of the Christmas preparations and the work schedule of the tutor. However it was agreed that a fortnight later on the same day and at the same time the researcher would return alone and video record the session again and give the debriefing. The tutor would then view the video and send notes and suggestions which might be helpful.

Mrs N. had been working with older pupils for several years until this point. Because there were a number of pupils with problems in the class she had found it difficult to get them to come and sit down on the mat to listen to the story or introductions to lessons although she really wanted to do this. She had been forced into the strategy of spreading the pupils around the large room and keeping them in their places but this was not an easy setting in which to teach and she wanted more intimate and informal sessions with the pupils close around her. The pupils however spent all their time on the mat annoying and interfering with each other and making a noise. The pupils were known to be drawn from a difficult local area with many deprivations.

As well as all this there was pressure from the school to improve the situation but it was felt that nothing constructive had been done to help with this. This was the context in which the following record was made. The researcher arrived before the class assembled and set up the video to take in a wide ranging view of the room and remained at the instrument to refocus if necessary. The register and so on were taken with the video present but not running so that the pupils would become used to the visitor and the recording.

Subject: History: Royal Family (Children all sitting at their desks)

9.29 Good, when I came in the children were listening very quietly. They were responding well to your questions. Good, you asked them by name to answer questions.

9.32 Their concentration is going and they are all talking to each other about what is going on. You have written a lot on the board; I wonder if they find this difficult as you switch your attention from them to it. As the board becomes fuller they may be finding it progressively more confusing, hence lack of attention.

9.33 Your first 'good' is followed by 'yes, well done'. This created a listening effect in the rest of the class. When one or two of them shout to each other, try asking the noisiest one a question. It helps them concentrate – can also just frown and ask someone who is quiet a question and explain why.

9.35 Sharpened your voice and said, 'Now , listen, I am going to give you some pictures to look at . . . ' Very good you ask Alan and Katy to fetch the pictures for their table. Good, you have enough for each table.

9.37 Having given them out you are moving round the tables. Have become stuck at the back talking to the girl who came in late (you dealt very kindly and well with her – well done) whilst boy at front table is calling, 'Look, look everyone!'. I think when you hear this you should look and frown and do one of the monitoring strategies. As you move quickly round each group try to settle them; start by keeping them talking only to their group. You are back at the front and have missed the two front groups. The children are now moving to the different groups to look at the other pictures and talk – their decision.

9.40 A number of them start to follow you, this is a good sign that they want to talk to you but not helpful in your organisation. They need some very gentle soothing and calming. I think this is one thing which you might like to work on.

9.41 Some of them are still looking interested but . . . 'Now class 7 will you go back to your places. Sarah put your chair leg down. Now I want somebody from each group to say which picture you have seen. A spokesman for each group . . .'

This is a good idea. I think you needed to give an inkling of this before they started looking at the pictures so that you could direct or focus their attention e.g. 'Look through your pictures and choose one. Then I am going to ask each one of you (as there are not too many of them) to tell us about one picture. They must do it without looking at the picture. (The rest of the children on the table might also have to guess which one they are talking about) This was a good try at language experience work.

9.46 Sharp voice, 'Now, put your pictures in a nice tidy pile on your table' Follow this up by saying such things as, 'Show me who's ready,' or 'Very good, Lisa's table are ready, look at them; so quiet and smart'. Give them models to follow.

Monitor gives out the books quite nicely – you could make sure he knows you are pleased with him. These children need a lot of support for good behaviour so they know what is acceptable.

Copying the notes from the board on the Royal Family will keep them quietish and it practises handwriting, what you need to consider is to what extent it 'engages their brains'. Why not follow the line you first started? Good, you use the copy writing quickly to stop the attention seeking behaviour.

Tactical lesson plan

Be brave! Try:

- Talking about the Royal Family with group (class)
- Looking at pictures individually
- Short 20 second talks on one picture of choice. Use a timer – they like this kind of challenge, each stand up and speak to the group. The very shyest need not be made to but allowed to when they become confident. Lots of praise and encouragement to the rest even if they do not complete the presentation and fill the time, praise for good ideas, funny talk, good vocabulary, fluent speech etc.
- Asking pupils to write down what they said about their picture and stick the picture in their books, e.g. they could pretend to be a TV broadcaster describing the snapshot to the viewers. If you do something like this next year you could in the meantime tape an extract from the radio and show how they conjure up the scene in words

for the audience. This type of work could be repeated with different ideas and the pictures can be passed round for them to decide if the description is a good one. They can also project what will happen next in the sequence.

(10.00 Children busy copying from the board, it certainly keeps them quiet)

• Those pupils who cannot write from inside their own heads can tell you what they want to say and you can write it for them, leaving key gaps so that they have to think to try to fill them in (e.g. study skill – deletion exercise).

10.04 Good, those who have finished copying are now filling in the family tree of the Royal Family. On questioning you will find that they fill it in by using the initial letter cues, not knowledge or understanding. e.g. Pr..... C...... unmistakable . They then look for these letters in the work they have copied and copy them from their history books onto the paper without necessarily understanding the construction and nature of the family tree. They are not necessarily using initial sounds to get the words either. It is a good idea but I think you are assuming too much prior knowledge – they mainly use an infill strategy without understanding. One or two of the more able ones might understand. Good, I noted you change to this because the children were restless and had to be given something to do.

• If you really wanted to check their understanding, as a game ask them to draw their own family (or the Royal Family) tree as a test. If they cannot do this then you need to consider how you would teach it. One way might be to start with your own family tree and show parents, siblings and children. Let them try and write theirs. One way which is easier than a family tree is the family circle e.g. this leaves out sibs but enables you to draw the tree from it and extend it to put in the relevant information.

  I know that you may need to be careful about their missing bits of tree but there are ways of getting round this – inventing an absentee in your own tree – saying that such things do not matter, just leave a space . . . or let pairs work on the task for one of them. or you could let them choose a family from East Enders etc. for a tree.

10.16 Clearing up. Why not have a lively one from each table tidy up rather than Lee, this will keep four or five of them occupied. Again, the 'show me who's ready' style will work. You did try a bit of it – 'Who's sitting up ready?' but you did not follow it up by saying, 'Good, look at . . .' 'Well done . . .' 'Perfect' etc. Try more praise for a task and on – target social behaviours to show them how you want them to behave. If you say 'don't' and 'stop' they do not know what to do next. You are very easily able to control them and also call them to attention, what you forget to do is to follow up and reinforce this, e.g. the monitoring and CBG.

Summary.

Try to introduce more CBG for social as well as task objectives. Remember to do monitoring from the 3 Ms. You are good on 'management' and 'maintenance'.

Try to introduce more P.C.I. and engage brain tasks.

You actually have a lot more control than you think you have, this will become apparent as you begin to follow the suggestions. Particularly the Tactical Lesson Plan plus cognitive engage brain strategies. I will send you a draft of some typical lesson plans based on a revision of today's session and the various ways in which it might be followed up.

Mrs N. Brief description of what was seen on the videotape two weeks later

The children are seen at their desks waiting silently. Mrs N asks them very quietly to come and join her. They are to sit quietly on the mat. They do so except one and he is asked very quietly to 'Come and sit down by me', he does so. The children wait expectantly all eyes on Mrs N and she begins the introduction to the lesson about Christmas cards and how they might explain the meaning of Christmas to someone who did not know about it, citing the example of a pupil from Korea of several years ago. Good control strategies were in use e.g. lots of CBG, calming gestures, questions asked instead of nagging, quiet naming, choosing one who is restless to do a task etc.

After the discussion the pupils are sent back to their places to do their writing. Key words are put on the board and Mrs N goes round helping individuals to get started. The lesson proceeds throughout in an orderly fashion. The pupils are very quiet and calm. They quickly became absorbed in their writing which they were going to read out later and were looking forward to the Christmas cards they were going to make.

The scene has been totally transformed. Mrs N's crisis in confidence is over. She is in full control and lessons are no longer a battle. The difficult children are still there but all of them are getting more attention and praise and so are working for this.

If pupils can feel they are learning this also contributes to their confidence and esteem and helps them concentrate on learning. More attention to the work enables them to progress. Mrs N kindly agrees for the videotapes to be used on the project training courses and books to help other teachers.

After the second video session the researcher interviewed Mrs N and the following was the result:

'How have things been since we visited you the first time?'

'I think there has been an improvement. I've relaxed and I feel much better. I needed to have someone from outside whose opinion I trust to tell me I was coping so I can believe it. I heard Diane lecture several years ago, and I've heard her speak since, so I really value the effort and the interest. I had a wonderful letter from her, full of marvellous ideas, which I will use. They will make some super lessons. I'm really grateful.'

In the record, as can be seen, time was spent on noting events as they happened in a factual way. Especially the difficult episodes and interventions and then suggesting positive strategies which might be used instead. In addition where the strategies used were effective these were detailed to show that Mrs N had all of them in her repertoire and when she used them systematically they worked. The good relationship she had with the pupils was emphasised, they wanted to work for her. If she could structure the learning experience in a tactical fashion she could get a better match to their needs. The result was she raised her praise, lowered her voice, engaged in tactical lesson planning and achieved the match. The pupils 'engaged brains' and together they created the busy hum of a learning environment.

Summary and Conclusions

These records have been selected from the development period of the Learning Difficulties Research Project (LDRP) Programme Four – The Evaluation and Enhancement of Teaching Performance and the subsequent research programme. This is to protect the teachers who have recently been observed from being identified. As can be inferred they are drawn from the period before the introduction of the National Curriculum. The records selected were from those in distinct difficulties or where some concerns had been raised. The improvements in each case were measurable after a period when there had been no improvement before the project interventions began. As can be seen it is difficult in field work to arrange for two observers, one of them a deputy head, to be at a school for a specific lesson and then repeat this with the same class a month or more later. In the main research study with the randomly assigned subjects this was only made possible by the recruitment of a research assistant.

These findings were also backed by studies with a range of satisfactory and good teachers in both primary and secondary schools with whom similar findings were obtained. There were improvements in general teaching performance in all of those who were not functioning at the highest level.

Those teachers who were already excellent found the process also extremely useful. First it affirmed in a constructive way that they were good teachers. It then explained to them why and how they were good which none of them seemed to know.

It gave them a language about teaching and a set of analytic skills which they could share with colleagues and so help in their development. It is this common language which seems to have been lacking over several decades.

Norma Hadfield and Nerys James, researchers with the programme, went on to undertake posts with advisory responsibility for appraisal and staff development and are still using the methods detailed here.

With the advent of renewed interest in performance appraisal and staff development in these last two years a new series of primary and secondary classroom observation appraisals have been undertaken for demonstration and retrieval purposes. The method does still work and in the same ways for the same reasons.

It was interesting to note in reviewing all the records that it is the Junior schools which are the most closed and not open to new initiatives and experiments such as this. Not one Junior School volunteered to join the project whereas many Infant and Nursery and Secondary Schools did. The method does work in Junior schools too of course . This was verified with students on ITT courses over a number of years.

Despite its effectiveness it is surprising that the method has not been more widely adopted. Some of the reasons for this perhaps lie in the criticism once made of it that it seemed to be too 'feminine' a method for many males to adopt. This presumably cuts out much secondary school use. The second reason was no doubt the problem of the investment of time. It takes at a minimum two hours for the observation and the feedback session, a review interview need only take about an hour, although the average has been found to be 30 minutes.

However the renewed interest in classroom observation generated by recent DfEE documents has meant that a wide range of schools have been given training in the use of the method and it has been accepted and adopted by male and female heads of both secondary and primary schools with good effects. The third reason is that it requires very intense concentration and rapid writing. It seems that in these days in particular, box ticking has been a preferred mode.

A fourth reason might have arisen from the excision of 'all that irrelevant theory' from courses of education under successive Governments which could have delivered us a cadre of anti-intellectuals in teaching. It is certainly true that many attending conferences demand that the school must receive a quantifiable return for the investment in terms of immediately usable materials. However there has been a significant upturn in interest in this method of classroom observation from a wide range of headteachers across the country and it is for them and their staffs that this book has been written.

Following on from this method of positive classroom observation it seems that the crucial elements needed to support this are an analysis of relevant theory and practice of learning and teaching. This is especially important in relation to the underpinning of the cognitive curriculum and PCI to support whole school development programmes.

In the next two chapters some consideration will be given to these topics under the headings of Effective Learning and Effective Teaching.

Chapter Four

Effective Learning

Introduction

The study of learning has had an intense and detailed history of theory and research especially during the 20th century. Yet it is only in the last two decades that the evidence from the various traditions and schools of psychology has been brought together to provide a more coherent account of what constitutes human learning, how it is acquired and what is needed to facilitate it. Despite this long history theories of learning took little account of what went on in classrooms and had little impact upon the practice of teachers (Ausubel and Robinson 1969; Eisner 1983; Desforges 1998).

School learning has been based much more upon custom and practice in association with the needs of mass education (Resnick 1987) rather than with the theory and practice of learning. Thus different traditions have grown which have not necessarily integrated theory and practice. Dichotomies in education, learning and teaching abound such as: progressive versus traditionalist teaching methods; formal versus informal methods; discovery learning versus directive teaching and so on. In the specific area of reading teaching a long-standing dichotomy was between meaning emphasis or 'look and say' versus code emphasis or phonics methods when what was required was a judicious mix of both at appropriate stages, plus other methods to support these basic strategies (Montgomery 1997a and b).

The theory and practice of learning and teaching have proved to be such complex areas that they have been difficult to integrate. In comparison, learning about a subject in order to prepare to teach it is relatively simple. Subject contents can be ordered, structured and defined for imparting to pupils as in the NC. The process by which we actually teach learners to learn it is much more complex. It hinges upon many intangibles and depends upon the complexities of social contexts, social control, motivation and human interaction in changing environments where there are no longer the same sanctions and overt controls as in the past. Jackson's surveys of classrooms (1968) showed that teachers took part in 200–300 exchanges every hour of their working day. Many of these were about the control of behaviour and events rather than about teaching interactions (Southgate-Booth 1986). Bloom

(1976) described it as teachers spending most of their time managing learners rather than managing learning. This was also noted in our case studies in classroom observation and is the reason for 3Ms and CBG being important parts of the sampling frame.

Learning is said to be any relatively permanent change in behaviour not due to drugs or fatigue (Hilgard and Bower 1981). This simple statement conceals how complex learning is. It is both a product, the memories, and the processes by which we commit things to memory. In contemporary studies of learning the most common approach is *schema theory and practice*. The schema is now used as the unit of analysis rather than simple stimuli and response connections. It is the mental representation of a person's organised experience and is specific to a setting or context. At the age of five years when children enter school they will have vast stores of schema representing all their experiences and knowledge up to that point. Learning in this context thus becomes a matter of growing or extending and modifying these schema.

To find if learning has taken place in schools it is traditional to use teacher assessments and attainment tests in reading and number. Now we also have national assessments called SATs (Standard Attainment Tasks) in mathematics, science and English at ages 7, 11 and 14 and of course public examinations such as GCSE's, GNVQ's and A levels. It was envisaged that all ten National Curriculum subjects would be assessed at each key stage but this burden of assessment proved too much and has been modified.

SATs and public examinations not only provide feedback for teachers to plan the curriculum, they also enable pupils, classes and schools to be compared. There are also hypothesised 'standards' against which these comparisons can be made. Standards are what pupils of a particular age and experience may be expected to attain. However, there are no absolutes or even research to show us what a distinct standard is, only historical and comparative profiles showing what some have achieved. What is not controlled are the methods by which these results have been obtained and what might have been obtained by other methods. In addition, what is set as a standard by comparison with other cultures and education systems is not necessarily what ought to be one.

Teachers need to assess pupils' work in an ongoing process so that they know how the work is going and whether it is of an appropriate standard so that it feeds back and feeds forward to both teachers and learners for the next part of the curriculum. What Savage and Desforges (1995) found, however, was that in busy classrooms teachers' capacity to assess work was limited and their assessments were often inadequate for work design.

Classroom observation shows that teachers move round the room monitoring pupils' work and spending time with difficult pupils or pupils with difficulties ignoring the rest. They have not done the systematic and detailed PCI so they do not have a clear grasp of what the pupils are achieving. Even when the books come in for marking the distinction between class and homework may not be clear and the marking may be cursory. The results of Bennett and Desforges (1984) can be seen often repeated throughout education. They found that 50 per cent of the work set to high achievers in primary school was too easy and 50 per cent of the work set to low achievers was too difficult. The problem solving tasks set often failed to achieve their desired result because the pupils were already familiar with the concepts and teachers failed to notice this.

When PCI is engaged in systematically during class time and is followed by detailed attention to marking and assessment of ongoing work these issues can be identified and this illustrates why PCI does work and belongs in the sampling frame.

Teachers themselves have been the subject of formal assessment over recent years through OFSTED inspections. These inspections which seek to determine the effectiveness of schools have, according to the NAHT (1999) survey, proved to be generally fairly conducted but because of the focus that they have on failure they failed to make any contribution to school improvement. It would be far more beneficial to have a system which focused upon strengths and motivated teachers to fulfil their professional duties rather than seeking to catch them out. To counteract such pressures schools do need to have their own supportive professional system of appraisal. We learn more from having our strengths identified and then know how to proceed. If our weaknesses are focused upon we only know what not to do not how to put things right.

Good examination results are used as a prime indicator in the evaluation of schools. However these do not necessarily mark successful learning or teaching. The intake of some schools is such that if they do little or nothing in the way of promoting learning the pupils will still achieve good results. It is for this reason that the notion of 'value added' has been introduced to try to determine which schools are making a difference. This will still, however, be defined by what tests can measure rather than what ought to be measured. It was more than fifteen years for example before the real value of the Headstart Programme became apparent (Hohmann *et al.* 1979). The differences did not show in annual tests of basic skills and curriculum attainments.

In the year when there was a prolonged teacher dispute and strike the pupils' national GCSE results in England and Wales continued an upward trend of improvement. Few people questioned whether the teachers were necessary or how the results had been achieved.

We need to question whether it really is reasonable to assess the success or otherwise of learning by a system of tests and examinations of school subject attainments. Indeed, should the results of these tests permit access to higher education and training in the absence of other considerations such as independence and autonomy in learning abilities, study capabilities, communication, creative and cognitive abilities? Entwistle (1998) found a predictive correlation of 0.38 (14.44 per cent) in pure sciences and 0.25 per cent (6.25 per cent) in social science between 'A' level and final degree results using regression analysis.

Personality was related to both study methods and degree performance. Motivation and study methods showed the highest correlation with degree performance. It was therefore concluded that variables that described behaviour and attitude within the academic curriculum context were likely to be better predictors of achievement. Could this also be true of pupils' performance in schools?

The achievements or results of school learning of our pupils is traditionally found to lag behind that of pupils in Germany and Japan and more recently behind that of other European and Far Eastern countries (Osborn 1997; Reynolds and Farrell 1996). These achievements are of course defined in terms of school curriculum subject content and skills. The researchers concluded that the 'successful' countries shared common characteristics. They valued education, which is shown in the greater respect for and status of the teacher. There was greater involvement and commitment from the pupils and the education and training system was not just for an elite. There was a greater stake in education and the workplace by the people and greater equality in literacy, skills and incomes in these countries than in the UK.

At face value this analysis seems to make sense. However it is unlikely that there is such a direct and transparent explanation for these differences for there are other contextual differences and traditions which might equally explain what is observed. In Germany for example there appears to be highly coercive system of didactics in operation which is punitively assessment driven and in the Far East the system of rote learning bodies of knowledge is much favoured. Content learning is the primary objective in these countries whereas in the UK the superordinate goal has been that pupils should be able to apply what they have learned to other situations and use the knowledge in some subjects to solve problems.

These differences did in fact emerge in the third TIMSS study (TIMSS 1997). The results of 19 countries were compared and showed that English pupils had done relatively well in written science tests at nine and thirteen. They were, however, below the international average in maths. In the TIMSS survey (1997) it was found that English pupils had done much better in applied maths and science. English pupils were among the best in the world at thirteen in applying their maths and science to real world problems and were second overall only to Singapore. Edge and Stokes (1997) found that much of the poorer performance could be accounted for by the smaller amounts of time devoted by our pupils to their subjects and the fact that our pupils learn a broader curriculum within these subject disciplines. In other words our pupils were not subject to a 'fair test' in scientific terms and the results were not correctly reported by the media. Yet our education system may well be changed on the basis of the misreporting of these results. The fact that there is pressure to change must result either from an incomplete analysis of the situation or a deliberate attempt to promote a particular philosophy of education despite the facts.

Most recently the National Primary Headteachers Association (1999) have undertaken a survey and have had SATs scores remarked for Key Stage 2 in a large number of schools across the country. They have demonstrated that there have been systematic inaccuracies among the front line markers in English and science and maintain that these League Tables should not be published as they reflect markers' incompetencies not pupils' attainments.

High school achievement is not necessarily the mark of a good education according to Rutter (1991). His extensive researches showed that in the pathways from childhood to adult life, 'It is not high school achievement that makes the difference, rather, it is positive experiences of a kind that are pleasurable and rewarding and which help children develop a sense of self worth together with the confidence that they can cope with life's challenges and can control what happens to them' (p. 8).

Earlier studies with which he was associated found that when there was an overemphasis upon academic goals and a neglect of the personal needs more children seem disposed to fail and become 'problem children' in the schools' eyes (Rutter *et al.* 1979). These differences could not be attributed to the catchment areas that the schools served (Hargreaves 1984). The number of pupils regarded as having special needs on the basis of their difficult behaviour depended more upon the school they happened to attend rather than on the pupils themselves or their families (Galloway and Goodwin 1987).

> Those pupils whom their teachers regarded as more successful tended to be given greater attention than others. The teachers interacted with them more frequently, paid close attention to their activities and they subtly structured and directed their efforts in ways which were noticeably different from the relationships with pupils less favourably categorised' (Sharpe and Green 1975, p. 115).

This can still be observed in classrooms today.

Academic pressures, coercive and didactic environments and negative teacher attitudes and behaviours can seriously dampen the will and motivation to learn in schools (Mongon and Hart 1989). Intrinsic motivation is fostered by a consistent, positive, supportive climate and positive constructive feedback (Deci 1988). In controlled studies it was found to be destroyed under pressure to reach and maintain standards and that pupils lost autonomy and self regulation in response to extrinsic motivation (Ryan *et al.* 1985).

Despite these research findings we have those responsible for education insisting on moving schools in the opposite direction. They are demanding a content approach to learning, more formal teaching, even in the earliest years in school, (and now in preschool it is threatened), more assessment of curriculum content learned and more strong discipline and stricter class control. It is important therefore that teachers learn to review the nature of teaching and learning so that they can evaluate these demands and balance them and so regain some control over their professional life and its concerns.

Education

Education is the system, structure, and organisation of learning as well as the processes and contents of that learning. Our system of education is thus the way we organise our children's experiences for learning as well as the curriculum and pedagogical methods used to achieve it. Although there might be many ways of approaching the same learning outcomes by different systems and educational processes we have adopted a compulsory system of primary and secondary education organised on an age cohort basis. Summerhill, a private school based upon a different system, of elective attendance and learning by interest and commitment rather than age preparedness is fighting closure against the State monolith. Education at Home is now the main alternative to the 'system' private and public but it is mainly only available to children of parents with considerable capital. The fact that the UK in common with many other countries has adopted a particular system does not mean that it is the best one. It probably means that it is seen as economically efficient for mass education whilst something better is always available to look after a country's 'élite', usually the privileged. But any system should be able to be made flexible to enable best practice to be developed or be adopted.

However, as the century turns what is at issue in the UK is that this flexibility is not permitted and that teachers are beginning to feel deskilled as they receive more and more prescriptions and policies which they must follow. As will be seen, many of these prescriptions arise from tradition and fly in the face of what research shows to be a 'good education' and one fit for the people of a new millennium.

What then is an appropriate education for the new millennium? It has traditionally been held that education should be the transmission to the young of knowledge and skills considered worthwhile in a particular culture. For the young people education should enable them to develop their potential to the full. Potential however is indefinable and children in any case have an enormous capacity to learn which no amount of schooling might fulfil. In addition to this, in this century knowledge and skills have vastly increased so that even an expert cannot know all there is to know in one subject much less across several as was the case in earlier centuries. It is thus that education for the young has to be a matter of selection of appropriate and relevant content and it becomes crucial who is permitted to select this content. Teachers in LEAs, by common consent and custom and practice, used to select curriculum content backed by training institutions and in-service programmes. Now Government appointees from business, commerce, the media and university subject departments excluding education do so.

In the past it was enough for the few to learn Latin, Greek and Hebrew to enable them to enter the Church. In the Merchant Schools mathematics was taught so that this would help boys with trade and navigation. Now it is not enough for children to learn just to read and write, calculate simple sums and be able to quote extensively from the Bible and poetry, the curriculum of the elementary schools at the turn of the century. Today the school curriculum is mandatory and broad based. It purports to transmit in large measure what our society considers relevant bodies of knowledge and skills. It is presented as the National Curriculum sectioned into ten subjects. This division is despite the fact that when subjects are approached from interdisciplinary perspectives the pupils' understanding reaches higher levels and enables them to apply their knowledge better in different situations.

The core subjects are English, mathematics and science. Each subject has a vast field from which the school curriculum has been selected by a panel who determined what it was the young should know. Characteristically, each of the ten panels drew up a subject curriculum which could in each case have taken up all the children's time in school if they were truly to learn it. The panels did not contain experts in teacher nor child education and very few classroom teachers. Even though the NC has been trimmed (Dearing 1994) and there are elements which may be selected, the teachers are now beset by an over-riding concern to 'cover the syllabus'. This used to be a phenomenon only observed in the later stages of secondary schools but now it is rife throughout schooling.

Despite this concern to impart subjects, when we look back on our own education it is seldom the subject content that remains with us. Instead it is the skills we learnt, the people who taught us, our peers and the things we did that we tend to recall. We may remember some of those poems and items that we were obliged to learn by heart but this does not mean that rote learning should be the primary vehicle for learning. Even the Koreans are rejecting this their favoured system as it has been found to handicap their society and limit its workforce's creativity and problem solving.

Donald Kennedy, a college principal in the USA drafted the following letter in 1987 on behalf of 36 college principals which was sent to all the rest. It was a warning of a national emergency for schools and the country and ran as follows:

> It simply will not do for our schools to produce a small élite to power our scientific establishment and a larger cadre of workers with basic skills to do routine work. Millions of people around the world now have these same basic skills and are willing to work twice as long for as little as one tenth our basic wages. To maintain and enhance our quality of life, we must develop a leading edge economy based on workers who can think for a living... If skills are equal, in the long run wages will be so too. This means we have to educate a vast mass of people capable of thinking critically, creatively and imaginatively.

The implications of such worldwide economics were already recognised in the UK and the Department for Employment commissioned a number of research projects to find ways of changing education and training for work. It emphasised the need for employees at every level to be workers, learners and managers. 'Business success depends upon the ability of educators to develop learners' self management, transfer and "learn to learn" skills' (p. 1, Foreword by Ann Widdecombe, Parliamentary Under Secretary of State for the D E, 1993). The CBI had the same perspective when they drew up the document *Towards a Skills Revolution* (CBI 1990) in which it was stated: 'All education and training provision should be structured and designed to develop self reliance, flexibility and broad competence as well as specific skills' (p. 1).

This message also seems to have reached our competitors in the Pacific rim and Eastern Europe for at international conferences over the last three years specific references to such needs have been made and examples given of ways in which their educational practices are being transformed. In the UK the school ethos and method have regressed since the introduction of the NC to subject specific learning of a large body of content.

What we do know is that such an overfilled content curriculum is not the best vehicle for developing the thinking capabilities of the large majority of learners. Nor is it motivating the lower attainers (Montgomery 1998a). In case studies in schools the pressure to cover the syllabus is beginning to show in increased alienation of pupils and resultant behaviour difficulties (Blum 1999). To counteract this, more attention will need to be paid to curriculum theory and practice by education planners.

The problem was clearly illustrated by Paul (1990) who developed an analysis of knowledge, learning and literacy which distinguished between 19th century learning and 21st century learning. The former concerns a process of education which he refers to as Didactic Theory, our formal methods and the latter as Critical Theory. He describes a Didactic education as one in which the fundamental needs of the students are to be taught more or less *what* to think not how to think. In Critical Theory the students are taught *how* not what to think. In Chapter Five on teaching Paul's analysis will be presented in more detail.

Learning

We know that the nervous system at birth is 'wired' to respond to certain external stimuli through reflex responses and there are a few innate behaviours such as the ability to respond to human facial patterns such as smiles from a very early stage. These are called ethograms and need little input to establish them. The rest of what we know is learnt in contact with our environment. The famous 'Kitten carousel' experiment (Hebb 1958) showed that the kitten that walked round in the carousel was able to see normally whilst the one which was carried round and was not in contact with the outside world appeared on release to act as though blind.

Human babies have a long developmental period when it would appear that they are laying down the fundamental patterns and neural connections upon which all the rest will be built. According to Kelly (1955) we are born as investigative problem solving organisms and operate on our environment like scientific investigators. Babies push, pull and suck things in their immediate environment and observe the results. As their capabilities become more complex with both maturation and learning so their ability to investigate and react becomes more and more complex.

Thus by the time most children arrive at school having had a typical infancy they are already repositories of a vast base of knowledge and skills and hopefully are ready for the new challenges of school learning.

At this stage they are essentially 'good learners'. They are keen, motivated, curious and full of zest for life and learning. They have already internalised vast complexes of learning schemas. They will have schemas for eating and drinking and hopefully for putting on shoes and coats as well as holding pencils and drawing. They may have already developed schemas about reading and writing and certainly for talking and listening and playing with toys. Some schemas may already have built-in errors. Other schemas are about self concepts both positive or negative which have been built up over time and experience.

If we develop a poor self image and a set of failure to learn schemas in the first weeks in school this can have profound effects for the rest of school life. Most of those who develop learning failure in school may only return to education if they really have to in order to develop their career prospects rather than as an end in itself. It is significant that there is a large number of pupils leaving school who never wish to have contact with education again despite the current commitment of Government to lifelong learning.

What then is it that we learn? Gagne (1975) identified five major categories of learned capabilities. These were verbal information, intellectual skills, cognitive strategies, attitudes and motor skills.

Verbal information consists of facts, names, principles and generalisations. It consists of the organised bodies of information such as in the National Curriculum and the learning of meanings (concepts). *Concepts* are the building blocks of learning (Anderson 1980).

The interaction with the environment from the early years enables us to build up mental representations of the external world which are termed 'concepts'. Concrete concepts refer to objects and events in the real world which can be seen and touched such as tables and chairs. A category concept can be derived from these perceptual referents using various key attributes of the group. Thus chairs, tables and settees make up a group, category or class which is termed 'furniture'.

Event concepts or *schema* can also be linked together and give concepts such as to 'chair a meeting' implying a whole set of related procedural concrete activities associated with the chairing. A range of concrete concepts and schemas can be linked together to form a constellation or abstract concept such as 'love', 'learning', 'justice' and 'education'. Individuals contribute their own idiosyncratic patterns of experiences to concept formation. Sets of concepts and hierarchies of abstract concepts are referred to as *constructs*. Hierarchies of constructs are referred to as *attitudes* or conceptual hierarchies within which emotions and feelings may also be bound. Thus it is that learning is often intimately bound up with feelings of anxiety or pleasure and can provoke intense feelings. It is often only the emotional content that causes things to be remembered.

When engaging in thinking at the simpler levels new concepts may be being constructed. This is the process of *concept and schema development*. This is particularly evident when learning new subject contents and skills. Programmes overloaded with content may occupy all of student learning time in the area of concept development so that on entering employment there is little competency and capability to do the work for which they are employed. They have too few applications schema.

Concepts themselves are not simple units, they are little complexes of relationships or schemas. For example, the verbal label 'chair' connects to its various images of chairs we have known and sat on, its spelling and writing feel. It links to notions of backs and seats and legs and crossbars, nails and glue and so on. The more experiences of 'chair' we have the bigger and more complex its schema structure. This is why the notion of schema theory has developed, concepts are themselves schematic representations. It has its origins in the works of Piaget (1952) in constructivist theory and the processes of *accommodation* in which the schemata are modified and extended to encompass new learning.

Organised bodies of knowledge, learning as a noun, are believed to provide the vehicle for thought. In problem solving a person thinks of many things and searches the stores of schema knowledge, information and concepts. It is thus easy for curriculum planners to fill students' time with content learning for concept development and omit thinking about their needs to learn to use this knowledge. Thus they have insufficient *application schema* and cognitive processes to make any sense of what they have learned or use it in real world problem solving.

Learning as a verb can be thought of as the process or processes of schema modification. Norman (1977) described three processes of schema modification as follows: 'accretion', 'tuning' and 'restructuring'. During learning there is the interaction of experience with the already stored schema.

Accretion according to Norman is the acquisition of new responses. The child may know the names of a number of fruits and recognise they can and have been eaten. In acquiring the name of a new one such as strawberry s/he may also acquire the category concept 'fruit' which puts all of them into a new and even more complex relationship.

Tuning is the process by which the use of a schema such as writing, problem solving, word processing, eating or riding a bicycle becomes more routine or automatic. The routine is run more efficiently and there may be short cuts found all of which free up the attention to learn new things. In tuning no new input is involved.

Restructuring involves the creation of new insights. We may give the thinking time and thus reorganise our knowledge or see it in a new and different way. All three of these processes of schema modification may and frequently do occur together during learning. However, this change in the schema really only occurs satisfactorily if we are engaged in '*deep*' learning and nothing much at all will happen unless the pupils actually *attend* to what is to be learned. Over the years in schools pupils frequently develop habits of inattention and non-attending so that at the outset of all parts of a lesson the pupils attention must be captured and maintained.

First there must come the teachers' attention gaining tactics as in the 3Ms, closely followed by interest, novelty, activity, personal involvement and whenever possible an open-ended problem to solve. Teachers can get into the habit of repeating everything three times before they expect pupils to listen. This sort of cycle needs to be broken. Pupils need to see the consequences of listening and not listening and this can be done by engaging in the occasional 'warm up' exercise to practice listening skills (Rawlings 1996).

Using the same format and procedures for lessons can give rise to habituation so that pupils' attention flags and they only begin to listen when the appropriate cues occur such as, 'Now this is what you are going to do.' They then 'do' but as they missed the explanation leading in to it their efforts may be of a trial and error nature and what they learn, if anything, is disconnected and remains unconnected with previous learning.

Deep and surface learning

This notion of learning was first developed by Marton and Saljo (1976). It seems to be a more easily understandable version of Piaget's (1952) accommodation and assimilation. In accommodation, new learning is incorporated into the old by modifying and adapting the existing schemata (now frequently referred to as 'Schema') to take account of the new information. In assimilation, the new may be adapted to fit in with the old learning or may be held in a sort of limbo capsule without being integrated. In accommodating we integrate the information into our existing concepts and schemas and in the process fully understand it, or understand it in our own particular fashion. This is also characteristic of deep learning and means we can use the knowledge in a variety of ways and different applications and we can use it to construct new knowledge. Surface learning remains essentially superficial, probably repeatable but not capable of transformation or enlightening. It tends to be the sort of learning without understanding which arises from rote or parrot learning. It may be the only level of knowledge achieved in revision sessions where strategies have concentrated too much on memorising as opposed to understanding.

According to Gibbs (1990), Biggs (1987) and Marton and Saljo (1976) there are a number of characteristics which result in superficial learning and these are:

- a heavy workload;
- relatively high class contact hours;
- an excessive amount of course material;
- a lack of opportunity to pursue subjects in depth;
- a lack of choice over subjects;
- a lack of choice over methods of study;
- a threatening and anxiety-provoking assessment system.

These as can be seen are typical of teacher education programmes and the National Curriculum in schools. If all these things lead to superficial learning of the school curriculum the consequences for teachers and learners are dire. The system is then set to favour the pupils who have very good memories and those who are more verbally skilled. This usually includes the more able and those pupils brought up in linguistically advantaged environments by the 'chattering classes'.

The oral language of pupils from other cultures and lower socioeconomic groups in this country is more distant from that of the school and so does not map easily onto its structures. These pupils' language is frequently abbreviated and content bound. For example a pupil looking at a series of stimulus pictures sees first a boy and girl playing football and then a broken window. The third picture shows an angry adult gesticulating at them. When asked to explain what the story is about the pupils with distant language usage might say: 'They broke it 'n 'es angry'. There is nothing wrong with the comprehension but the form does not help them with school work. It is too closely dependent on having the pictures present. Lack of practice in listening to and using extended oral language gives them little opportunity to understand the language schemas that teachers and textbooks use, discover and then implicitly make use of them in their writing.

If we can teach lower attainers what other pupils pick up from their ordinary listening and reading and apply them in their writing then this could be a significant support to them. A grammar of listening and writing schemas can then be taught to pupils (Montgomery 1998a).

Good writers and successful pupils in school learn about the internal organisation of texts spontaneously from reading; others do not. These others tend to be the slower learners, the learning disabled such as dyslexics and those with subtle language difficulties with verbal CATs scores being 15 points lower than non-verbal scores (Mellanby *et al.* 1996). Brown and Palinscar (1984) attributed these differences to a difference in learning style and Torgeson (1982) suggested that it was because they were inactive learners. The inactivity was attributed to a problem in *metacognition*.

The deficits in metacognition were a lack of awareness and use of organisational strategies. This lack of awareness prevented them from using the schemas for writing. Hence dyslexia teachers find that with very much older pupils they are still having to remind them to use the basic story schema – beginnings, middles and ends – whereas very much younger good readers will already have absorbed this.

It could be argued in the case of all these pupils with learning difficulties and lower attainments that they are so effortfully preoccupied with the mechanics of reading they fail to grasp the overview of the organisation of what they read. This then has implications for their writing and they are doubly handicapped for they are then struggling with the mechanics of spelling and handwriting as well as content so that they have little cognitive time and space for higher order aspects of processing.

Culturally different pupils frequently lack the standard text knowledge of the school. The closer the match of the language of the home to the formal language of the school then the closer will be the match to school texts making it easier for this group of pupils to acquire writing grammars.

Making these implicit understandings explicit or directly teaching pupils to use and respond to them can enable them to move from superficial to deeper learning for then they are not so dependent on rote memory but can use the schemas to aid both retention and recall. This is one aspect of teaching for metacognition and can make learning more efficient.

To foster a deep learning approach we need the reverse conditions from surface learning – relatively low class contact hours; an intrinsic interest in the subject; freedom in learning in content and method; scope for intellectual independence; experience of 'good' teaching. These conditions are easy to state but rather more complex to create, for example 'intrinsic motivation'. In this the pupils should want to learn what the teacher sets for them rather than what already interests them and this learning is self motivated. Creating the environment for making pupils want to learn is one of the key roles of the teacher and will be more fully explored in the next chapter. Regrettably pupils in our education system do not always come with an enormous desire to learn anything the teacher cares to teach whereas this is still the case in many developing countries. In these places class sizes may be 55 or more, there are few text books and the sessions are didactic, relying on extensive rote memorising. In Arab countries this form of education is highly valued.

Making explicit and teaching listening and writing schemas to pupils is one of a range of learning strategies which can be imparted to help all learners become more effective. Regrettably, learning strategies are often confused with memorisation strategies which tend to be far more tedious as they do not have power for generalisation nor the power of 'chunking' and relating information to existing frameworks.

Intellectual versus cognitive skills and schemas

Intellectual skills are about 'knowing that' and 'knowing how'. They include converting printed words into meaning, fractions into decimals; knowing about classes, groups and categories, the laws of genetics, how to form sentences, adverbs and adjectives and so on. Concepts are the substance of intellectual operations from which we derive rules and principles and higher order rules. The general aspects of these skills are tested in intelligence tests. Thus these tests have a major component of 'that which has been learned' or acquired in contact with a particular cultural and schooling environment.

Cognitive strategies are internally organised capabilities (Gagné 1975, p. 64) which the learner makes use of in guiding his or her attending, learning and remembering. These capabilities make possible the executive control processes that activate other learning processes. He thus distinguishes between cognitive skills and intellectual skills in that intellectual skills enable us to deal with the numbers, words and symbols of the world 'out there'. Cognitive strategies are directed to internal operations. The learner uses cognitive strategies in attending to what is being learned or read; in thinking about what has been learned we use cognitive strategies (Gagné 1975 p. 66).

Sophisticated thinking involves the manipulation of various levels of schema by what we call *cognitive processes*. These may involve searching through concepts and constructs in sequential order, ranging through hierarchies of concepts, for critical features, probing deeply into a construct, focusing on 'key' concepts with similar tags of reference, re-ordering and reconstructing to develop new constructs, scanning data and schemas, missing key attributes and using personal or idiosyncratic attributes. It may also include retrieving old, well-tried schemas and strategies to solve a new problem or using part of an old strategy to help in the process. On appropriate occasions analogies may be used to solve old problems in an entirely different context in an imaginative and new way. Broad reading and broadening experiences can facilitate creative modelling and analogous thinking but only where there is flexibility in thinking and time for reflection. Many processes occurring simultaneously, drawing on many conceptual hierarchies, is typical of this kind of multilogical thinking. An overfilled curriculum and pressure to cover the syllabus is thus a handicap to thinking and problem solving. This then damages the students' ability to gain competency and capability in real world problem solving.

Remembering

Some learning inputs have been found to be more effective than others in single presentations. For example in the *passive reception* mode we remember 10 per cent of what we read; 20 per cent of what we hear; 30 per cent of what we see; and 50 per cent of what we see and hear at the same time (AVA News 1985). This only of course applies in schools if the pupils are literate – can understand what they read with the same facility as what they understand when something is read to them, which is not always the case. However, the teacher's talk, direct instruction, supported by visual and other material is crucial for maximum learning possible before repetition is entered into. When pupils are *actively engaged* in constructing the message themselves then they of course remember much more. We remember 80 per cent of what we say and 90 per cent of what we say and do at the same time. Thus it is that teachers are often the ones who are learning the most and feeling the most satisfied. They also find it hard to give up this active role to facilitate the learning of their pupils. If they are not talking and explaining they think they are not teaching.

In undergraduate learning the amount remembered is cited in Race (1992) as follows: from the lecture 5 per cent; books 10 per cent; audio visual presentation 20 per cent; dramatic lecture with A-V presentation 30 per cent; discussing 50 per cent; explaining 75 per cent; teaching 90 per cent; assessing 95 per cent. This further reinforces the points already made about active and constructive learning and was supported in our studies with teacher education undergraduates (Montgomery 1993,1995 1998c). When we changed our programme to enable them to learn by the active methods which we were advocating that they use with the pupils (Cognitive process methods, see Chapter 5) their final exam grades rose exponentially whilst the tutor input was dramatically reduced. By the end of the programme the students had almost entirely taken over the regulation and conduct of their own learning. and had enjoyed the experience.

Intrinsic motivation as already indicated is fostered by a consistent, positive and supportive climate and positive constructive feedback. It is destroyed under pressure to reach and maintain standards. Pupils and their teachers lose autonomy and self regulation in response to extrinsic motivation – the 'carrot and stick' methods. In cognitive process pedagogies and PCI, positive and constructive feedback are essential input in maintaining motivation and keep it running intrinsically.

Real world learning and learning in classrooms

In any analysis of learning in school it is necessary to distinguish between 'real world learning' and that which takes place in classrooms. The former is normally self initiated, self regulated and the learner is actively engaged in solving problems posed by life situations. In the latter the learner is essentially passive and the learning is mediated verbally by the teacher. It is also mainly teacher directed and organised. It is not surprising therefore that real world learning tends to be intrinsically interesting and motivating and lasts lifelong whereas much of school learning is extrinsically motivated and temporary.

Educators concerned with effective learning in classrooms are thus not infrequently seeking to change the processes of school learning from passivity to activity and to cause it to be more regulated and directed by pupils so that they can become more motivated particularly intrinsically so. Because school learning is very much concerned with the transmission of knowledge stored in books and on disk in verbal and pictorial forms, real world scenarios are often difficult to construct from it in classrooms. In the real world the knowledge and skills we learn are essential and have to be put to use as soon as possible. An example of this might be the fast learning curve in knowledge, skills, vocabulary, stories, histories, and maritime geography that one needs to know and suddenly acquire when estuary sailing a boat for five hours. This is in contrast to what might be learned in the same time in a schoolroom. The closest we might get is in the virtual classroom or simulator but five hours of that would still need to be accompanied by real world experience. Desforges (1998) expresses this problem as follows:

> More fundamentally pupils are expected to learn to use and apply their knowledge and skills in situations outside schools, in their domestic and professional lives, for example. These different learning outcomes require very different learning processes which in turn would be promoted through different teaching processes as might be expected.' (p. 12)

Because knowledge has been traditionally stored in books teachers have resorted to presenting it in the form of abstracts and verbal summaries or illustrated lecturettes. These verbal transmission methods are supported by question and answer sessions to check on pupil recall followed by paper and pencil exercises to represent learner activity and help the material be assimilated. These techniques enable the material to be repeated in three different ways so that the majority of the pupils absorb it. Later they may be required to revise it and repeat it in written form in an exam. This is then the evidence used to award certificates for amount remembered and applications learned or derived. The better the pupils' memories, the more efficient the teacher analysis of questions and drill, the more efficient the revision strategies, the higher the grades obtained. This all applies of course as long as the pupil can spell adequately and can write quickly and legibly to get enough of the ingested material down and is motivated to learn in this way.

There have been a number of longterm research studies which have looked at how best children may be educated and the most effective ways in which they learn. One of the most important and well documented is the Perry Preschool Project now called the Highscope Project. David Weikart established it in 1968 as a Cognitively Orientated Preschool Curriculum in Ypsilanti, Michigan. It was a response to finding in 1962 that 50 per cent of pupils in one 'working class' school were retained in grade by the fourth grade while only 8 per cent in a 'middle class' school had been retained. The majority of so-called mentally retarded students, discipline cases and referrals to outside agencies were from the lower socioeconomic population, both black and southern white.

The purpose was to reduce alienation and juvenile delinquency by offering pre school education. However the theory and practice of early education and research on its effectiveness were not then available and so the team engaged with teachers, parents and pupils in a programme of continuous development (Hohmann *et al.* 1979).

The later studies compared the progress of former students at intervals in academic and social terms. Three types of preschool curriculum learning experiences were evaluated. It was found that those who had experienced a form of free play education based upon the 'cognitive curriculum', developed into well adjusted adults with positive attitudes to their education and lifelong learning. In this free play setting the adults encouraged the use of student language expression and thought. This was compared with children in the DISTAR method classrooms (Direct Instructional Systems in Teaching and Remediation – highly structured sequences of learning derived from task analytic approaches, Carnine and Engelmann 1982) and the traditional group who received the more formal teaching in teacher directed groups as found in many nursery and Reception classes today.

The pupils at the outset of the experiment were from disadvantaged backgrounds and the groups overall had low measured IQs. The typical student product of these other classrooms at 35 years was one with a career in social deviance, a dislike of what had been experienced at school and an aversion to education. However it was demonstrated (Weikart 1998) that only the cognitively orientated free play form of schooling protected them from their disadvantaging environments and enabled them to develop into well adjusted, stable and achieving adults. They also grew in cognitive capabilities, took on work responsibilities and engaged in further college training.

Similar results have just become available from an English study into nurture groups (Bennathan and Boxall 1998). The nurture groups were small classes set up in primary schools with about one dozen pupils, one teacher and three assistants in each during the 1970s and early 1980s. The pupils engaged in self-directed free play whilst the adults modelled and made explicit pro social behaviours in their own and the pupils' interactions. Head teachers in the London schools which set up these nurture groups were convinced that they had a remarkable effect. The majority of the pupils referred to the nurture groups because of their disordered behaviour were able to be reintegrated into the normal classroom after a year. The rest of the classes from which they were drawn were able to function properly again when the disturbed individuals had been removed.

The data showed that 20 years later 82 per cent of those children who had been in nurture groups had maintained their place in mainstream school and had not acquired a police record and resorted to crime. This was in contrast to only 29 per cent of children who had been selected for the nurture groups but had not been permitted to go because most of these special classes had been closed down with the demise of ILEA and the GLC and the prevailing views of those in command of the education service at the time, notably male and secondary orientated.

This is of course data on disadvantaged and disturbed children from disadvantaging environments. However Roberts (1986) reported similar findings about her studies of normal nursery and reception class children. The four year olds put into formal reception classrooms as 'rising fives' showed many distress behaviours in the formal work; they were frightened of the 'big' children (the five year olds!) and bullied by them. When asked what they had learned, they were preoccupied with things like knowing what was in the teacher's head, and 'you mustn't cry, or tell lies like Samantha'.

They presented a sad little spectacle when compared with their Norwegian peers who do not experience formal schooling until they are seven and who within two years quickly outperform our pupils who have been at school learning to read and write since five. Silva (1998) is currently engaged in a long-term international study of comparative preschool education which is already showing signs of the value of free play and the cognitively orientated curriculum.

If we can establish this special form of free play preschool education then reception classes too will need to become more flexible and permit greater autonomy for pupils as they demand greater independence of thought and action within the more formal framework. This then follows throughout the school. What has recently been proposed is that now the NC should reach down into Nursery schools and preschool education providing a foundation of basic skills, the reverse of what children need.

A senior teacher in a secondary school before the introduction of the NC in a disadvantaged inner city area, persuaded a team of teachers to work together with the whole Year 7 intake as mixed ability groups on interdisciplinary projects. This lasted the whole year and was based on a primary classroom model. The pupils were very comfortable with it and the staff saw big improvements in literacy and study skills, social and behavioural skills in comparison with previous years. The project was discontinued mainly because the staff receiving them in Year 8 complained that they were always asking questions and were unmanageable, moving about the rooms just as they pleased. A little autonomy too far! It is frequently found that pupils lose motivation as they go through year 7 (Alexander 1998; James 1984). They continually move from room to room and teacher to teacher hardly known by anyone unless they misbehave. It is not surprising that their interest declines as teachers fail to take an interest in them. This transfer year into secondary school is a crucial one as important as reception class and in both class sizes of 15 would be more appropriate to counteract the alienating effects of mass education.

Effective learning

The nature of learning and learners' needs of which teaching methods have to take account, based on De Corte's (1995) analysis of research in instructional psychology, is as follows:

- Fundamentally *learning is constructive*. This means that pupils are not passive recipients of information. In order to learn they have to participate in the construction of their own knowledge and skills. This he contrasts with the implicit view current in teaching practice that learning is the transmission and passive absorption of knowledge gained and institutionalised by past generations.
- *Learning is cumulative* and it is on the basis of what they already know that pupils construct new knowledge and derive new meanings and skills.
- *Learning is best when self organised*. This is related to the metacognitive nature of effective learning especially the managing and monitoring of learning activities – self regulation.
- *Learning is generally goal oriented* although a small amount of learning is incidental. An explicit awareness of and orientation towards a goal facilitates effective and meaningful learning especially when the learners can choose the goal and define their own objectives.
- *Learning is situated*. This means that learning essentially takes place in interaction with the social and cultural environment. It follows from this that learning which is collaborative is more effective because the interactions can induce and mobilise reflection and thus foster the development of metacognitive knowledge and skills.
- Finally, *learning is individually different*. Individual differences in ability, skills, needs, interests and learning style etc. mean that we each construct our learning of the same experience in different ways. Learning styles such as whether a deep approach or a surface approach (Marton and Saljo 1976) is adopted can mean very different learning outcomes.

When learning is collaborative many of the above principles are realised. Interaction and cooperation induce reflection and so foster the development of metacognitive skills and constructive learning.

Teaching methods which have bound into them an automatic recognition and fostering of the principles of human learning will be far more effective than didactics and will provide greater opportunities for differentiation at all levels of ability. These are methods of teaching for learning.

According to Jones (1998 p. 39) there is a wealth of evidence to indicate that participation for democracy in education and training is linked with enhanced learning and efficiency. She linked enhanced performance in schools to the development of democratic skills displayed in whole-class teaching. In the UK apparently we have hierarchical systems of organisations in business and schools. This acts against the exercise of the democratic skills seen in team building and teamwork. She lists broad team skills as discussion, communication, problem solving, decision-making, self and team development. Functional skills were defined as initiating, consulting, informing, presenting, supporting, requesting, seeking information and advice, receiving critical questioning and feedback, evaluating, revising, linking, suggesting, expressing, describing, clarifying, planning, inferring, delegating, producing, promoting etc.

She argues that the student centred approach to learning creates 'deep' enquiry based learning which is characterised by:

- life/work – ties theory to relevant practical examples;
- hands on – simulated/real practical activity;
- collaborative – coaching, mentoring role of teachers.

She identifies collaborative interpersonal skills which are essential for team work such as – listening, openness, non-abrasiveness, non-judgmental tolerance, genuineness, consistency, objective rationality, self reflection. The core of these are collaborative interpersonal attitudes of respect, trust, honesty, humility, fairness, justice, empathy, liking of people etc. Genuine teamwork is characterised by reciprocal or collaborative relationships (Jones p. 29). Without the core attitudes we cannot involve others as equals and engage in the broad skills. Other labels have been used for these core skills such as critical thinking skills, people skills and life skills.

> In males a lack of respect for others, arrogance and lack of humility, an inability to listen acts as a major factor in undermining performance in classrooms, democratic skills such as described are downgraded as 'soft' or feminine and further lack of respect (Jones 1996 p. 23).

Her argument is that traditional hierarchical teacher/learner, manager/employee relationships undermine democracy and are anti-learning, blocking it so that the focus is on individual gain at the expense of others. She criticises the general failure to tackle the authoritarian hierarchical relationships between teachers and pupils for preventing the move towards *student centred learning*. Small group work restricts communication and cooperation between individual pupils and the rest of the children, according to Jones, and encourages them to do their own thing. She favours the horseshoe and the circle setting of chairs and worktops. There are some significant points presented in this view and it would seem important that there should be a place in all classrooms for student centred learning experiences of the kind she outlines. She comes to this from an industrial training perspective and it is typical of management and business training programmes to engage in student centred learning.

The differences between this and school learning is that often in the training setting there is a problem to identify, data to collect and issues to resolve whereas in much of school learning there is a specified curriculum and no overt problems to resolve. This does not mean that we should not at times create these learning situations within the National Curriculum. It might even make a valuable experiment to turn over the curriculum learning to this method and find if at the end of a year groups differently learning have made the requisite progress. It would not work well, however, if the student centred learning had to fit into the lesson timetable of the ordinary school. Such learning does not suddenly end when the bell rings.

Rudduck (1995) summarises the ways in which we can make a significant difference to pupils' learning. She states that it is necessary to have respect for pupils as individuals; to be fair to them irrespective of gender, ethnicity, ability and class; to give them autonomy and responsibility; to offer intellectual challenge with learning presented as a dynamic and empowering activity; to provide social support for academic and emotional concerns; to ensure there is a lack of threat to self-esteem and that there is security in the physical and interpersonal setting of the school. How precisely can we do these things in a busy classroom?

Capability

After a successful launch of Education for Capability in 1978 little seemed to happen as a result in schools and thus attention was turned to higher education to try to get the movement for change underway by influencing the planners and leaders of the future.

'Education for Capability' believes that capability is best promoted and motivation enhanced if learners exercise responsibility, take initiatives, are creative, and cooperate within learning programmes. Real experience of these activities, and of exploring and accounting for the relevance of their learning to themselves and to the society of which they are part, can build learner's confidence: in their ability to take effective action; in their worth as individuals and members of groups, and in their capability to learn (Stephenson and Weil 1988). These will help develop abilities to:

- acquire and apply knowledge;
- communicate ideas and information;
- listen to and collaborate with others in mutually planned activities;
- set achievable and relevant goals;
- assess the effectiveness of their actions;
- be critical of and creative in their thinking and actions;
- see both success and failure as opportunities for learning;
- take account of their feelings and intuition;
- show respect and concern for others;
- reflect on their values.

It is possible to distinguish between general capabilities, knowledge and skills which are transferable across fields such as problem solving, social and communication skills and specific capabilities. Specific capabilities are those aspects of knowledge and skills which are specific to a discipline or a type of work. This might be how to plan a lesson for teaching knowledge of disease symptoms in medicine, how to prepare wood and make joints in carpentry and so on.

In school learning with the curriculum divided into separate subjects each teacher spends the time developing specific knowledge and skills only sometimes with reference to general capabilities. English and drama teachers often do work to promote some aspects of general capability. However, a review of the cognitive curriculum and its application in capability will show that this learning is very patchy and sometimes negligible. Schools are not yet equipping pupils for the world of work or for a future of non-work.

Hemispheral differences in learning and cognitive style

The different hemispheres of the brain are set up to engage in different forms of data processing. The sequential ordering processes are thought to be typical of the left or language orientated hemisphere. Imaginative, inductive and appositional thought processes (Gazzaniga 1967; Bogen and Bogen 1969) are found to be characteristic of right hemisphere activities. The most creative of our scientists and artists appear to have had great facility in the use of both hemispheres. Regrettably Western Education has been accused of only valuing and educating the left hemisphere linguistic functions (Ornstein 1982). This tends to permeate attitudes to all the subjects in the school curriculum e.g the so called 'academic' versus the 'non-academic subjects'.

Some tests of cognitive abilities by Gagné's definition consist mainly of tests of right and left hemisphere intellectual skills and some of only one hemisphere. Teachers of science, maths and technology frequently claim to be developing problem solving abilities but now it would appear that this may not be so, they are posing problems to be solved mainly using intellectual skills. Examples they give might be to plan a party menu for four people with £10 to spend, or design a bridge from straws and paper to carry the weight of a can of coke.

Cognitive style

Personal style describes the way in which a person habitually approaches or responds to the learning task. It has two aspects – *cognitive style* which reflects the way the person thinks and *learning strategies* – the processes used by the learner to respond to the learning task. Cognitive style according to Riding and Rayner (1998) appears to be present at birth or fixed soon after. They argue on the basis of a meta analysis of research that style has a physical basis and can control the way individuals respond to the events and ideas they experience.

They identified two orthogonally related dimensions of style. The *wholist-analytic* and the *verbal-imagery* dimensions. The former represents whether an individual tends to organise information into wholes or parts. The latter whether during thinking the individual tends to represent information verbally or in mental pictures. These styles also relate to preferences for attending to and analysing information in the preferred mode. Thus some subjects will say they cannot understand information in figures such as graphs as well as they might if the information was in words. This is after problems in dealing with graphs are controlled.

The *wholist-partist* style is often reflected in people's approaches to problem solving such as how to assemble a model from a kit, complete a jigsaw and so on. The Partist will lay out all the parts, read the instructions and follow them as in a recipe in the prescribed sequence. The Wholist (holist) will take out the parts and immediately begin the assembly without doing more than look at the picture. Only if this strategy begins to fail will the holist get out the instructions and begin to follow them. In these examples one can see the elements of the different hemispheral processing preferences.

Most people tend to approach such a task with a preference for one or other strategy but in the end may use a mixed method as appropriate. Anxiety, learning experiences and minimal cerebral dysfunction may make people adopt an extreme reliance on one or another style as a compensatory mechanism. On the whole we should be educating people to be able to select the most appropriate strategy and dimension to gain the particular learning outcome most efficiently. Flexibly switching styles between holistic and sequential processing styles and verbal and iconic imagery should be an important part of the learning process. It is this flexibility that highly creative individuals appear to enjoy.

Because of the importance of style preferences for some learners it is necessary for teachers to make sure they make their materials accessible to learners by supporting verbal input with visual and iconic representations and by allowing pupils some choice and determination of methods of learning and recording.

Transfer of learning

The results of the five DE projects were summarised by Blagg *et al.* (1993). One of the key issues arising was that of transfer. They found that all too often learning was highly specific and did not transfer to new circumstances and situations. The DfEE argues that the NC is a prescription for offering a broad and balanced curriculum for every child. However in application, in the way it is 'delivered' it does not result in the appropriate learning outcome of transferability. Thus it is that a broad and balanced curriculum does not necessarily lead to a broad and balanced education.

Transfer means to learn something in one context and be able to apply it to another. In expansion experiments in science the pupils lower a ball through a ring, then heat the ball and find it will not go through until it cools down again. Transfer questions are later posed such as why are there gaps in railway lines, why the lid is taken off a tin of beans before cooking and why telegraph wires are put up slackly in summer. Large numbers of pupils find it hard to transfer the principle of expansion to these simple examples. Even when they do solve one problem they may not solve the others or relate them to other similar problems they might meet in daily life.

Three models of transfer were identified by Blagg *et al.* as follows:

- The Bo-peep theory: this is that transfer will take care of itself. However, their research showed that this was not the case. Learners too often failed to deploy or adapt their intellectual resources in unfamiliar circumstances.
- The Lost Sheep theory: Transfer rarely occurs so most new problems are likely to require additional training.
- The Good Shepherd theory: Transfer does occur if it is shepherded, nurtured and mediated. Their researches showed that there were certain kinds of learning and teaching activities that are likely to foster the ability to transfer. In a wide range of industrial and training contexts they found the following were needed for transfer:

  - thinking and problem solving skills need to be made explicit;
  - holistic tasks should be used;
  - occupationally relevant simulations should be used;
  - attention needed to be given to the key aspects of training and delivery.

'Increasingly it is recognised that learning about and gaining control over one's thought processes is fundamental to improving the ability to learn and transfer.' (Blagg *et al.* 1993, p. 5)

Learning and transfer using problem solving techniques

In terms of school learning Blagg and Lewis's work as well as that of Swartz and Parks (1994) indicates that thinking and problem solving skills must be made explicit as well as situations set up so that they may be applied.

The simulations need to be set in the subject context. Thus in history, the topic of the Battle of Hastings can provide a ground plan of the troops and the problem might be to decide how to use them to predict who should win. This can be followed by reading accounts of what was reported to have happened and follow up discussions. Comparisons can then be made with the same setting, the same problem and modern warfare weapons. Pupils should be allowed to share their ideas with each other in pairs before contributing to class discussion. There are several reasons for this:

- It allows them to identify what they know, for often we do not know what we think until we try and explain it to someone else.
- It enables them to work over the material, making sure they have covered or included all the points.
- It helps develop their communication skills for they will need to question each other and use extended language.

- They will each engage in a small element of teaching their peer which ensures learning takes place at deeper levels.
- They will learn to link what they are working on to their previous frameworks of understanding and this helps to make the learning secure.
- They will engage in problem solving and thinking not just waiting for other pupils to tell the rest the answers to the teacher's questions.
- They will practice some social and negotiation skills.

As can be seen the original problem is 'fuzzy' and its resolution also has to be part of the problem. At the end of any such session it is therefore important for the teacher to make explicit what were the best problem solving protocols in this case, using the pupils' examples. These can then become part of the repertoire too for later problem solving.

Surface learning strategies

These are usually defined as post-study activities. The pupil reads the material or listens to the teacher's exposition; then at a later date, even although practice exercises have been undertaken, a number of post-study activities are recommended to help reinforce the strength of the learning and aid later recall. Examples are: rereading, note taking, essay writing, diagramming, charting, concept mapping, mnemonics, and SQ3R (*Survey* the information, raise *Questions* about each part, then *Read, Recite and Review* – 3R). Each of these when first introduced can be interesting to the learner but as time wears on, interest wanes. Creating a mnemonic such as SQ3R or its counterpart 'Richard Of York Gained Battles In Vain' to remember the colours of the rainbow is a device known as clustering. The sentence is mildly more memorable than the separate colours, a semi-cognitive activity but the end product involves rote learning and of course is wrong as there are only six colours in the rainbow. (Early scientists were influenced by the so called mystical properties of the number seven and felt there must be seven colours adding indigo to fit in with this notion.)

The typical content of study skills programmes is illustrated by Pascal (1998) in his One Day courses for NASEN. The programme covers *Active Classroom Revision; Examination Skills* such as question analysis, answer planning and proof reading; *Specific Skills* – organisation of notes and study time, note taking, note making, essay planning; and finally *Learning Techniques*. These activities are directed to organising memory for better recall and are useful end strategies.

Most revision strategies involve rote learning activities after the event whereas if the initial learning task was involving and constructive, directed to some real purpose the learner wanted to achieve, then there would be little chance of forgetting. It would be better if we did not start from there. If we can make the original learning more effective detailed and extensive revision would not be required. Revision is required in inverse proportion to the effectiveness of the original learning.

Deep learning and transfer strategies

Learning strategies are often called study skills or even DARTs (Directed Activities Related to Texts). They may also be referred to as higher order reading or learning strategies. The important aspect is the process in which the learner is involved which causes him or her to engage with the material at deep cognitive levels so that what is already known is linked to the new or is changed by it. The learner in the process learns the relevance of the content and how it may be applied, perhaps in a modified form, to another situation. In 'the Information Age' information is so readily available that key words can summon it up from disk and no search skills are necessary. What is becoming increasingly important is to know how and where to find information when it is needed and then how to understand, manage, organise, use and communicate it effectively to meet specific purposes such as in decision making and problem solving.

Study skills are a form of self directed learning and are used whenever material is read or viewed in order to use in a communication.

In the Schools Council Project (1980) to promote literacy in the secondary school, reading was defined in two ways – *receptive reading*, a running read such as we use when reading a novel, and *reflective reading* a more complex activity in which we use study skills to glean information and ideas from the text. In fact it is equally possible to apply the same terms – *receptive or reflective viewing* of video and screen data or real life events. One of the major concerns of the project was that pupils did not distinguish between the two forms and tended to apply the same strategy, receptive reading, to all their study tasks.

In their Reading to Learn Project Thomas and Harri-Augstein (1975) found similar results. First year students on degree programmes who were ineffective readers engaged in several rapid read throughs of text. They were later unable to summarise what they had read or complete satisfactorily a short answer factual recall test on it. Successful readers engaged in reading through the text but rolling forwards and backwards in order to check up on points and they also paused for thinking and reflection time as well as to organise their notes. Partially effective readers engaged in slow runs through the text stopping to make notes as they did so. These students were only successful on the objective test and not the summary. It is typical of the strategy which students learn to collect information for an essay. They do not do a survey read to get an overview but just do a note taking run expecting by this means to understand what is written. The result is that the essay looks like a neatly written version of the original note taking exercise and is not organised to answer the question or written in a coherent form.

DARTs were devised in order to encourage pupils to slow down and engage with the text in more reflective reading. The activities illustrated different ways in which pupils could be obliged to give detailed attention to text and the results could be discussed with them to show the value of adopting different study strategies.

Reflection helps them gain metacognitive control over their mental processes of which they may initially be unaware but then can promote and control them better in subsequent activities. Watson (1996) showed the value of such reflection to her groups with moderate learning difficulties.

Different types and levels of study skills are needed for different tasks from simple note taking to writing a report or doing research. The first thing which should be done is to survey the information by scanning the title, subtitles, looking at the pictures, reading the summaries, flipping through each page, using the index to locate specific information. Most pupils are unaware of these skills and they need to be specifically taught. They may even feel they are cheating if they do not start at the beginning and read through.

In addition to scanning a text Anderson (1979) found that there were other activities going on. He found that nearly all his students were trying to answer three additional 'how' questions. These were:

1. How much do I already know about this topic and text? If anything is already known it can act as advance organisers (Ausubel *et al.* 1978) to make later acquisition more effective.
2. How interested am I in it?
3. How difficult or time consuming will it be for me to learn what I need to know from it?

If by scanning they could not answer all these questions they went on to read sections in more detail or the surveying would break down and they turned to another book or another activity. Each subject area will have its own deep learning techniques; some general ones used in study activities follow.

Some cognitive activities used in studying

In reading for information surveying, locational and reference skills may be used. In reading for the main idea or to understand the logic of a piece, interpretive skills are needed to understand structure and sequence, to find meaning and to understand tables, graphs, illustrations and ideas. If it is necessary to understand the overall structure of something then information has to be organised, summarised, outlined and perhaps labelled. Critical comprehension will involve the use of thinking strategies at literal, interpretive, critical and creative levels. In the process we may reflect on ideas presented, tap into the writer's organisational plan, relate new ideas to old using mental imagery. All of these activities are potentially at work together and as can be seen it is essentially a constructive learning activity. It is constructive in the sense of the learner or reader being actively engaged in making meaning.

Study skills and the curriculum

Even though pupils might know how to survey text there was no guarantee that they would use the skills and save themselves time (Neville and Pugh 1977). They needed systematic teaching in primary and then again in secondary school. There was also little correlation between reading ability and the ability to use effectively a range of study skills.

In the last ten years partly because of the information revolution and more particularly because of a concern to ensure that students at all levels really *learn how to learn* and can become self organised learners the conception of study skills has been significantly developed beyond a consideration of the narrow confines of information skills (Weinstein and Goetz *et al.* 1988).

Main points

The teacher organises the pupils' learning, setting them to learn how to learn by organising the material and the tasks in various ways. For example instead of taking a poem or a piece of prose and asking the pupils to read it silently in sections and then question them about the content trying to get at their factual and inferential comprehension the teacher might ask them to read it and then in pairs identify the *main point* or main idea. The strategy is *read – think – pair – share*. After their deliberations they then can present their main ideas to the rest of the class and they can be evaluated by all. Similarly the rest of the structure can be explored in like fashion. Pictures can be examined and ideas about them discussed using this procedure. Identifying main and subordinate ideas can lead on to producing flow charts and chronologies or time lines whatever method of recording and representing might be appropriate. The pairing and sharing ensures that all the pupils have an opportunity to express their own ideas in complete sentences not just one word responses to the teacher. There is also opportunity for pupils to question each other and where necessary engage in teaching the other how they arrived at their main ideas.

Concept mapping comparisons

Concept mapping is related to the notion of identifying main points. Now the mapping links them and also includes related ideas in the net attached to each main idea. The essence of the map is that it represents one's own ideas about a subject and by representing these on paper they can be inspected, compared with those of others and discussed. As new knowledge is accumulated it can be incorporated into the map and a new map may need to be drawn showing a complete change in the whole structure so that developments in learning can be seen.

It is a useful strategy for finding out what pupils bring to a topic and getting this recorded. Subjects might be: castles, settlements, rivers, weather, flowers, fish, food, tools – any subject in the school curriculum and the process can be begun with a 'brainstorm'.

After several teaching inputs, readings and so on the pupils can be asked to draw another concept map to show their current thinking. From this the teacher can see conceptual developments without having to read large volumes of notes which may or may not reflect knowledge or understanding. To help the pupils reflect upon what they know and have learned ten differences between the pre- and post-teaching maps may be asked for together with their reflections upon these. Again pairs work can help focus the attention as each discusses the work with the other and tries to explain it.

The rationale behind all this is that we so often do not know what we think until we try to explain it to someone else. Brainstorming and drawing the concept maps enables the pupils to bring to the forefront of the mind the previous knowledge and experience and inspect it to try to establish connecting links. Having heightened awareness in this way there is a better chance that the information in the new learning will be integrated into the past structures.

Concept completion

Cloze procedure is used in comprehension tests. Gaps are introduced every e.g. seven words and the pupil must complete the sentence. In concept completion the gaps are not at regular intervals but defined by the concepts the teacher wishes the pupils to focus upon.

In pairs the pupils read the text and discuss it to try to fill in the gaps to reconstruct the author's meaning. On completion they can be asked for reasons why they produced their particular words An example of a concept completion activity for pairs of pupils might be to read the poem by Stephen Spender and try to reconstruct the author's original intention:

Ultima Ratio Regum (first verse only here)
The guns spell money's ultimate reason
In letters of _____ on the Spring hillside.
But the boy lying _____ under the olive trees
Was too young and too _____
To have been notable to their important eye.
He was a better target for a _____ .

Assessment

If learners take on an assessment role then their learning of the material is likely to be as high as 95 per cent (Race 1992) and is able to reach deep levels so that it is available for transforming and using in various creative ways. ITT students were asked to evaluate one of the tests of reading set out in a workshop and to use the criteria set out in a lecture on 'What makes a good test'. In-service students on a distance programme were asked to write a short answer exam paper on Dyslexia worth 100 marks. It had to consist of True or False, multiple choice and sentence completion items. The main bulk of the questions had to be based upon three recent research papers and their own knowledge of the subject.

In general science and biology teaching pupils were asked to work in small groups to produce an end of year exam paper. They then had to draw up answer plans and assign marks to model answers to each question. Younger pupils did similar activities but in relation to two questions. They were all given previous exam papers to base their ideas upon and all their text and notebooks.

Editing and marking

Pupils' writing from previous years can be used as edit material. Good and poor examples can be used for comparison to discuss what makes quality writing. The subject can be a story or a narrative such as an account of the Wars of the Roses. The original can be used as a *scaffold* for producing a good account and pupils can learn from assigning grades based upon subject criteria. They can use these scaffolds to build their own accounts, for homework for example.

Older pupils working for public exams can be given the task in pairs to mark an exam essay using a criterion referenced grading system given. They then have to justify the mark they have given and write some positive points of guidance on how the writer could have improved the essay. Again content is learned incidentally in this process as well as exam technique.

Summarising

There are many summarising strategies which can be used as part of study skills to enhance learning. Most study material contains information of various kinds such as facts, opinions, methods, steps, ideas and so on. A quick assessment by the teacher can enable such questions to be asked as:

Identify the five (ten etc) *main points* in the chapter about e.g. the role of the church/monarchy/peasantry. Extra marks and special praise can always be given for finding more points. Write the points in *order of importance* from most to least important.

Ask the pupils to write a summary of a book/chapter they have just read in exactly 50 words, a *minisaga*. This really causes them to focus on the essentials of the text and to consider each word of their sentences carefully.

A book or a section of work can be recorded as a *summary*. Pupils often do not know how to summarise something and so the introductory techniques of stating how many main points there might be or how many words they are to use can be helpful training exercises. They have to stop copying out sections verbatim and think over the sections of the content. Discussing how they approached their task will give helpful clues on how to develop their techniques further. Many careers such as police investigation work, travel agency, travel guiding, advertising, teaching, research, journalism, medical practice and so on require summarising skills. The value of the technique should be emphasised.

Writing summaries for different *audiences* can help pupils understand the deeper structure of learning contents. For example, a section of historical information might be written up in the style of a modern day newspaper such as *The Sun*. Pupils can have a lot of fun with this as well as secure their knowledge of an historical topic.

They might be encouraged to put all their work together as an historical newspaper, or present it as a version of the 'Today' Programme on radio or a news broadcast on TV. The National Curriculum is still so full that much of the development work on such projects would be need to be done independently, outside lessons but the enthusiasm which can be generated is usually sufficient for this to happen. Writing the same information for different audiences can also help it to be learned in a pleasurable way rather than by rote. The audiences may be real, historical, or in different registers for different cultures and sub-cultures.

Critical reviews of topics will include a brief description of the key aspects with some appropriate evaluation. Examples of the structure of such reviews can be used as models for the pupils to follow. They have to gain more than a knowledge of the content in order to do any summarising task such as this. It is also important to identify the overall structure of the ideas and their relations to each other. Different review perspectives can also be adopted such as in relation to gender, ethnicity and class not only in English classes but also in technology, science, art, geography, mathematics and history.

Comparing and contrasting information is another approach to identifying main points and summarising the key issues in many subjects. Sometimes it can be helpful to *tabulate* such data. At other times the differences can be represented *diagrammatically.*

Organising, tabulating, classifying, ordering, diagramming, categorising are all strategies for reducing information into smaller manageable and more meaningful chunks. The process of doing so is also very useful for assisting learning at deeper levels to take place especially where the learners have done the work for themselves.

Time lines, lists, critical incident analyses, and *chronologies* are in their own ways summaries which can be useful processes to aid learning.

Teaching

In order to help pupils to learn it is sometimes helpful and interesting to provide them with learning materials and set them to design a short teaching session on some aspect. This can be prepared in small groups and then the mini teaching session can be given to the group. Some might be encouraged to give their presentation to the class. Nothing concentrates the mind more on getting down to the essentials of a subject than when it has to be taught to someone else, as every teacher knows. After assessment it is one of the best methods for ensuring something is learned. Teaching sessions need careful structuring so that the same material is not repeated and the class do not have to listen for long periods to topics which the teacher could present better. This is where group work is an important substage and all presentations must have a time limit. An alternative may be for the presentations on what they have learned to be offered at Parents' Evenings as a change from wall displays and neat books. Both parents and pupils gain an enormous amount from these teaching sessions.

The 'jigsaw classroom' approach is based on teams presenting different parts of a topic to the class as a whole.

Exhibitions and Posters also summarise achievements and can be accompanied by pupils giving mini presentations on their work and what they were trying to achieve. Even the youngest of pupils can do this.

Other types of summary might be to *make two overhead transparencies* to illustrate the main points of a topic. Only seven words to a line are permitted and only ten lines to be used so that it is large enough for all the class to see easily and compare summaries. They can learn from this that the best method is to put as little on the OHT and then the presenter uses these key points to elaborate upon.

On another occasion they might be asked to produce their summary notes as an A5 *four page leaflet* for visitors or as a *cartoon sequence*. Pin men drawing needs to be taught for those who would rather not exercise or exhibit their artistic repertoire. Personal computers can be used to support this if pupils prefer.

Sequencing

Pupils can read a research paper/story/chapter or piece of poetry or prose to identify its main and subordinate points, separate these out and then put them in an order which reflects the meaning of the text. They can then be asked to make this into a flow chart. Alternatively the teacher can take a *flow chart* designed by another class, empty it of its contents and give it to the new class to puzzle out what goes in the empty boxes. In each case a puzzle or problem is given for the pupils to resolve. In the process they will have to give the content their most detailed attention and they learn it very well without any apparent effort, enjoying themselves in the process especially if they are allowed to work in pairs and are not made to feel it is some kind of test.

Any process or procedure in a subject area can be made into a sequencing activity, for example there is a *set sequence or procedure* to lighting a Bunsen burner in science or following a routine or recipe in technology, geography and maths. Once the procedure has been demonstrated and practised it can be useful to say, instead of 'Now write down that procedure', 'Now look at this work sheet with your partner and you will see that someone does not know how to do it at all. Write down the number of the sentences showing the order in which they should be'. This means that the poorer writers are not handicapped and can focus on the real issues. Scissors can be provided if they need to cut the text up and move it about physically. If there is a fear that scissors would be too big a distraction then prepared cut slips can be given out in envelopes which adds to the little bit of mystery.

The same technique can be applied to paragraphs or short stories. What sometimes results is that the pupils may produce a better order than the original author. Very young pupils enjoy being given puzzle envelopes in which the lines of a nursery rhyme have been cut up and jumbled. In pairs they can then practise their reading skills whilst they try to reconstruct the nursery rhyme correctly. Self correction can be built into the task by having a picture on the reverse of the card which is only complete when all the lines are in the correct order – a self checking device.

Cooperative learning strategies

Dansereau (1988) gave student dyads scientific content to master. He broke the cooperative learning strategy down into six stages which he found facilitated co-operation and learning and labelled them MURDER i.e. establishing the positive Mood for studying; Understanding while studying, Recall – summarising what is read; Detecting errors and omissions; Elaborate to facilitate learning and Review. The *think – pair – share* collaborative strategy is a much less formal procedure than Dansereau's but none the less valuable for younger learners.

The main problem in classrooms at present is that the desks are often arranged in groups but pupils are engaged in individual work whilst at them. Their talk then tends to be social chat (Bennett 1986) not problem solving or collaborative. It is therefore the teachers' responsibility to set the task in such a way that the pupils do share their knowledge and that they do this in a purposeful manner which has an appropriate outcome. Teachers need to legitimise the talk which goes on in class-rooms by defining it as purposeful activity leading to more productive solutions and learning outcomes. It is these sorts of experiences that can prepare pupils for team-work in their careers.

Summary and Conclusions

An outline has been given of the nature of learning and current learning or schema theory. There are many different learning processes and each learner on entry to school has a vast repertoire of knowledge, skills and applications, schema or learn-ing skills at their disposal.

In order for learning to occur pupils must attend to what has to be learned and then by the processes of accretion, tuning and restructuring the schemata may be modified to encompass the new information and skills. A distinction was made between deep and surface learning linking them to particular teaching methods. Surface learning tends to be more superficial and cause little or no change in the schemata. The degree of surface learning is indicated by the amount of revision and reinforcement required to induce recall by the learner. The conditions for effective learning or deep learning were identified and linked to particular learning strategies. These are often referred to as higher order reading skills, higher order cognitive skills and Directed Activities Related to Texts (DARTs).

Motivation, particularly intrinsic motivation, is essential for effective learning to occur and suggestions were made as to what encourages and discourages this. It was suggested on the basis of research with learners that opportunities for self organisation in learning, planning and working in collaboration with peers, and problem orientated approaches can induce this motivation.

In the final section details of particular learning strategies which foster surface and deep levels of learning were exemplified.

Chapter Five

Effective Teaching

Introduction

In 1995 Jim Rose, the Director of Inspections at OFSTED, reported on teaching problems found at Key Stage 2 in the following manner. The 'below the line lessons', lessons of unsatisfactory standard, demonstrated factors that stood in the way of pupils making better progress and reaching higher standards. Of these, three factors were more prevalent in these lessons than in others. First, the pupils in some lessons received little direct teaching because the teachers were preoccupied with controlling too many group activities at once. In others teachers pursued a programme of individual work that was self defeating because teaching time available to each pupil was insufficient. In these cases the high teacher work rate was in direct contrast to pupil work rate. Similar circumstances and results were found in the teaching of reading by Southgate-Booth *et al.* 1982; Southgate-Booth 1986. Pupils might expect to receive only about 30 seconds actual reading time per day and even then the teacher's attention might be shared out on controlling pupil behaviour. She advocated that teachers should work less hard and engage in individual, group and whole class reading teaching, strategies which have been incorporated into the literacy hour.

The second problem in unsatisfactory teaching sessions found in the OFSTED reports was that the assessment of pupils' capabilities left much to be desired. The pupils rarely received the critical and supportive feedback and 'feed forward' or developmental advice that they needed and were left unsure of what they had to do to improve their work.

The third problem observed was that the teacher's subject knowledge was insufficient to match the developing abilities of their pupils. In a sense this is not surprising, especially in the Junior school stage, for, although there is some subject specialisation by teachers, many still have to spread their knowledge across more than a dozen subject areas with at least six of them being the content areas of the National Curriculum. The Chief Inspector for Schools Chris Woodhead (1998) annually presents his report and makes similar points arguing for more direct teaching or more formal methods as a result.

However, the results obtained may lead us to different conclusions and strategies for there may be many ways to improve teaching other than the modes advocated in the official reports. The causal connections made in them do not appear to be established in or supported by research.

The impact of these OFSTED inspections and reports over the years has been to drive teachers to rely more and more on verbal transmission modes which could be creating problems for a wide range of learners (Montgomery 1998a).

Already the demotivation of the grading system is being felt by teachers. A teacher who is generally working at a very good level on the days of the inspection may only be seen to teach for the second half of two sessions when the interactivity with the class is not in operation. The resultant grade will be good/satisfactory the same as that of someone who has performed at a marginally competent level who is not then a failure but known to be underperforming during the rest of the year.

Teachers are currently graded on a seven point scale but the feedback is in three categories – excellent/very good; good/satisfactory; fail. If the teacher is not seen engaging in interactive teaching the grade cannot be more than satisfactory even though the pupils demonstrate that they have learned and are following up the work in a highly motivated manner. The message is that 'real teaching' is interactive and direct and anything else is not of significance. Thus it is that when teachers organise group work because this is an appropriate method for enabling the pupils to learn a particular part of a topic, they do not feel they are teaching and do not value the pupils' learning in the same way as if they had done most of the talking themselves. This is despite the fact that we know that the more we as teachers talk the less the pupils tend to learn.

The overfilled curriculum also creates pressures on teachers to cover the syllabus by engaging in more and more direct teaching at the expense of the learners' learning. There is no time to take account of local phenomena such as floods and gales – or the death of the hamster – the syllabus must be covered.

This content curriculum is required to be assessed at frequent intervals. Such a system leads, according to the researches of Feller (1994), to a lowering not a raising of standards. This is in direct contrast to what we are continually told by the quasi governmental agencies (quangos).

The system of didactics also has to be bolstered by spoonfeeding of critical information as well as a regular régime of testing and reinforcement of the information. The tests act as external or extrinsic motivators to keep the pupils' attention on the tasks however irrelevant they might perceive them to be. Achieving good test results can become an end in itself.

In Asian cultures where memorising and rote learning have dominated there is now a move in many of them to seek to enable their learners to begin to think and problem solve and learn how to be more creative. English Education however is being measured by their content standards and is being driven towards their methods. Such rote forms of education are more in the mode of brain washing and make the learners vulnerable to the irrationalities of emotion and social pressures. This releases fundamentalism.

Teaching

But what is teaching? According to Curzon (1992) it is 'a system of activities intended to induce learning, comprising the deliberate and methodological creation and control of those conditions in which learning does occur' (p. 18). The critical points here are the activities inducing learning.

Despite what is continually presented as the accepted wisdom we do not teach subjects, we teach pupils *how to learn* subjects. Thus instead of the dichotomy continuously being proposed that we must get teachers to become better and better subject teachers and stop them, particularly primary teachers, from all that child minding, we should be focusing upon a *learner centred curriculum* and *teaching for learning.*

Let it be proposed that effective teaching is occurring where the majority, preferably all the pupils, learn most of what the teacher intended. Good teaching is occurring where the pupils want to learn and do not have to be made to. It is seen when the pupils want to continue and do continue with the study long after the lesson ends. They are to be seen animatedly talking about the subject during and long after the session ends. All the pupils complete their assignments and may do extra studies and investigations with enthusiasm and creativity. The classroom ethos is a hive of energy and activity presided over by a positive and supportive teacher playing many different roles. These roles may be teacher, follower, leader, facilitator, coordinator, manager and so on, not continuously didactic as we are frequently told they should be by those who do not teach and have never trained a teacher.

School effectiveness is seen to be in larger measure, a direct result of the learning and teaching taking place in classrooms (Reynolds 1992). The success or failure of the teacher-student relationship has been identified as a critical factor in setting standards of learning performance, as well as greatly influencing positive or negative individual behaviour (Riding and Rayner 1998 p. 167).

Work presented by the teacher which is too difficult or irrelevant may create learning difficulties and problem behaviour. Mortimore *et al.* (1988) also found that the pedagogy and curriculum process played a significant role in generating and preventing EBD. The markers they found associated with effective schools included – consistency among teachers; structured, well-planned lessons; intellectually challenging teaching; a work-centred focus in lessons; an easy dialogue between teachers and pupils; good record keeping (personal, social and academic); and a positive attitude.

The ethos of a classroom and a school, the quality of staff-student relationships, a structured and purposeful learning situation with adaptive flexibility within which individual contribution is encouraged and acknowledged are arguably prime factors in the successful classroom. Their absence will make for difficulties, troublesome behaviours and learning failure. Such conditions may also produce EBD or at the very least, reinforce such behaviours and result in learning failure (Riding and Rayner 1998).

For Eisner (1983) teaching is both a skill and an art. The teacher must perform with skill and grace; must exercise qualitative judgments in achieving qualitative ends regarding tempo, time and pace; this involves a tension between automaticity and inventiveness, and as a result many ends are emergent, not preconceived. However for others it has been considered as *either* a skill or an art. Depending upon in which frame the research is set the results obtained will be likely to confirm the hypothesis, thus demonstrating that teaching is both art and skill and more than each individual part.

Another method used by researchers to demonstrate effectiveness or otherwise of the teaching activity is to measure the amount of time that the pupil spends on task, the amount of time spent attending or looking at the task, and/or the amount of the material taught which has been learnt. What is seldom taken into account is what has also been learnt that was not directly or specifically taught. There is a tendency to concentrate only upon the curriculum content and skills when assessing learning as a result of teaching. Pupils may also be learning a wide range of social and communication skills, ethics and values, attitudes and intents.

Effective teaching practices for inclusive education are suitable for teaching all students according to Knight (1999). Effective teaching as outlined in the National Competency for Beginning Teaching (Commonwealth of Australia 1997) includes:

- being sensitive to students' academic and emotional needs;
- negotiating goals and expectations with students;
- making the intent of activities explicit and clear to students;
- selecting, adapting and sequencing learning content to suit individual students;
- using a wide range of teaching approaches and pacing to meet students needs;
- actively teaching strategies to students;
- setting appropriately challenging tasks;
- modifying materials and assessments to suit students needs;
- adapting instruction to appeal to different learning styles; and
- continually monitoring teaching programmes and student learning.

When we compare this list to the everyday practices in classrooms where didactics reign and the teacher controls all aspects of interaction and task work and students are all undertaking the same tasks in the same way from the standard text or work-sheet we can see that if this was to be promoted as effective teaching in the UK, there would be a mismatch between expectation and reality.

Explicit teaching for inclusion is also important. Students with special needs do not develop skills incidentally, these have to be explicitly taught so that they can later be applied in new situations. The teacher is working with the pupil within each students' 'zone of proximal development' – ZPD (Vygotsky 1978). Knight describes the process of working with students within their instructional level and ZPD as 'guided internality' (Knight 1994). It encourages students to be active learners in control of their own progress.

A guided internality teaching process is generated by:

- the teacher modelling and making thought processes overt;
- the teacher in collaboration with individual students setting realistic goals;
- promoting students' active role in the learning process in decision-making and risk taking;
- giving students sufficient practice to ensure the mastery of skills; and
- teaching strategies which match students cognitive abilities so that the task is first analysed to check that the students have the requisite skills (Knight *et al.* 1998 cited in Knight 1999, p. 6).

Teacher education

All these recommendations and attributes are far removed from class teaching procedures which may be generally observed. Not that it is the fault of the teachers. How is it possible for undergraduates trained to teach their subject to adapt what they do to teach pupils how to learn it? Even after many years of experience teachers may be using the same practices and repertoire of skills which they used in their first year of teaching and find it hard to adapt them to suit new situations. Changes of school can promote development in teaching but a career in the same school may not. The single training day and short course are not effective in promoting changes in practice (Montgomery 1998c, Barker 1998) Long courses of systematic in service training with systematic assignments in classrooms linking theory and practice can induce development and change in teacher thinking and practices (Montgomery 1993, 1994, 1998c)

The 'good' graduate with a PGCE has had a course of training to teach lasting nine months, two thirds of which is spent in a school where experience and training can range from 'sitting by Nellie', a weak form of the apprenticeship approach, to prescriptions from personal practice. The three months training, marginally longer than the time it takes to put a policeman on the beat, has to equip them for the most complex job anyone can ever do. They have to be taught the contents of and how to teach the National Curriculum, a curriculum remote from their degree programmes and which occupies most of the 18 hours per week contact time which they might be required to undertake. This is hard effort after their more relaxed low contact hour degree programmes where attendance was mainly optional.

Theory and practice of education which is used to underpin teaching programmes in most countries has been mainly expunged from the programmes in the UK. In the decade following the introduction of the NC theory was regarded as irrelevant to learning to teach and institutions were gradually obliged to remove it from their programmes, leaving method to be taught by the subject tutors. Thus it is that a decade of teachers have nothing rational in the way of theory and research upon which their teaching is based.

It has resulted in the expansion of the reflective practitioner movement particularly in the inservice field to attempt to compensate for this. In PGCE programmes students from a wide variety of institutions have complained that they are not taught to teach and that a single lecture on classroom management and a few on special needs are not sufficient (Hadfield 1990). Most NQTs in their own schools questioned by my postgraduate students had not heard of the Code of Practice (DfEE 1994) in 1995 and 1996 and the few that had did not actually know what it was about.

The primary PGCE students' task is even more broad ranging and complex than that of the secondary subject teacher and so it is not surprising that their skills are found wanting. It is of great credit to them that they make such huge efforts to catch up. In other countries a two year specialisation in teacher education after an undergraduate programme is considered essential. Even the four year BEd, now the BA QTS, has been converted to a subject degree programme on the PGCE model, interspersed with concurrent practice. It was found that teacher supply could be switched off and on more effectively (and economically) in this 'three plus one' training model.

Teachers who have no grounding in relevant professional theory become vulnerable to fashions and fads for they cannot bring an appropriate critique to what they are told. The proposed contractual obligation to engage in regular professional updating (DfEE 1999) seen in this light is essential but it is also proposed to control this centrally so we can expect more problems for both learners and teachers.

Currently we have seen the introduction of the National Literacy hour which specifies how and what teachers will teach and soon there will be the National Numeracy hour. The Literacy hour training and materials have been very helpful to many young teachers according to Moriarty (1999). It demonstrates that they have simply not been properly trained in the first place and that it is also a case of 'Back to the Future' since primary teachers taught 'Basic Skills' for two hours each morning before the National Curriculum was introduced ten years ago.

In the HMI document *Teaching Quality* (DES 1983) we were told, 'Teaching and educational quality go together. It is the teachers who have to shoulder most of the task of giving the children and young people in our schools the education which attempts to measure up to the nation's aspirations. They are performing that task with professionalism and skill. But still further progress is needed'. (para 93). Two years later we learn in *Better Schools* (DES 1985) that teachers are suddenly not up to scratch at all. 'The Government view, in the light of reports by HMI is that a significant number of teachers are performing at a standard below that required to achieve the objectives now proposed for our schools' (para 138). These quotations illustrate what can be done with the same data. The first presents the positive supportive view directing teachers towards self improvement. The second shows a complete change of attitude towards the negative and punitive. It is this climate which has pervaded ever since and in which teachers as learners themselves find it difficult to remain positive and, like pupils, find such a regime stressful and leading all too easily to bullying and scapegoating. What is needed is a supportive and constructive ethos to promote teacher development. We grow best from our strengths.

Mentoring in ITT

Since 1992 British legislation has given schools the prime responsibility for teacher training practice. Schools can now develop their own teacher training programmes with HE or independently and once they obtain accreditation they can carry them out on their own. There has always been a tension between schools supervising the teaching practice of ITT students and able to spend considerable time with them in the classroom and the HE institution sending out the supervisor for the weekly visit. Some supervision schedules might only permit funding of one or two visits per practice. Subject specialists were very often ill-equipped to supervise primary teaching practices or even their own subject areas in secondary schools if they were not engaged in research on teaching and learning in their subject areas.

The role of the mentor was seen as overcoming many of these perceived deficiencies. Mentoring is based on the idea of supplanting the imperious visitation by a transfer of responsibility to on-the-job, in house personnel in daily contact with children and the curriculum. It should offer the novice teacher full and free daily access to relevant, real and practical advice, criticism and guidance (Batteson 1998). However, the administrative burden upon teachers in schools is such that observation of teaching and mentoring duties frequently become lower order priorities.

Batteson (1998 p. 29) describes mentoring as the Faustian embrace:

'... within this shift from the ivory tower to the classroom there are inherent tensions. Pre-eminent amongst these is celebration of the role and power of 'real' teachers in reproducing the nation's teaching workforce whilst a fairly remorseless moral panic has clustered around convictions that schools and teachers have contributed to declining standards of literacy, numeracy and behaviour. It is odd that schools which politicians and the media allege, have contributed to a levelling or lowering of standards, can increasingly take on the task of training new, improved teachers (and can apparently avoid – to paraphrase the 1992 Three Wise Men report – recycling their inadequacies).

There have been a number of reviews of the partnerships arising in this new purchaser-provider framework and they also do not give cause for optimism that mentoring and the school-based training model have solved any of the former problems. They may in fact have introduced new ones. It was found by Edwards and Collison (1997) that:

- Schools were treating the training as 'projects' and had not developed an overall rationale to give it a status in everyday school life. Mentors felt unable to link the responsibility to pupils with their responsibility to students
- Teachers valued theory but said they could not provide it and would not risk discussions which went beyond task setting and performance. For secondary teachers, theory meant subject not educational theory.

- Teachers were providing model lessons but did not expose their practice to further scrutiny and discussion. They did not explore problematic events or engage in co-enquiry.
- The tutors acted primarily as trouble shooters and did not take part in any development activities.
- The mentors had not developed any identity as mentors.
- The relationship was one of 'colonisation' of the college by the school.

Furlong (1996) found that in 45 courses genuine partnerships were rare. They were very much constrained by the economics of the system in that the costs of teacher and tutor time militated against the scheme. It appears to be a less economically efficient system than the old one. Even the claims of the course leaders to follow the reflective practitioner model were seen as problematic for in practice the move from disciplinary theory was supporting a very superficial level of personal reflection.

Good teaching

The teaching techniques used by teachers carry ideological beliefs and are thus more than just classroom behaviours (Fenstermacher 1986; Jackson 1968). The dominant view of teaching is that effective teachers have a broad repertoire of skills and techniques which they use in skilful ways to meet the changing needs of classroom demands (Glaser 1977, Gagné *et al.* 1988). However these optimistic views are not borne out by the research.

Goodlad (1984) observed 1000 classrooms and Cuban (1984) 7000. They concluded that teaching was mostly a teacher-centred activity. The teachers lecture and the students practice. Student-centred teaching made up only a small per cent of the observations. The methods changed slightly with mathematics or social sciences contents (Stodolsky 1984). In maths there was more recitation, teacher control and skill organisation; in social studies the work was more varied and included group work, student reports and a variety of cognitive levels were identified.

Joyce and Weil (1986) identified four families or models as follows: information processing; personal; social and behavioural in which the theory guided the style. Joyce and Shower (1988) found that the more effective teachers:

- taught the class as a whole;
- gave an animated presentation;
- were task orientated;
- gave non-evaluative relaxed instruction;
- had high expectations of the more able and for them the pace was faster and created alertness; and
- related comfortably to pupils and so got fewer problems.

Scheerens (1992), looking at effective schools in an international analysis found that effective teachers:

- made clear what had to be learnt;
- managed learning units in a considered sequence;
- gave much exercise material for pupils which involved use of hunches and prompts;
- gave regular tests with immediate feedback.

The data from each of these investigations shows a bias towards the notion of the reproducibility of knowledge. It also indicates a conception and construction by the researchers of effective teaching as what effective teachers do. Whereas what teachers do, even successfully, is not necessarily what they should be doing. This is well illustrated by Paul (1990) in his summary of didactic versus critical thinking theory and its influence on the educative process. In the following sections three of his seventeen categories are summarised to illustrate these differences.

The Fundamental Needs of Students in didactic theory are to be told *what* to think. They are given details, definitions, explanations, rules, guidelines and reasons to learn. In critical theory the fundamental needs of students are to be shown *how* not what to think. They learn that it is important to focus on significant content and this is accompanied by live issues that stimulate them to gather, analyse and assess that content.

About the Nature of Knowledge the students learn in didactics that knowledge is independent of the thinking that generates, organises and applies it. Students are said to know when they can repeat what has been covered. They are given the products of someone else's thoughts. In Critical Theory classrooms students learn that all knowledge of content is generated, organised, applied and analysed, synthesised and assessed by thinking; that gaining knowledge is unintelligible without such thought. Students are given opportunities to puzzle their way through to knowledge and explore its justification as part of the process of learning.

In his *Model of the Educated Person* Paul identifies those from didactic education as literate people who are fundamentally repositories of content analogous to an encyclopaedia or a data bank, directly comparing situations in the world with facts in storage. This is a true believer. Texts, assessments, lectures, discussions are content-dense and detail-orientated.

An educated literate person from a critical theory background is fundamentally a repository of strategies, principles, concepts and insights embedded in processes of thought. Much of what is known is constructed as needed, not prefabricated. This person is a seeker after truth and a questioner rather than a believer. In such a system teachers model insightful consideration of questions and problems, and facilitate fruitful discussions.

It can be inferred that in the world of the 21st century and the Internet where all the data in the world is available on line there is very little sense in having an education which has as its main preoccupation the stuffing of childrens' heads with facts.

The era of 'What we want is facts' has passed. What we want is knowledge and understanding and the ability to apply what we know in appropriate situations. We also need to be able to construct new applications and solutions and apply them creatively. It is difficult to see how the current State system of education in the UK is going to meet the needs of the new millennium. Perhaps the process of development in education and learning has only been temporarily set back. However, within a few years more it will need to be set in motion again if the UK is to maintain its current position in the world much less improve it.

Teaching methods

Over time during the 20th century two different teaching and learning traditions were seen to evolve. Subject teachers, mainly those in secondary schools, adopted methods which involved the verbal transmission of material to be learned in the didactic subject-centred form using a watered-down method such as they themselves might have experienced in their university education. The primary school movement favoured a more child-centred learning organisation with much more practical and self directed learning activities by the pupils. This was rooted in theories of child development and education based upon the work of early childhood educators such as Friedrich Froebel, Lilian de Lissa, Margaret and Rachel MacMillan, Maria Montessori and so on. It did in fact have a substantial base in theory and practice whereas secondary education did not.

Secondary education grew by extension of education into the later years of adolescence and an extension of the number of curriculum subjects to fill this time. After the 1944 Education Act when the tripartite system was established the secondary modern schools tended to adopt a mixture of the two approaches to fit better the learning needs of their pupils as they saw them and the grammar schools offered more in the way of didactics. Of course within these general trends there were individual variations as teachers and schools experimented with both curriculum and method. They had more time for this up as far as Year 9 when pupils might begin formal study for the public examinations such as O and A levels.

In subsequent years a number of significant attempts were made to influence these traditional teaching methods and heated arguments reigned with the battle lines drawn between keeping up traditional standards and not succumbing to the progressive ideologies of the 'great unwashed'. These were the terms used to disparage the suggestions of a new generation of teachers and lecturers who might wear jeans and have long hair (especially of the men). In the 1960s and 1970s three new models of teaching and learning emerged. These were the Behaviour Control methods of Skinner (1957) underpinning task analysis and programmed learning, the Discovery Learning method of Bruner (1968) and the Cognitive Orientated curriculum of Weikart (1967) which did not emerge in the UK until much later. In the UK we had the Logical Constructive approach proposed by the philosopher Hirst (1968). His papers and lectures set me thinking and working on a psychological model by which to express his general principles and then to convert these into practical applications for my students in teacher education. This was the basis of the 'modern model of teaching' which follows in a later section. Skinner's ideas and principles underpinned the work on CBG and 3Ms especially in relation to positive behaviour management in schools.

Discovery learning

Bruner undertook a considerable amount of practical work in classrooms and established some principles which many constructivists have incorporated into their own themes and theories and practices. He coined the term 'Discovery Learning' and it is worth looking at some of the issues he raised in more detail.

According to Bruner (1968) the class teacher has the responsibility of ensuring the methods of teaching and learning are realistic in that they allow discovery activity. He states that purely expository teaching on its own is of little value for it does not help a student acquire the capacity to think creatively and critically.

Discovery learning is an inquiry training so that pupils gain the most fundamental understanding of the underlying principles that give structure to a subject. The pupils in discovering the meaning of the principles learn in the process the concepts and relationships. This can be compared with what Bloom (1956) describes in the process of Analysis in his Taxonomy of Educational Objectives. The fact that Bruner is suggesting that very young children can engage in this form of activity as well as teenagers should in their curriculum subjects, was bound to upset a lot of people, even though he may have been right! He found that when pupils worked in these ways there was:

- growth in intellectual potency;
- intrinsic motivation
- mastery of principles which enabled them to apply the learning;
- gains in memory as a result of the organisation of their own knowledge.

Bruner also insisted that pupils needed training in the plausibility of guesses. If teachers or parents suppress guessing they are inhibiting a process inherent in discovery or as Kelly (1955) might suggest, we would be preventing them being scientists and hypothesisers, our natural selves. Parents in particular tend to stop their children guessing seeing it as wrong and correcting them with the truth or facts.

Bruner maintained that if there was a de-emphasis on extrinsic motivators then the learners needed steady feedback on performance giving them accurate knowledge of progress. This can be seen as a fundamental reason for PCI: it feeds intrinsic motivation and that is why it is important to construct it in a positive format or use it to raise questions for the learner.

One of the important programmes which was developed by Bruner and his co-workers was the curriculum project 'Man A Course of Study' (MACOS) which became very popular in the 1980s with tutors in ITT and Humanities students. In the process he also introduced the modified notion of 'Guided Discovery Learning' to counteract the major criticism that no one lived long enough to rediscover for themselves the first principles of all the subjects they needed to study.

Taba (1963) identified four steps in discovery learning, which can also be used as a teaching/learning protocol as follows:

- the problem creates bafflement;
- the learner(s) explore the problem;
- the learners are prompted to generalise and use prior knowledge to understand a new problem or pattern;
- there need to be opportunities to apply the principles learned to new situations.

Another significant researcher and thinker in the teaching field at that time was Ausubel (1968). He criticised Bruner's notions of discovery learning, claiming that not all discovery was or could be made meaningful. In his view beginning learners learn more effectively by 'Reception'. This involved presenting the entire content of what is to be learned in its final form. The learning is meaningful if it allows reproduction with understanding at a future date. He rejected the idea that discovery learning engendered intrinsic motivation. Reception method is common throughout the education system. It places a great emphasis on the teacher's skill in structuring the subject content to be learned. The NC could be seen as an important contribution to underpinning reception teaching by teachers.

Ausubel coined the term '*Advance organisers*'. These consist of a short arrangement of the whole material introduced before the lesson begins. It might consist of a list of the main points or the main topics or side headings to be covered showing the structure of the lesson or lecture. It is popular at the moment to state the 'learning outcomes' of programmes and lessons. These organising principles form a Gestalt which both aids learning and later helps recall. The advance organisers for the classroom observation method are given as CBG, 3Ms and PCI.

Progressive differentiation is a system recommended by Ausubel for teaching the most generally relevant concepts first followed by second order concepts and so on. This process gives stable hooks to which the learning may be attached. He rejects the notion that the learner might have some autonomy in selecting what might be learned. For Ausubel it is the teacher's role to determine the subject of teaching.

It can be seen that there is room for both reception teaching and discovery learning as part of the teachers' repertoire of skills. At present pupils are suffering from too much reception method and not enough eclecticism.

Reflective teaching

The development of effective teachers is the primary goal of teacher education programmes. Smyth (1989) described the emergence of reflectivity as a conceptual thrust in teacher education. There is currently a general consensus that reflectivity leads to professional growth (Van Manen 1991) and according to Widman *et al.*

(1990) professional growth is unlikely without it. Reflective teaching is currently viewed as a paramount vehicle for enhancing the development of effective teachers (Allen and Caspergus 1997, p. 741). However, considering the minuscule amount of time initial teacher education students have to devote to reflection on their activities it is in-service education in England and Wales which has provided a better opportunity for it to be fostered.

Systematic reflection allows the teacher to be self directed. It facilitates the growth from novice to expert. It enables the teacher to view teaching from a more interpretative and critical perspective. Reflective teaching is the process of assessing the origins, purposes and consequences of one's teaching at a variety of levels. These Van Manen (1991) identified as follows:

Level one: technical rationality, efficient and effective application of pedagogical knowledge.
Level two: practical action learning concerned with explicating and clarifying the assumptions and predispositions underlying competing pedagogical goals and assessing the educational consequences of a teaching action.
Level three: critical reflection, moral and ethical criteria, such as whether important human needs and purposes are being met, are incorporated into the discourse about practical action.

Once again it has to be pointed out that teachers' practices are not always the best sources for reflective analysis. What a teacher may be doing may not be what they ought to be doing which can lead to problems for extrapolation and for mentoring and so on.

Text methods

Zahorik (1990) studying reading teaching and social studies teaching identified three different teaching approaches which were described as follows:

Text coverage: In the reading lesson there was an introduction of new vocabulary and pupils were briefly told the content of the story. The story was then read by the pupils, next they took turns in oral reading. There was then a discussion of the story focusing on the recall of events. The pupils then did word attack or comprehension practice in their work books or on worksheets.

Text extension: In this method there was text content teaching with an acquisition focus at a level mostly beyond the knowledge level and it was indirectly related learning activities that extended the textbook content as well as activities directly related to the text. The skills of story writing, drawing on listening to records, additional reading and genuine discussion were developed.

Text thinking: In this method the text content plus other content was used with a development of thinking focus at Bloom's (1956) analytic, synthetic and evaluation levels. These were used both directly and indirectly related to the learning activities. Thinking critically and creatively were encouraged and independent thinking was fostered and rewarded. Open questions were used and children were encouraged to give opinions and support them with evidence.

This last method is presumably another version of interactive teaching with more challenging questions favoured by Government inspectors.

A set of teaching methodologies was described by Curzon (1992) writing for teachers in Further Education. However there is less on method and more on organisation of settings and presentations. For example:

- the formal lesson – a teaching/learning sequence based on mastery of intellectual skills;
- the skills lesson – motor skills teaching to a required standard requiring demonstration and practice;
- the lecture- a one way communication;
- the discussion group – a small number of students discuss a problem set by the tutor;
- the seminar – a class member presents a thesis or topic for scrutiny;
- team teaching – a group of teachers collaborate and teach a topic together;
- tutoring – learners and tutor discuss problems presented by the tutor;
- Audi visual instruction – used as parts of an instructional sequence;
- programmed instruction – self administered program on the basis of stimulus response connections presented in small steps;
- computer based instruction.

(Curzon 1992, p. 237)

There are, of course, many variations on these themes, for instance there can be 'demonstration lessons' and seminars in which all the students are set to read a paper and then produce the main ideas, issues and sequences without reference to their notes. This is more challenging than having one or two students reading their prepared notes ending up as a very poor version of the formal lecture. Tutorials may be with individual student and tutor who discuss problems raised by either the pupil or the tutor; or the student may read an essay and discuss the points in it which the tutor may raise.

There has been a move in FE to introduce more methods based on 'good primary practice' (FEU 1987) so that there is more action learning. Gibbs (1990) introduced the concepts and techniques of experiential learning (Kolb 1984) and linked these with methods necessary for 'deep learning' encouraging them to be applied in both further and higher education (Gibbs 1995, 1996). These methods have much in common with the Education for Capability movement (Stephenson and Weil 1988, Yorke 1995).

Britzman (1991) in her study of teacher education programmes and how students learn in them showed that the foundations and sources of theory lie in teachers' practice. She claimed that 'educational theorising is situated within the lives of teachers, in values, beliefs and deep convictions enacted in practice, in the social context that encloses such practice, and in the social relationships that enliven the teaching and learning encounter' (p. 50). The field is the direct site of theorising and it is the irrelevancy of much academic theory to field settings which has led to so much hostility in practitioners.

However, irrelevant theory was not promulgated in all teacher education courses (Montgomery 1993, 1998b). There is a coherent theory and practice of teaching to be found now. During the previous 25 years it has been in development. Education tutors in that period were employed because of their teaching expertise to complement the subject expertise of other staff. Much of the theory and practice of teaching framework is to be found in constructivist and instructional psychology with which these practitioners were not usually conversant. They were seldom engaged in research in the problem areas of pupil's learning. Without research on learning and teaching and especially grounded research to test theory and practice many programmes lacked application and relevance.

A grounded theory is one that is inductively derived from the study of the phenomenon it represents. That is it is discovered, developed, and provisionally verified through systematic data collection and analysis. Practice and theory stand in reciprocal relationship with each other. One does not begin with a theory, then prove it. Rather, one begins with an area of study and what is relevant to that area is allowed to emerge (Strauss and Corbin 1990, p. 23).

In the final section of this chapter some examples of teaching methods promoting enhanced learning outcomes are given. These are based upon grounded research in classrooms across the country and in the international field.

Curriculum

The curriculum is all those planned experiences of the school (Neagley and Evans 1967) and consists of programmes of activities to enable pupils to attain, as far as possible, educational ends and objectives (Hirst 1966).

The National Curriculum purports to be broad and balanced. However this must be questioned as it is only one aspect of the curriculum of schools though of course an important one. It should consist of all the information and skills that the culture thinks important to transmit to its young people bound up in the ten subject syllabi.

Despite it being cut by 20 per cent by the efforts of Sir Ron Dearing (1994) teachers complain that there is still too much content to be able to teach classes of pupils effectively. Interactive teaching only allows them to 'cover' this content. In terms of providing an education for the nation's future the NC can be regarded as a narrow vehicle for transmitting the culture to the young. In 1998 after ten years it has been discovered that the English curriculum is not the best vehicle in primary schools for transmitting literacy. The literacy hour and soon to follow, the numeracy hour are being reintroduced.

There are at least seven different curricula which the pupil might be learning and aspects of all at once although these may not be being directly taught. These seven curricula are as follows:

- *The National Curriculum:* English, mathematics, science, RE, geography, technology and IT, history, music, art and PE.

- *The basic skills curriculum:* reading, spelling, handwriting and number skills. These underpin the other subjects and may be the main vehicles for reinforcement and learning.

- *The extra curriculum:* These are all the out of school activities such as orchestra and chess clubs which the school provides and also those extras which parents and the local community may provide.

- *The hidden curriculum:* This is the system of attitudes and values transmitted by the ways in which pupils, teachers and staff in general are treated and treat each other. Remedial tutorials in scruffy corridors and rooms with broken furniture transmit a hidden agenda.

Despite the kindliest intention of teachers, fear is the central debilitating characteristic of many pupils' school lives (Mongon and Hart 1989). They found that the effect of the hidden curriculum was to exert a destruction of dignity which was so massive and pervasive that few pupils subsequently recovered. The sad thing was that it was never intended by the teachers to be thus. Its effect is a legitimate criticism of the schooling process. We need to add to this that the majority of girls come through the process with a diminished sense of self-esteem and self-worth whilst boys overestimate their abilities and yet underachieve by comparison in co-ed institutions because they feel they must preserve a macho image and not be seen to try. All this means that the schooling process is less than facilitative. There is also widespread bullying and denigration of any pupils who have learning difficulties or who are ethnically different so that their sense of self-worth is even further diminished.

- *The personal and social skills curriculum:* After the NC had been designed it was then realised that several important areas of learning had been omitted. They were reintroduced as cross-curricular issues in the context of PSE. Other aspects such as equal opportunities and meeting the needs of the more able were bundled into cross-curricular themes. Civics is currently looking for a place as is education for parenthood.

- *The moral and ethical curriculum:* Having specified a Eurocentric Christian approach to RE despite the range of religions followed by pupils in schools there was little opportunity to consider moral development in general and wider ethical issues.

- *The cognitive curriculum:* The most neglected of all has been the cognitive curriculum. Childrens' cognitive development has been regarded as incidental to learning the school curriculum. Teachers in the past learned about cognitive development but seldom was this integrated with what they might teach and how they should foster cognitive development. It is not surprising therefore that two thirds of the population may not achieve the intellectual independence of abstract thinking. It was this that Donald Kennedy was concerned about in writing to all college principals in 1987. It is the same issue raised by Paul in 1990 and by many educational thinkers before and since. In the final section of this chapter an attempt will be made to tackle these issues. It will deal with the problems of differentiation, cognitive challenge and the nature of a cognitive curriculum.

Teaching the cognitive curriculum would mean that every teacher would be expected to be developing thinking skills and study skills in the medium of their own subject. This would offer the cognitive stretch that all pupils need. It enables them to work independently and alongside peers in a variety of different ways. It offers all pupils more flexibility in learning, giving them greater autonomy to learn more and to learn at deeper and more secure levels. This has been shown to be beneficial to all learners (Montgomery 1998a).

It was Bloom (1956) who first established what he called a taxonomy of educational objectives in the intellectual domain. These were cross-curricular and have begun to play an important part in the development and design of learning methods and teaching materials (Montgomery 1995).

Differentiation

This is the term reserved for individualising the curriculum task so that individual needs and difficulties are catered for. There are a number of strategies which may be used and they can be grouped under two main headings. There are those methods which are structural and which are generally applied across the school for grouping pupils for teaching. An example of this technique is streaming by ability, now commonly replaced by 'setting' or streaming for ability in a limited number of curriculum subjects such as English and mathematics. Acceleration involves moving highly able students up a year or two, known as 'grade skipping' in the USA. Although teachers worry about the social implications of this strategy individual pupils may cope remarkably well with this situation. The choice should be left to the pupil rather than the teachers – it is a case of pupils know best as they directly experience the advantages and disadvantages and know how with support to balance them.

Differentiation is concerned with the delivery of the curriculum and its assessment in practice. Figure 5.1 shows diagrammatically the two categories. In integral approaches it is the basic curriculum which is individualised and forms in the best examples a whole life-style approach. The structural approach deals mainly with groups and it is less certain in that system that the same basic curriculum is available to all.

Structural methods all involve accelerating or decelerating the learner through curriculum contents in various ways and include methods such as 'grade skipping'.

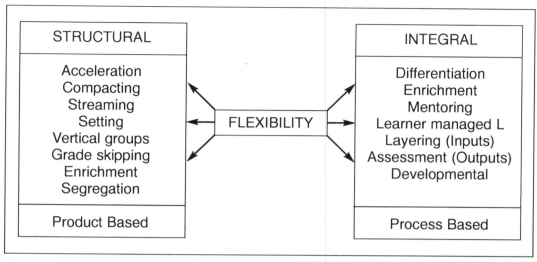

Figure 5.1 A model of methods of differentiation

Even some enrichment materials merely teach what the learner could expect to learn in another phase of education. For example, primary pupils might be given sections of the secondary school or even university curriculum in the periods allocated to 'enrichment'. This form of provision is 'bolted on' to the normal classroom activities whereas a more sophisticated form which is integral to the normal curriculum is what is required. Content enrichment is really not enrichment at all but content acceleration.

If differentiation is integral or built in to the mainstream work *all children* can have an opportunity to profit from the enrichment. Most structural approaches tend to be product or content based whereas integral approaches have to be concerned with process, in particular cognitive processes in which there is both content *and* method.

The integral approach has the enrichment or the differentiated work built into the daily curriculum and so is inclusive education. There is however a serious problem in that not all differentiation is inclusive. It actually segregates pupils from others giving them a separate and different curriculum usually in the same classroom.

Three Models of Integral Curriculum Differentiation

By inputs – the setting of different tasks at different levels of difficulty suitable for different levels of achievement (layering).

By outputs – the setting of common tasks that can be responded to in a positive way by all students (assessment).

Developmental – the setting of common tasks to which all students can contribute their own inputs and so progress from surface to deep learning and thus be enabled to achieve more advanced learning outcomes.

The first two offer little more than the formal or didactic methods of teaching to the middle with their inbuilt disadvantages of which teachers need to be aware. These two forms of differentiation are no more than a within-class selective education system.

The form of differentiation by which higher cognitive abilities and skills have been achieved (Montgomery 1990, 1996) has been termed *developmental differentiation* and it was cognitive process methods which enabled an inclusive education to be offered to all the class in a form which could be enriching for all.

It is termed developmental differentiation because pupils gain access to the curriculum at a level suited to their linguistic, cognitive and other developmental levels. Through their studies the activities enable them to progress towards higher levels of skills both in the cognitive and subject curriculum and in general developmental terms. Developmental differentiation is shown diagramatically in context in Figure 5.2.

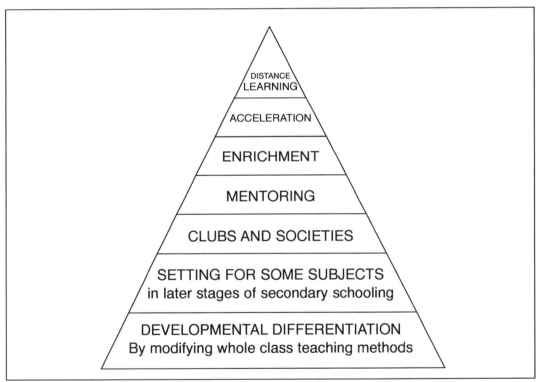

Figure 5.2 Diagram to illustrate the seven types of curriculum provision which should be on offer in every school

The basic plan should be that every teacher would use a range of teaching methods which offer developmental differentiation. This would mean a modest change at times in their teaching methods so that they taught both the National Curriculum but at the same time the Cognitive Curriculum.

Critical thinking theory as a background to cognitive process teaching methods

Critical thinking is the art of thinking about your thinking so as to make it more precise, accurate and relevant, consistent and fair (Paul 1990). This had been expressed as 'metacognition' by Flavell in 1979. He argued that thinking about how we are thinking and learning whilst we are doing so contributes in a major way to intelligence.

Teaching the cognitive curriculum would mean that every teacher would be expected to be developing thinking skills and study skills in the medium of their own subject. This would offer the cognitive stretch that all pupils need. It enables them to work independently and alongside peers in a variety of different ways. It offers more flexibility in learning giving them greater autonomy to learn more and to learn at deeper and more secure levels. This has also been shown to be beneficial to all learners. It is also possible, given the right sort of preparation to get five and six year olds to function in abstract thinking modes. This is not to deny Piaget's (1954) work on stages of intellectual development but to suggest that intellectual development can be promoted by encouraging more reflective teaching and learning.

Intellectual skills are about 'knowing that' and 'knowing how'. They include converting printed words into meaning, fractions into decimals, knowing about classes, properties, groups and categories, laws of e.g. genetics, how to form sentences and so on. Intellectual skills enable us to deal with the world 'out there'. These refer to the contents and skills of the subjects of the National Curriculum.

Cognitive skills are internally organised capabilities and are directed to internal processes such as thinking, planning, organising, problem solving, creativity, self regulation, reflecting upon and monitoring one's own learning. Their development is at present incidental to most school learning but needs to be made explicit and the subject of systematic development if we are to enhance the capabilities of our future work force for the challenges of the new millennium.

Research by Wang and Lindvall (1984) showed that self monitoring and self regulatory activities not only contributed to improved acquisition of subject content but also to improved generalisation and transfer of knowledge and skills. They also gave students a sense of personal agency, a feeling of being in control of their own learning. Self regulatory activities were defined by Brown *et al.* (1983) as including planning, predicting outcomes and scheduling time and resources. Monitoring included testing, revising and rescheduling with checking to evaluate outcomes using criteria developed by the individual and also those which were externally defined.

There was, however, a failure to develop higher order cognitive or thinking skills in schools and colleges according to Resnick (1989). Schools had historically been most conservative, uncritically passing down from generation to generation outmoded didactic, lecture and drill-based models of instruction. The result was that students, on the whole, did not learn how to work by, or think for themselves. They did not learn how to gather, analyse, synthesise and assess information. They did not learn to enter sympathetically into the thinking of others nor how to deal rationally with conflicting points of view. They did not learn to become critical readers, writers, speakers or listeners and so did not become literate in the proper sense of the word. They did not critically analyse their own experience and would find it difficult to explain the basis of their own beliefs and so did not gain much genuine knowledge. They therefore lacked the traits of mind of a genuinely educated person, such as, intellectual humility, courage, integrity, perseverance and faith in reason (Paul 1990).

Fortunately Paul identified a means of overcoming these problems which he called the application of Critical Theory. He emphasised the fact that normal individuals do not naturally think critically nor are they inspired by rationality. They do not engage in reflective thinking automatically. They have to be encouraged and helped to do so at all levels of education. It is thus applicable to *how* people learn with teachers as models of the investigator after truth and fairness, the reflective questioner, the opener of minds. Unfortunately minds seem happy to adopt biases, prejudices, stereotypes and short cuts to thinking and will state these authoritatively, quite genuinely believing them to be truths.

In a previous decade Flavell (1979) had established that metacognition was a highly important contribution to higher order learning. Metacognition was defined as the process by which we think about our cognitive machinery and processing mechanisms (Flavell 1979). These metacognitive activities underpinned the development of the self regulatory and self management skills already referred to as well as the sense of personal agency. Failure to develop learning conversations inside the head, or metacognitions, left the learner in 'robot mode' according to Thomas (1976). This was a state of learned helplessness where the response to problems was to use old well-worn strategies even if they had little hope of success and to profit little from experience. He estimated that some 80 per cent of the population might be in robot mode.

Failure to develop higher order cognitive skills in schools and colleges was, according to Resnick (1989), not surprising for it had never been the goal of mass education to do more than develop basic skills of literacy and numeracy and core subject knowledge.

Paul maintained that as societies become less isolated and more complex, lack of rationality at both global and local level becomes increasingly dangerous for the maintenance of human existence. To combat these dangers of didactic education which brings with it its own kind of ignorance and prejudice, education worldwide needed to change.

If teachers work together on a whole-school basis it is possible to achieve the goals of critical thinking either with a small amount of extra time or frequently with no additional time. It could be equivalent to each curriculum area offering one cognitively orientated training session per term. The orchestration of this would be an important task in developing the cognitive curriculum.

The cognitive curriculum

There are five main aspects to developing the cognitive curriculum. These are:

a. Developmental differentiation

This is the setting of common tasks to which all students can contribute their own inputs and so progress from surface to deep learning and thus be enabled to achieve more advanced learning outcomes.

b. Positive cognitive intervention

This is the information which the teacher gives to the pupils when on task, explaining how the work in progress is going, how good it is and what steps might be taken to make it even better. This was given more detailed treatment in Chapter 2.

c. Cognitive process pedagogies

These are the core of developmental differentiation and PCI and they enable it to be achieved. Cognitive process teaching methods are based in Critical Thinking Theory (Paul 1990; Resnick 1989) and are the means by which higher order thinking and metacognitive skills can be developed through the ordinary curriculum. These are given more detailed treatment in a later section as are the following.

d. Explicit teaching of cognitive protocols

There are general rules and procedures which can usefully be followed when engaging in decision making and problem solving. When these protocols are made explicit students can use them in a variety of new and different situations to improve their learning and problem solving.

e. Creativity training

In this area there are also protocols which can be followed to facilitate opportunities for creativity, as well as giving more open ended problems and activities to 'capture' any creative notions that might be presented. It is more difficult to ensure there will be a truly 'creative' response or outcome. Something truly creative has to be not only new in terms of the individual but also in terms of the society at large and be a recognisable product.

In order to adjust to teaching the cognitive curriculum the teachers' own theory or theories about teaching need to be changed. Without change in the guiding perceptions the resultant lesson plans and teaching methods will not really change. The teacher will use the appropriate vocabulary but teach in the same old ways or relapse back into them very quickly.

The central objectives in teaching need to be redefined as follows:

To enable students to think efficiently, and to express those thoughts succinctly. This reframing can be represented in the form of a model as in Figure 5.3.

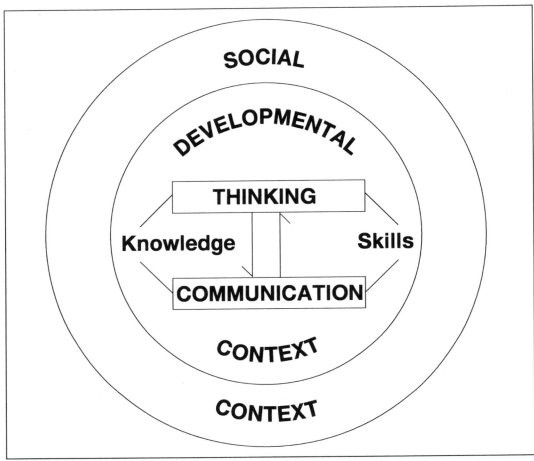

Figure 5.3 Model of modern teaching (Montgomery 1981)

Teaching for learning using cognitive process strategies

i. Games and simulations

In the non-simulation game students work in groups and have to know certain facts, perform skills or demonstrate mastery of specific concepts to win or be successful. The participants agree objectives and there are sets of rules to obey. Typical of this form is the card game which can be adapted to educational purposes such as 'Phonic Rummy', 'Alphabet Snap' and so on.

Simulation Games contain the elements of real situations and students individually or in groups interact with and become part of the reality. Role playing is often an important feature of the game. For example in working with a class of children on the problems of bullying or stealing it is often very useful to organise small group work role play so that individuals can practice expressing their own and other's feelings about the subject as well as analyse the issues and suggest solutions or resolutions of the problem. Characteristic of all games is that they must be followed by a discussion-debriefing session to discuss what transpired so that emotional, educational and metacognitive objectives can be achieved.

The castle task below is not only an example of problem solving it is also a simulation game in which roles are played.

ii. Cognitive study skills

The following examples can apply to textual, visual and performance material: Locating the main points and subordinate ones; flow charting; completion activities; prediction activities; sequencing; comparing and contrasting; drafting and editing; organising – tabulating, classifying, ordering, diagramming, categorising; drawing inferences and abstractions; recognising intent, bias and propaganda. Some of these have been exemplified in Chapter 4.

Cognitive study skills are a form of self directed learning and involve active work on textual and other material. Although reading skills are taught it is not usual to teach higher order reading and cognitive skills although they are considered to be essential to the educated person and a requirement for success in higher education. Even able children do not automatically develop them. It is important to incorporate study skills into *all* curriculum subject areas rather than try to teach them in a separate skills course. Bolt-on provision has been shown to be ineffective and non-transferable.

iii. Real problem solving and investigative learning

Human nature is such that if you present a person with an open ended situation in which the answer to a problem is not given the mind automatically tries to solve it. This notion of the human as scientific problem solver and investigator from birth was put forward by Kelly (1955). Although not everything can be converted into a problem there is considerable scope for doing so across the curriculum.

Characteristic of the approach is that there needs to be plenty of content material around to research to help develop ideas and strategies or verify solutions. Because the activities start from the children's own ideas and knowledge each is building up their own cognitive structures and knowledge hierarchies and can interrogate the various sources. The teacher is not only a resource but is also the manager and facilitator of learning.

The essentials of 'real problem solving' (RPS) and 'problem based learning' (PBL) are that the initial problem is *'fuzzy'*. According to Gallagher (1997) PBL has been around for more than two decades and its evolution has resulted in four elements: an ill structured problem; substantial content; student apprenticeship; and self directed learning. He confirms that research supports the view that PBL is better than traditional instructional methods for:

- long term retention of information;
- conceptual understanding;
- self directed learning.

The research of Dods (1997) showed that didactic methods tended to widen the content coverage whilst understanding and retention were promoted by PBL. However, because of their previous training it was found that students frequently demanded more information. Teachers and pupils on our courses behaved in a similar fashion (Montgomery 1993) until we were able to prove to them that our methods were powerful inducers of learning. The crucial concept was that if they had to spend a lot of time revising then they probably had not learnt and understood the material the first time. Only a minimal amount of revision as a reminder should be necessary even for those who lack very good or photographic memories. Verbal instructions from the teacher, direct teaching, can set the scene and define a structure or a procedure in a quick way but only those with gifted memories will retain it. Even then they may not be able to use it efficiently, that is, transfer their learning.

The real problem solving approach in relation to an NC topic such as Saxon Settlement might be to start with the 'fuzzy' problem. In pairs the pupils should look at map a) to note where settlements occurred and in pairs put themselves in the position of the settlers and try to hypothesise why they might choose those spots. They should try to form a description of each from the map details and find any common factors. This task should occupy 5–10 minutes and then they should share their ideas with the rest of the class and agree a best fit hypothesis.

In phase two new information should be presented and this can consist of a page or two of information so they can employ some study skills. Pictures of artifacts, and drawings of the life of the Saxons could now be presented. The pupils are asked to consider the following questions working in pairs or groups of three. First they should raise a hypothetical answer to each question before looking at the study materials.

a. How did they come?
b. Why did they come?
c. Why were they permitted to settle?
d. Given the tools and materials available what sort of settlement could they build?

At intervals for a change of activity the pupils can share their findings and hypotheses with the rest of the class.

The key topic of what sort of site they will need to find can then be addressed now that they have the background. They can be given different maps and should identify in their groups five or six essentials which a site they now choose for settlement should fulfil and then apply these to their study of the map to decide on the best site. In the final session groups should explain which site they have chosen and give reasons for their choice. This procedure will take slightly longer but the final section could be set for individual homework.

As a follow up they might focus on a particular aspect of Saxon life such as boats, tools, clothes, food for research. Thus not every lesson must be problem based but it is helpful to begin a series with such a lesson to excite interest and motivation, treating it all perhaps like a big detective story. There are a wide range of resource which can be used to reinforce the learning once they know something and they can learn more from a video tape with such advance organisers than if it is used as the primary and initial source of information. Preparing the mind for the new information is important if deep learning is to take place. Ensuring there is pupil discussion before more public sharing of ideas will help them to be clarified and expressed more succinctly.

Comparisons of real settlement sites with modern maps can bring it into the present and careers in archeology, history and geography can be mentioned as well as using such knowledge as a backcloth to novels. The idea of introducing these things is to extend the pupils' interests and experiences beyond the school walls.

Other PBL example topics

When the subject of Homes in different environments, in history and in different countries is considered the subject of Homes on Stilts may become a focus. Instead of being told the title the pupils are given details about climate, monsoons terrain, general physical geography, flora and fauna and tools available. In groups of three they are asked to examine the resource materials and slides etc. and then discuss and design the sort of home which would take account of the setting. They usually come up with homes on boats and homes on stilts. They should then be asked to present their arguments for and against their chosen designs. At the conclusion of the session they can be shown pictures of how the locals solve the problems.

In a study of the local area pupils seldom have an overview or an understanding of how others may view it. Even in an historical study it can be important to start from the here and now before probing into the local past. A collection of holiday brochures can be brought in to show pupils' ideal locations for a vacation. Pairs should then research the brochures to identify the types of information and the language register in which they are written. Using similar headings they should then apply these to a selected part of their home area and document it with Polaroid photographs and cut outs from local newspapers and magazines. At intervals the teacher can call them all together to share aspects and to develop points. They can paste up their four page leaflets and word processing for homework and then hold an exhibition in which they can offer to do verbal presentations of their holiday offers. Follow up work on other peoples' views and comparative studies of the photographs can lead into further work on the same area in the Victorian era, plus a new brochure and language register and interviews with their oldest relatives born in the area. It can also lead to the usual work on local survey and to visits to the local museums and libraries for research.

As a 20 minute problem-based introduction to mediaeval castles pupils can be shown a pictorial map on which five or six sites are under consideration for building a castle – a hilly area; a high circular plateau; an island in the middle of the river; a plot of land near a village in the fork of the river; a plot near the forest and some quarries and so on.

In groups of five, pupils have to imagine that they are the site agent for the place designated for their group and then have to produce a marketing brief to try to persuade the teacher (now titled the Lord or Lady of the Manor) in 1200 AD to purchase their particular site. After 10 to 15 minutes discussion (some may like to record a few notes) one of each group with the help of the rest has to make a presentation. When these are over the teacher can help them to develop the criteria for a good castle site and then by comparing and contrasting the features of each site they can decide on the best one. The teacher can next factor in such things as cost and give details of the actual period labour charges for walls, slits, crenelations and so on, plus the master mason's rates and those of the work people. As the study proceeds they can begin to compare their hypothetical site and castle with some of those in existence and then select one to study in further depth. This should preferably be one close by so that a visit can be arranged for more intensive study and some measurements. This links PBL to experiential learning. Pictures and ground plans of some of the more important castles of the period can be studied together with their owners and how and why they came to be where they were.

In science it is usual for pupils to study separation as a set of scientific processes culminating in pupils being given a mixture of sand and salt to separate. As they are frequently given the diagram to draw first and then get out the apparatus and set up the 'experiment' there is little experimentation or problem about it except the enjoyment of doing it all. It was found to be far more memorable as a learning experience when the pupils, after studying various forms of separation, enter the laboratory one day to be given little piles of an unknown mixture which they are asked to separate. There are two substances which someone has stirred up together.

In pairs the pupils are asked to hypothesise what the substances might be and to design some apparatus to finish up with two piles of dry clean substances. Ask them to consider what the dangers might be in not knowing what the substances are and how they would avoid them. When they have designed their apparatus and it has been checked to see if it is safe they should then set it up even if it is wrong and try it out. At the end of the session in the review a number will have modified their designs and now have semi-separated substances but know what they should have done to clean it. A few who went off on the wrong tack will want to set it up again in the lunch hour so that they can have the satisfaction of completing the task successfully. They remember this lesson very well.

A mathematical example of this sort of thinking is illustrated in the following: Three numbers 3, 6 and 9 represent a rule which I have in my head. In order to find out what my rule is you can generate some numbers too and each time I will tell you either, 'Yes that is an example of my rule', or, 'No that is not an example of it'. As soon as you feel you know what the rule is you can propose it and you will be told whether or not you are correct. If you are incorrect you can go on and propose more examples. This can prove to be a useful exercise in examining metacognitive events in relation to number work.

iv. Experiential Learning

Experiential learning involves learning by doing or *action learning* but the learning is not circular, returning the learner to the same point each time. Instead, at each turn, the experience, the talking about the experience and the reflecting upon the learning and doing adds to the sum of knowledge and changes the processes and the understanding in an additive way. The result is a *learning spiral* (Montgomery 1994), progressing from surface to deep learning (Marton and Saljo 1984) often with the mediation of the teacher (Feuerstein 1995). See Figure 5.4.

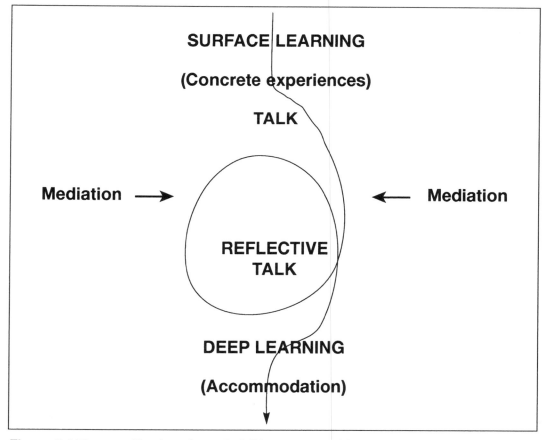

Figure 5.4 The cognitive learning spiral (Montgomery 1994)

Experiential learning can be based on a wide range of activities from visits to the local fish market or quay, the farm, church, and castle, to town centre visits. They can equally include theatre and cinema visits and the study of TV and radio programmes as well as journeys and holidays.

On return from one of these experiences it is not enough to simply talk and write about them, recording the events. It is essential to talk about and reflect upon the thinking and learning experiences and processes which were engaged during and after the event.

v. Collaborative Learning

Collaboration means that students work with each other towards the framing and design of problems and strategies as well as in their resolution or solution. Each contributes some part to the whole. Quite often the process is called 'cooperative learning'. *Think – pair and share* is a powerful vehicle for promoting learning. Pupils are frequently arranged in groups at tables but are only doing their own individual work (Bennett 1986). In real group work they are sharing the tasks, questioning and negotiating with each other and sometimes teaching each other. Collaborative work can be most effective when pairs work is arranged. It is more difficult to have groups of three or five with everyone contributing although some tasks need the larger groups.

vi. Language experience methods

These involve the pupils composing and compiling their own textual materials. It began as a method of creating reading books for poor readers in which they would discuss topics and experiences with a tutor and then the tutor acted as a scribe and wrote down the story which the pupil told. This was then word processed and used as reading material. More recently pupils in pairs can work together at the word processor composing a story and writing up reports. Equally they can work alone with the support of the word processor drafting and editing their own material.

It will be seen that the various forms offered in the cognitive process methodologies have the objective of training in metacognition and in organising what one knows to take account of new knowledge and skills. The objective of training in metacognition is thus to make one a skilful user of knowledge. Nickerson *et al.* (1985) concluded that if training in metacognitive skills is done effectively it should have considerable pay off so that learners learn better and begin to behave like experts. The learners also take on different roles during the activities as many of them are collaborative. Collaborative work by pupils stimulates their thinking processes. As there is an element of open endedness to the tasks there is also a large amount of creativity involved both for learners and teachers.

Over a period of seven years more than 120 experienced teachers on two MA Distance Learning programmes have been given a range of different teaching techniques to evaluate with their pupils. These were methods such as games and simulations, real problem solving, experiential and collaborative learning. None of them were using these techniques prior to the programme. The tasks were to use the set materials or design and implement similar tasks of their own within NC content.

They then evaluated the learning outcomes for themselves and with the direct help of the students. In every case they were able to obtain better learning outcomes from the students than with their traditional methods and the pupils behaviour improved and they became highly motivated and interested. This is ongoing research for the Learning Difficulties Research Project (Montgomery 1998b).

Explicit teaching of protocols

Asking pupils to think about a topic does not teach them to become skilful thinkers. The first task would be to discuss with them the nature e.g. of *skilful decision making* and a graphic organiser can be provided to show where they should arrive but it can be in their own words:

Skilful decision making

1. What makes a decision necessary?
2. What are my options?
3. What are the likely consequences?
4. How important are the consequences?
5. Which option is best in the light of the consequences.

(Swartz and Parks 1994, p. 39)

An example science lesson might be about renewable energy sources and what a country should rely upon for the future. Pupils will have developed their plan for taking good decisions and are asked to review their previous knowledge on energy sources in the thinking actively section. Here the teacher uses reflective questioning techniques and explicit prompts such as asking why people today are concerned about energy; what are some of the optional sources available; what information might the pupils need to research. They make lists of known information with factors such as cost of production which might need to be taken into account. Groups then pick two sources of energy to research and fill in a data matrix with headings such as Options – Relevant Consequences and under this the Factors to Consider e.g. ease of production; environment; cost; availability. From this each group decides which is the best source of energy and discusses why. They then have to prepare an oral or written recommendation giving the reasons for their choice.

In the next phase they are encouraged to think about their thinking, describe it and draw a flow chart to represent it. The flow charts should all contain the five key questions. They then discuss any difficulties experienced, the pros and cons of the procedure and compare it to the ways they ordinarily take decisions.

In the final phase they apply the strategy to a decision they are dealing with at the present, they consider other imaginary issues and later in the school year reinforcement activities are introduced and examples given are on pollution, endangered species, immigration and so on. Skill extension activities are also suggested such as work on determining the reliability of sources for decision making.

Skilful problem solving

In their approach to this Swartz and Parks (1994) make the argument that good problem solving can improve the quality of the lives it affects. Advances in science, medicine and technology have improved the standards of living of people today because problems were identified and solved. Everyday life as well as curriculum topics can present problems to be solved such as what to do when we get lost, cannot start the car, develop a rash, become too hot and so on. They then identify shortcomings in problem solving such as, we do not recognise the situation as a problem; we make hasty choices or consider too narrow a band of solutions; we may fail to consider the consequences of our choices or the feasibility of them, and the result is a poor solution. They show how the pupil can learn to be a skilful problem solver and by the same method as before go through the problem solving protocol beginning with the advance organiser:

1. Why is there a problem?
2. What is the problem?
3. What are the possible solutions to the problem?
4. What would happen if you solved the problem in each of these ways?
5. What is the best solution to the problem?

(Swartz and Parks 1994, p. 76)

The curriculum for infusion of critical and creative thinking which they identify and give detailed treatment is:

Skilfully managing thinking tasks

- decision making;
- problem solving.

Understanding and retention: clarifying ideas

a. Analysing ideas:

- comparing and contrasting;
- classification;
- determining parts-whole relationships;
- sequencing.

b. Analysing arguments:

- finding reasons and conclusions
- uncovering assumptions

Creative thinking: generating ideas

a. Alternative possibilities:

- generating possibilities.

b. Composition:

- creating metaphors

Critical thinking: Assessing the reasonableness of ideas

a. Assessing basic information:

- determining the reliability of sources.

b. Well-founded inference:

i) Use of evidence

- causal explanation;
- prediction;
- generalisation;
- reasoning by analogy.

ii) Deduction

- conditional reasoning.

Of special interest is their approach to creative thinking. They use the brainstorming technique first and then generate further possibilities by listing and considering aspects of the topic and recombining ideas to form new ones. They illustrate the use of concept maps as another way of generating possibilities and suggest that in asking the question, 'Are any of these original ideas?' this also often promotes further and more original suggestions. The example on metaphors shows how they may be constructed by considering amongst other things the key characteristics which the object, person or event has in common with other things which might indeed make the metaphor e.g.'All the world's a stage'. Throughout the pupil is helped to understand what are the errors or defaults in our thinking in order that they can be avoided.

Examples of similar protocols and sets of lessons may be found in de Bono (1983) in his Thinking Action programme. Although it is run as a separate course of thinking lessons the strategies and example lessons can be fitted into the normal lessons based in the National Curriculum. Fisher (1994) also gives examples of problem solving and curriculum thinking activities. He advocates the *scamper* protocol for creative thinking.

Planning and managing one's learning and keeping it on task and on schedule

There are many activities which can be designed to help pupils learn and develop these skills. They need to start with small projects in which they have autonomy to try things out and to learn from their mistakes. Some of the activities already described can provide the initial training ground. An intermediate sized project might be to set small groups to design and develop a school handbook on study skills for Year 7 pupils. They can begin by discussing in their groups their first two weeks in their new school and how they felt and what they needed to know. They can review what they know of study skills across the subjects so far and draw up a check list of skills cross matched with subjects. This can form the basis of a small scale research project using presentational skills of various kinds including statistics. It can form the basis of a useful audit of the degree of permeation of study skills.

A newspaper project. Designing a class or year newspaper using PBL and modelling the processes and roles in a newspaper office can be undertaken with pupils across the age ranges. A full description of how to set this up has already appeared in Montgomery (1985, 1996) and illustrated with pupils' work some five years old and some much older.

Teaching for creativity

Creativity refers to an innovative, ingenious and productive response to ordinary problems. This is often characterised by a flexible approach to thinking, the capacity for induction and use of analogies and models in new and productive ways. According to Simonton (1988) the creative person is particularly good at producing associations and then recognising the significance of the new configuration which has occurred. There is hence a need for inclusion of flexibility and creativity training and experience in education if the country is to maintain its economic position and even improve it.

Recently Yashin-Shaw (1994) suggested that there are three orders of schemata or cognitive process underlying creativity:

> The first order schemata represent familiar knowledge, skills and procedures that have been mastered, and checked and assimilated.
> The second order are the knowledge, skills and procedures used for relatively unfamiliar schemata and need conscious control. Operations in this order possess a high cognitive load.
> The third order represents metacognition which is the cognitive control mechanism enabling the operation to switch between knowledge as it is needed.
> Creativity is not located in any one order but results in a combination of all three being used in various degrees. Synergy is created where the combination exceeds the sum of the constituent parts.
>
> (Yashin-Shaw 1994, p. 35)

Teachers who fostered creativity were found by de Alencar (1995) to encourage pupils and students to:

- be independent learners and thinkers;
- formulate their own ideas;
- be motivated to think and reason;
- cultivate their interest in new knowledge and discoveries;
- ask challenging questions.

The teachers presented them with challenging tasks, stimulated analyses of different aspects of a problem, respected students' ideas (so that they could risk sharing them), were enthusiastic, accepted their students as equals and rewarded them for creative behaviour.

Summary and Conclusions

In this chapter the subjects of effective and good teaching have been grappled with. To some extent it is still a personal construction for there is a flood of influential official publications presenting a different view. However this does not make the official view correct and the didactic mode it presents is in direct contradiction to the research on how people, especially children, are best enabled to learn.

An outline has been presented of what is effective teaching and how teachers may plan their teaching using a variety of different methods to teach. The assumption is that if we teach, the pupils are automatically learning. They will learn effectively only if the methods we use help them to get below surface issues to the deeper levels. Each learner has to be enabled to construct their own knowledge and it is here that the cognitive curriculum becomes essential.

It is only when thinking, reflection, decision making and problem solving are built into daily teaching that learning the subject curriculum becomes relevant and effectively learned.

Five key elements in teaching the cognitive curriculum were identified and exemplified. These were: developmental differentiation; positive cognitive interventions; cognitive process pedagogies and explicit teaching of cognitive protocols; teaching for creativity, all within the subject contents of the ordinary curriculum by every teacher in the school.

Epilogue

In classroom observation appraisal three main types of purpose were identified. These were for staff or professional development, for reward and for promotion. There are also three main forms of assesement that might need to be made – summative, formative and diagnostic for intervention sometimes called diagnostic-prescriptive.

Difficulties can arise when a school elects to use one form of assessment such as the checklist for all three purposes. It can be used summatively and formatively. It may even be used diagnostically to identify strengths and weaknesses. However, it has been shown in the appraisal researches that it cannot be used effectively for intervention to improve classroom performance.

For helping schools with their development and teachers with their professional development a sampling frame method of classroom observation was introduced which was backed by trials in both primary and secondary schools. Because of the detailed approach the method can be used as a coaching system to improve teaching performance across subject disciplines and also can contribute to identifying general and specific in service training needs. The method can also be used in nursery classrooms and in further education. With modifications to the classroom management section it has also been shown to be capable of enhancing performance in higher education although details of this work have not been included.

Whole school appraisals have been undertaken using the method and the results revealed that the majority of schools had similar general in service needs. These were significant areas for whole school approaches and three common targets were:

Target One
To address the cognitive curriculum and engage in systematic development.

Target Two
To address the behaviour management of classes as groups and to increase the amount of CBG to promote a more positive school ethos.

Target Three
To address the needs of learners, in particular the issue of handwriting. All pupils entering secondary school should be able to write at the speed of at least 25 words

per minute if they are to cope with the curriculum recording demands made upon them. This must include teaching a full cursive writing form where necessary. All pupils in Year One should be able to write simple sentences using a full cursive style unless they have mild handwriting coordination difficulties when they must be taught cursive but will take longer to become fluent. Further details of how these targets may be addressed and a fuller rationale for cursive may be found in other texts by the author in the reference list.

References

ACAS (1986) *Teachers' Dispute: ACAS Independent Panel, Report of the Appraisal and Training Working Group*. London; ACAS.

Adelman, C. (1990) 'Teacher appraisal, collaborative research and teacher consortia', in Simons H. and Elliott J. (eds) *Rethinking Appraisal and Asessment*: 36-43. Milton Keynes: Open University.

Alexander, C. (1998) 'An investigation into the voluntary reading practices and attitudes towards teaching of year 8 pupils in a London Secondary School'. Unpublished MA dissatation, London, Middlesex University.

AMMA (1985) *Trick or Treat?* London: AMMA.

Anderson, T.H. (1979) 'Study strategies and adjunct aids', In Anderson, R.C., Osborn, J. and Tierney R.J. (eds) *Learning to Read in American Schools*, 483–502. Hillsdale NJ; Erlbaum.

Anderson, J.R. (1980) *Cognitive Psychology and its Implications* 3rd Edition. San Francisco: Freeman.

Ausubel, D. P. (1968) *Educational Psychology. A Cognitive View*. New York; Holt Rinehart and Winston.

Ausubel, D.F. and Robinson, R.G. (1969) *School Learning. An Introduction to Educational Psychology*. New York: Holt Rinehart and Winston.

Ausubel, D. P., Novak, J.D. and Hanesian, H. (1978) *Educational Psychology. A Cognitve View* 2nd Edition. New York: Holt, Rinehart and Winston.

AVA News (1985) 'Table of percentage learning times' *AVA News* p. 23.

Bandura, A and Walters, R.H. (1963) *Social Learning and Personality Development*. London: Holt, Rinehart and Winston.

Barker, J. (1998) 'A study of ways of developing professional skills and literacy teaching through cross phase inservice training'. Unpublished MA SEN dissatation. London: Middlesex University.

Batteson, C. (1998) 'Empowering or enslaving? Speculations on the mentoring of trainee teachers', *Management in Education* **12** (1), 28–30.

Becker, W.C., Madsen, C.H., Arnold, C.R. and Thomas, D.P. (1967) 'The contingent use of teacher reinforcement and praise in reducing classroom behaviour problems', *Journal of Special Education* **1**, 287–307

Bennathan, M. and Boxall, M. (1998) 'The Boxall Profiles and underpinning research' Speech by M. Bennathan at the November Conference of the *European Association for Special Education (EASE)*. Prague: Benesov.

Bennett, N. (1986) 'Cooperative learning. Children do it in groups, or do they?' *Educational Child Psychology* **4**, 7–18

Bennett, N. (1998) 'Learning to teach. The development of pedagogical reasoning', pp.130–42. In Mcbride op. cit.

Bennett, N. and Desforges, C. (1984) *The Quality of Pupil Learning Experiences*. London: Erlbaum.

Bennett, N. and Jordan, A. (1975) 'A typology of teaching styles', *British Journal of Educational Psychology* **45** (1) 20–28.

Biggs, J.B. (1987) *Student Approaches to Learning and Studying*. Melbourne Australia: Australian Council for Educational Research.

Biggs, J.B. (ed.) (1991) *Teaching for Learning: The Viewpoint from Cognitive Psychology*. Hawthorn: Australian Council for Educational Research.

Blackham, G.J. and Silberman, A. (1971) *Modification of Child Behaviour*. Belmont: C.A. Wadsworth.

Blagg, N., Lewis L. (1993) *Effective Learning: A Report of Six Funded Projects*. Sheffield: Department for Employment.

Bloom, B.S. (ed.) (1956) *Taxonomy of Educational Objectives* Vol 1. London: Longmans.

Bloom, B.S. (1976) *Human Characteristics and School Learning*. New York: McGraw Hill.

Blum, E. (1999) 'An investigation into the effects of recent legislation on the process of integration of pupils with SEN at the H. high school'. Unpublished MA Thesis. London: Middlesex University.

Bogen, J.E. and Bogen, G.M. (1969) 'The other side of the brain. III The corpus callosum and creativity' *Bulletin of the Los Angeles Neurological Society* **34** (4) 191–220.

Bollington, R. Hopkins, D. and West, M. (1990) *An Introduction to Teacher Appraisal*. London: Cassell.

Borich, G. (1997) *The Appraisal of Teaching*. Reading, Mass: Addison-Wesley.

Bradley, H.W. *et al.* (1989) *Report on the Evaluation of the School Teacher Appraisal Pilot Study*. Cambridge: Cambridge Institute.

Britzman, D. (1991) *Practice Makes Practice: A Critical Study of Learning to Teach*. Albany: State University of N Y Press.

Broadhead, P. (1987) 'A blueprint for the good teacher the HMI/DES model of good primary practice' *British Journal of Educational Studies* **35** (1) 37–71.

Brown, A.L., Bransford, J.D., Ferrara, R. A., and Campione, J.C. (1983) 'Learning, remembering and understanding' in Flavell, J.H. and Markham, E., (eds) *Carmichael's Manual of Child Psychology* Vol 1. New York: Wiley.

Brown, A.L. and Palinscar, A.S. (1984) 'Teaching and practising thinking skills to promote comprehension in the context of group problem solving', *Remedial and Special Education,* **9** (1) 53–59.

Bruner, J. (1960/1977) *The Process of Education*. Cambridge. MA: Harvard University Press.

Bunnell, S. (ed.) (1987) *Teacher Appraisal in Practice*. London: Heinemann.

Burgess, R.G. (1990) 'A problem in search of a method or a method in search of a problem? A critique of teacher appraisal', in Simons, H. and Elliott, J. (eds) *Rethinking Appraisal and Asessment,* 24-35. Milton Keynes: Open University.

Buzzing, P. (1992) *An Effective Return to Secondary Teaching*. West Sussex Co Council Print Unit.

Callaghan, J. (1976) Prime Ministerial Speech Oxford: Ruskin College.

Cantor, L. and Cantor, M. (1976) *Assertive Discipline*. London: Behaviour Management Products.

Cantor, L. and Cantor, M. (1991) *Assertive Discipline*. London: Positive Behaviour Management Products.

Carnine D.W. and Englemann, S. (1982) *Theory of Instruction: Principles and Practice*. New York: Irvington.

CATE (1983) *CATENOTE 1*. London: DES.

CATE (1991) *Teacher Competencies*. London: DfE.

C.B.I. (1990) *Towards a Skills Revolution*. London: C.B.I.

Cheeseman, P. and Watts, P. (1985) *Positive Behaviour Management: A Manual for Teachers*. Beckenham: Croom Helm.

Chisholm, B., Kearney, D., Knight, G., Little, H., Morris, S. and Tweddle, D. (1986) *Preventive Approaches to Disruption: Developing Teaching Skills*. London: MacMillan.

Clift, P. (1982) cited in Turner G. and Clift, P. (1985) *A First Review and Register of School and College Based Teacher Appraisal Schemes*. Milton Keynes: Open University Press.

Commonwealth of Australia (1997) *National Competency Framework for Beginning Teaching*. Canberra: Australian Government Publishing Service.

Cuban, L. (1984) *How Teachers Taught. Constancy and Change in American Classrooms 1890–1980*. New York: Longmans.

Curzon, L.B. (1992) *Teaching in Further Education* 4th edition. London: Cassell.

Dadds, M. (1987) 'Researching teacher appraisal'. Paper presented at the BERA Conference, Manchester Polytechnic, September.

Dansereau, D.F. (1988) 'Co-operative learning strategies', in Weinstein, C. F. Goetz, E.T. and Alexander, P.A. (eds) *Learning and Study Strategies* Chapter 7, 103–20. New York: Academic Press.

Dare, C. (1982) 'Techniques of consultation' *Association of Child Psychology and Psychiatry; Newsletter* **11**, 5–9.

Darling-Hammond, L. (1985) 'Valuing teachers. The making of a profession' *Teachers' College Record* **87**, 205–18

D.E. (1993) See Blagg and Lewis (1993) op. cit.

de Alencar, E.M.L. Soriano ((1995)) 'Developing creative abilities at the university level', *Journal of High Ability* **6**, 82–90.

de Bono, E. (1976) *Lateral Thinking*. Harmondsworth: Penguin.

de Bono, E. (1983) *CoRT Thinking Programme*. Oxford: Pergamon.

De Corte, E. (1995) 'Learning and high ability.A perspective from research in instructional psychology', in Katzko, M.W. and Monks, F.J. (eds) *Nurturing Talent* 148–61. Assen: The Netherlands, Van Gorcum.

Dearing, Sir Ron (1994) *The Final Report. National Curriculum and its Assessment*. London, School Curriculum and Assessment Authority (SCAA).

Deci, E. L. (1988) 'Motivating the highly able to learn'. Lecture to the 10th International Symposium, Plovdiv, Bulgaria, October.

Deci, E. L. and Ryan, R.M. (1983) *Intrinsic Motivation and Human Behaviour*. New York: Plenum Press.

Desforges, G. (1998) 'Learning and teaching: current views and perspectives', in Shorrocks-Taylor D. (ed.) *Directions in Educational Psychology*, 5–18. London: Whurr Publishers.

DES (1983) *Teaching Quality*. Command Paper 8835, London: HMSO.

DES (1984) *The CATE Criteria*. London: HMSO.

DES (1985a) *Better Schools*. Command Paper 9469. London: HMSO.

DES (1985b) *Education Observed 3. Good Teachers*. London: HMSO.

DES (1987) *The National Curriculum 5–16. A Consultation Document*. London: HMSO.

DES (1989) *The National Curriculum. From Policy into Practice*. London: HMSO.

DfE (1991) *Education (School Teacher Appraisal) Regulations*. London: HMSO

DfEE (1994) *Code of Practice*. London: DfEE.

DfEE (1997) *Excellence for All. Meeting Special Needs*. London: DfEE.

. DfEE (1999) *Teachers, Meeting the Challenge of Change*. London: DfEE.

Dods, R.F. (1997) 'An action research study of the effectiveness of PBL in promoting acqui- sition and retention of knowledge', *Journal of the Education of the Gifted* **21** (1), 18–25.

Edge, A. and Stokes, E. (1997) *Quality and Assessment in Secondary Education. An Exploration of Curriculum and Examinations Year 1*. London: LSE Centre for Educational Research.

Edwards, A. and Collison J. (1997) 'Partnerships in school-based teacher training. A new vision? *Teaching and Teacher Education*. **13** (5), 555–61.

Eisner, E. (1983) 'Can educational research inform educational practice?' Paper presented to the annual meeting of AERA, Montreal, Canada.

Elliott, J. and Labett, B. (1974) *Teaching Research and Teacher Education*. Norwich: University of East Anglia CARE mimeo.

Elliott, J. (1990a) 'Teachers as researchers: Implications for supervision and for teacher education', *Teaching and Teacher Education* **6** (1), 11–26.

Elliott, J. (1990b) 'Appraisal of performance or appraisal of persons? pp. 80-99 in Simons, H. and Elliott, J. *Rethinking Appraisal and Asessment*. Milton Keynes: Open University.

Elliott, J. (1990c) 'Conclusion, rethinking appraisal' in Simons, H. and Elliott, J. (eds) *Rethinking Appraisal and Asessment*, 180–93. Milton Keynes: Open University.

Entwistle, N.J. (1998) 'Understanding academic performance at university. A research retro- spective' in Shorrocks-Taylor, D. (ed.) *Directions in Educational Psychology*, 106–127. London: Whurr Publishers.

Eraut, M. (1990) Teacher appraisal and/or teacher development: friends or foes?', in Simons, H. and Elliott, J. *Rethinking Appraisal and Asessment*, 106–27. Milton Keynes: Open University.

Evans, A. and Tomlinson, J. (1990) *Teacher Appraisal*. London: Jessica Kingsley.

Feller, M. (1994) 'Open book testing and education for the future', *Studies in Educational Evaluation* **20** (2), 225–38.

Fenstermacher, G.D. (1986) 'Philosophy of research on teaching. Three aspects', in Wittrock, M.C. (ed.) *Handbook of Research on Teaching* 3rd Edition, 37–49. New York: MacMillan.

Feuerstein. R. (1995) *Mediated Learning Experience Training Conference*. London: Regents College.

Fisher, R. (1994) *Teaching Children to Think*. Hemel Hempstead: Simon and Schuster.

Flavell, J.H. (1979) 'Metacognition and cognitive monitoring', *American Psychologist* **34**, 906–11.

Furlong, L. (1996) 'From integration to partnership. Changing structures in Initial teacher education', pp. 121–129 In Mcbride, op. cit.

Gagné, R.L. (1975) *The Essentials of Learning*. London: Holt, Rinehart and Winston.

Gagné, R., Briggs, L. and Wagner, L. (1988) *Principles of Instructional Design* 4th Edition. New York: Holt Rinehart and Winston.

Gallagher, S.A. (1997) 'PBL. Where did it come from? What does it do and where is it going?' *Journal for the Education of the Gifted*. **21** (1), 3–18.

Galloway, D. and Goodwin, C. (1987) *The Education of Disturbing Children*. London: Longmans.

Gazzaniga, R. (1967) 'Split brain in man', *Scientific American* **217**, 24–29.

Gibbs, G. (ed.) (1995) *Improving Student Learning*. Oxford: Oxford Brooks University, Centre for Staff Development.

Gibbs, G. (1990) *Information Sheet*. Summary of Courses and Contents. Oxford: Oxford Polytechnic Centre for Staff Development.

Gibbs, G. (ed.) (1996) *Improving Student Learning Through Assessment*. Oxford: Oxford Brooks University, Centre for Staff Development.

Glaser, B.G. (1977) *Adaptive Education. Individual Diversity and Learning*. New York: Holt Rinehart and Winston.

Glaser, B.G. (1978) *Theoretical Sensitivity*. Mill Valley CA: Sociology Press.

Goodlad, J. (1984) *Teachers for our Nations' Schools*. San Francisco CA: Jossey–Bass.

Graham, D. (1985) *Those Having Torches: Teacher Appraisal, a Study*. Ipswich: Suffolk Education Department.

Graham, D. (1987) *In the Light of Torches: Teacher Appraisal, a Further Study*. London: Industrial Society.

Hadfield, N. (1990) 'Survey of probationary teachers' experiences of ITT in one LEA: Unpublished Report. Kingston Polytechnic. Learning Difficulties Research Project.

Hadfield, N. (1999) Personal communication.

Hancock, D. (1985) 'Staff appraisal in Schools and Colleges. A view from the DES' Speech given at a seminar on Appraisal hosted by the Industrial Society, 25th February.

Handy, C. (1972) in Handy, C. and Aitken, R. (1986) *Understanding Schools as Organisations*. London: Penguin Books.

Hargreaves, D. (1984) *Improving Secondary Schools*. London: ILEA.

Harrop, A. (1984) *Behaviour Modification in the Classroom*. London: Unibooks.

Hebb, D.O. (1958) *The Organisation of Behaviour*. New York: Prentice Hall.

Hilgard, A.H. and Bower, G. (1981) *Theories of Behaviour*. New York: Prentice Hall.

Hirst, P.H. (1968) 'The contribution of philosophy to the study of the curriculum', in Kerr, J.F. (ed.) *Changing the Curriculum*. London: University of London Press.

Hohmann, M., Barnet, B. and Weikart, D.P. (1979) *Young Children in Action: A Manual for Preschool Educators*. Ypsilanti Mich: Highscope Press.

HMI (1982) *The New Teacher in School*. London: HMSO.

HMI (1983) *Teaching Quality*. London: HMSO.

HMI (1985) *Better Schools*. London: HMSO.

HMI (1989) *Developments in the Appraisal of Teachers*. London: DES.

HMI (1997) *Annual Report of the Senior Chief Inspector for Schools in England*. London: HMSO.

Horne, H. and Pierce, A. (1996) *A Practical Guide to Staff Development in Schools*. London: Kogan Page.

House, E.R. and Lapan, S.D. (1990) 'Teacher appraisal', in Simons, H. and Elliott, J. (eds) *Rethinking Appraisal and Asessment*, 55–63 Milton Keynes: Open University.

Husbands, C, (1996) 'Change management in ITT. National contexts, local circumstances and dynamics', in Mcbride, R. (ed.) *Teacher Education Policy. Some Issues Arising from Research and Practice, Chap 1*. London: Falmer.

ILEA (1977) *Keeping the School Under Review*. London: ILEA.

Jackson, P. (1968) *The Practice of Teaching*. New York: Teachers College Press.

James, N. (1984/1989) Report on appraisal research in an LEA cited in D. Montgomery and N. Hadfield (1989) *Practical Teacher Appraisal*. London: Kogan Page.

Johnson, G. (1997) 'Reframing teacher education and teaching: From personalism to post personalism', *Teaching and Teacher Education* **13** (8), 815–29.

Jones, S. (1998) 'Whole class teaching, democratic skills and improving performance', *Mangement in Education* **12** (1), 22–24.

Joseph, Sir K. 1984 Speech at the North of England Conference Sheffield, January 6th.

Joseph, Sir K. (1985a) Speech at the North of England Conference Sheffield, January 4th.

Joseph, Sir K. (1985b) Speech at the 'Better Schools' Conference, Birmingham November 15th.

Joyce, B. and Weil, M. (1986) *Models of Teaching* 3rd Edition. Englewood Cliffs NJ: Prentice Hall.

Joyce, B. and Shower, B. (1988) *Student Achievement Through Staff Development*. New York: Longman.

Kelly, G. (1955) *The Psychology of Personal Constructs* Vols 1 and 2. New York: Norton.

Kennedy, D (1987) Draft of letter to College Principals.

Knight, B.A. (1999) 'Towards inclusion of students with special needs in the regular classroom', *Support for Learning* **14** (1), 3–7.

Knight, B.A., Paterson, D. and Mulcahy, R. (1998) *SPELT. A Cognitive and Metacognitive Approach to Instruction*. Melbourne: Hawker Brownlow Education.

Kolb, D.A. (1984) *Experiential Learning. Experience as a Source of Learning and Development*. New York: Prentice Hall.

Kounin, J. (1970) *Discipline and Group Management in Schools*. New York: Holt, Rinehart and Winston.

Lawrence, R., Steed, D. and Young P. 1984 *Disruptive Children – Disruptive Schools?* London: Croom Helm.

Luton, K. and Booth, A. (1991) *Positive Strategies for Behavioural Mangement*. Windsor: NFER–Nelson.

Maier, N.R. (1976) *The Appraisal Interview: Three Basic Approaches*. New York: University Associates.

Makins, V. (1991) 'Five steps to peace in the classroom', *Times Educational Supplement 1* November, p.23.

Marton, F. and Saljo, R. (1976) 'On qualitative differences in learning I. Outcome as a function of the learner's conception of the task', *British Journal of Educational Psychology* **46**, 4–11.

McBride, R. (ed.) (1996) *Teacher Education Policy. Some Issues Arising from Research and Practice*. London: Falmer.

McCulloch, M. 1979 *School Experience in Initial B.Ed/B.Ed. Hons. Degrees Validated by the Council for National Academic Awards*. London: CNAA.

McIntyre, A. (1980) 'The contribution of research to quality in teacher education', in Hoyle, E. and McGarry, J. (eds) *Professional Development of Teachers,* 295–307. World Yearbook of Education. London: Kogan Page.

McIntyre, A. (1985) *After Virtue* 2nd Edition. Notre Dame Indiana: University of Notre Dame Press.

McIntyre, D. (1990) 'Criterion-referenced assessment of teaching' in Simons, H. and Elliott, J. (eds) *Rethinking Appraisal and Assessment,* 64–71. Milton Keynes: Open University Press.

McNally, F., Cope, P., Inglis, B. and Stronbach, I. (1997) 'The student teacher in school. Conditions for development' *Teaching and Teacher Development* **13** (5), 485–98.

Mellanby, J., Anderson, R., Campbell, B. and Westwood, E. (1996) 'Cognitive determinants of verbal underachievement at secondary school level', *British Journal of Educational Psychology* **66**, 483–500.

Mongon, D. and Hart, S. (1989) *Improving Classroom behaviour: New Directions for Pupils.* London: Cassell.

Montgomery, D. (1998a) *Reversing Lower Attainment.* London: David Fulton Publishers.

Montgomery, D. (1998b) *Appraisal and Staff Development (2nd Edit) MA SEN and MA SpLD Module Ten.* (1994 1st edn) London: Middlesex University.

Montgomery, D. (1998c) 'Teacher education and distance learning', *Education Today* **48** (4), (Dec) 39–46.

Montgomery, D. (1997a) *Spelling: Remedial Strategies.* London: Cassell.

Montgomery, D. (1997b) *Developmental Spelling. A Handbook of 100 Spelling Lessons.* Maldon: Learning Difficulties Research Project.

Montgomery, D. (1981) 'Education comes of age. A modern theory of teaching', *School Psychology International* **1**, 1–3.

Montgomery, D. (1983) 'Teaching thinking skills in the school curriculum', *School Psychology International* **3**, 108–112.

Montgomery, D. (1984) *Evaluation and Enhancement of Teaching Performance.* Maldon: Learning Difficulties Research Project.

Montgomery, D. (1985a) 'Appraisal: The nub is credibility', *Education* 22 March, p 259.

Montgomery, D. (1985b) 'Oxbridge influences' *Education* 29 March.

Montgomery, D. (1985c) 'A positive approach to appraisal', *Inspection and Advice* **2** (1), 16–19.

Montgomery, D. (1988) 'Appraisal', *New Era in Education* **68** (3), 85–90.

Montgomery, D. (1989) *Managing Behaviour Problems.* Sevenoaks: Hodder and Stoughton.

Montgomery, D. (1990) *Children with Learning Difficulties.* London: Cassell.

Montgomery, D. (1991) 'Appraisal: A review of 10 years work', *Management in Education* **5** (3).

Montgomery, D. (1993) 'Fostering learner managed learning in teacher education', in Graves, N. (ed.) *Learner Managed Learning*, 59–70. Leeds: Higher Education for Capability/World Education Fellowship.

Montgomery, D. (1994) The role of metacognition and metalearning in teacher education', in Gibbs, G. (ed.) *Improving Student Learning*, 227–53. Oxford: Oxford Centre for Staff Development.

Montgomery, D. (1996) *Educating the Able.* London: Cassell.

Montgomery, D. and Hadfield, N. (1989) *Practical Teacher Appraisal.* London: Kogan Page.

Montgomery, D. and Hadfield, N. (1990) *Appraisal in the Primary Classroom.* Leamington Spa: Scholastic.

Moriarty, M. (1999) 'An hour a day helps them spell, read (and play!)', *Teachers* **1**, Spring, pp. 6–7 London: DfEE.

Mortimore, P., Sammons, P. Stoll, L. *et al.* (1988) *School Matters.* London: ILEA.

NAHT (1999) an interview with the national President of the NAHT on Radio 4, News February.

Neagley, R.L. and Evans, N.D. (1967) *Handbook for Effective Curriculum Development.* Englewood Cliffs NJ: Prentice Hall.

NC (1989) *National Curriculum.* London: DES.

Neill, A.S. (1883 –1973) Founded Summerhill School in 1929 in Suffolk. A self-styled 'Progressive School'.

Neville, M. and Pugh, A. (1977) 'Ability to use a book: the effect of teaching', *Reading* **11** (3), 13–18.

Nickerson, R.S., Perkins, D.N. and Smith, E.E. (eds) (1985) *The Teaching of Thinking*. Hillsdale, NJ: Erlbaum.

Nisbet, J. (1986) 'Appraisal for improvement', *Appraising Appraisal*. London: BERA Publications.

Norman, D.A. (1977) 'Notes towards a complex theory of learning', in Lesgold, A.M. Pellagino, J.W., Fokkema, S.D. and Glaser, R. (eds) *Cognitive Psychology and Instruction*. New York: Plenum.

NPHA (1999) 'Survey of marking of SATs at Key Stage One' Reported on Radio 4 You and Yours, 22 February.

NUT (1997) Statement by Director of NUT Reported in *Times Educational Supplement* 26 October, p.1.

OFSTED (1997) *OFSTED Report*. London: HMSO.

Ornstein, R. (1982) *The Psychology of Thinking*. 2nd Edition. San Francisco: Freeman.

Osborn, M. (1997) 'When being top is not seen as best' *Time Educational Supplement* 10 Jan., p. 14.

Pascal, L. (1998) Study Skills Training Course leaflet. Stafford: NASEN.

Patterson, W. (1985) 'Appraisal of schoolteachers. An Industrialist's perspective from HAY/MSL' NUT Conference, London: NUT.

Paul, R. (1990) 'Critical thinking' Chapter 3 in *Critical Thinking Handbook*. Sonoma, Sonoma State University Centre for Critical Thinking and Moral Critique.

Piaget, J. (1952) *Origins of Intelligence in Children* 2nd Edition. New York: International Universities Press.

Pollard, and Tann, S. (1994) *Reflective Teaching in the Primary School*. London: Cassell.

Poster, C. and Poster, D. (1991) *Teacher Appraisal: A Guide to Training*. London: Routledge.

Prawat, R.S. (1989) 'Promoting access to knowledge, strategy and disposition in students. A research synthesis', *Review of Educational Research* **59** (1), 1–41.

Race, P. (1992) 'Developing competence', in *Professorial Inaugural Lectures,* 1–53. Glamorgan, University of Glamorgan.

Ramsden, P. (1997) 'The context of learning', in Marton, F., Hounsell, D.J. and Entwistle, N.J. *The Experience of Learning* 2nd Edition. Edinburgh: Scottish Academic Press.

Rawlings, A. (1996) *Ways and Means Today: Conflict Resolution, Training and Resources*. Kingston: Kingston Friends, 78 Eden Street, Kingston KT1 1DG.

Renzulli, J.S. (1986) 'The three ring conception of giftednesss. A development model for creative productivity, in Sternberg, R.J. and Davidson, J.E. (eds) *Conceptions of Giftedness*, 332–57. New York: Cambridge University Press.

Resnick, L.B. (1987) 'Learning in schools and out' *Educational Researcher* **16** (9), 13–20.

Resnick, L.B. (ed.) (1989) *Knowing, Learning and Instruction Essays in Honour of Robert Glaser,* pp. 1–23 Hillsdale NJ: Erlbaum.

Reynolds, D. (1995) 'The effective schools. An Inaugural lecture', *Evaluation and Research in Education* **9** 2, 57–73.

Reynolds, A. (1992) 'What is competent beginning teaching? A review of literature', *Review of Educational Research* **62**, 1–36.

Reynolds, D. and Farrell, S. (1996) *Worlds Apart? A Review of International Surveys of Educational Achievement Involving England*. London: OFSTED.

Riding, R. and Rayner, S. (1998) *Cognitive Styles and Learning Strategies*. London: David Fulton Publishers.

Roberts, M. (1986) 'The education of preschool and nursery children'. Seminar given at the *World Education Fellowship Conference (GB Section)*. London: Kingston Polytechnic.

Rogers, W. (1994a) 'Teaching positive behaviour to behaviourally disordered students in primary schools', *Support for Learning* **9** (4), 166–70.

Rogers, W (1994b) B*ehavioural Recovery: A Whole School Approach for Behaviour Disordered Children*. Melbourne: Australian Council for Educational Research.

Rose, J. (1995) *OFSTED Inspections Report*. London: OFSTED.

Rosenshine, B. (1979) 'Content, time and direct instruction,' in Peterson, P.L. and Walberg, H.J. (eds) *Research on Teaching*. Berkeley CA: McCutchan.

Rudduck, J. (1995) 'The effective teacher', *Evaluation and Research in Education* **9** (2), 74–83.

Rutter, M. L. (1991) 'Pathways from childhood to adult life'.

Rutter, M.L., Maugham, M., Mortimore, P. and Ouston, J. (1979) *Fifteen Thousand Hours*. London: Longman.

Ryan, M.L., Connell, J.P. and Deci, E.L. (1985) 'A motivational analysis of self determination and self regulation in education' in Ames, C. and Ames, R. (eds) Vol 2 *Research on Motivation in Education: the Classroom Milieu, Chap 1*. New York: Academic Press.

Sammons, P. (1998) 'Diversity in classrooms: effects on educational outcomes', in Shorrocks–Taylor, D. (ed.) *Directions in Educational Psychology*, 39–66. London: Whurr Publishers.

Samuel, G. (1983) 'Evaluation as a way of life' *Education* **162** (14), 272.

Samuel, G. (1987) 'Appraisal: A rose by any other name?' in Bunnell, S. (ed.) *Teacher Appraisal in Practice*. London: Heinemann.

Savage, J. and Desforges, C. (1995) 'The role of informal assessment in teacher practical action', *Educational Studies* **21** (3), 433–46.

Schon, D.A. (1983) *The Reflective Practitioner*. New York: Basic Books.

Schools Council (1980) *Study Skills in the Secondary School. Project Handbook*. London: Schools Council.

Scriven, M. (1986) 'New functions of evaluations', *Evaluation Practice* **7** (1).

Scott-MacDonald, W. (1971) *Battle in the Classroom*. Brighton, Intext.

Sharpe, R. and Green, A. (1975) *Education and Social Control. A Study in Progressive Primary Education*. London: Routledge and Kegan Paul.

Silva, K. (1998) 'Report of an international comparative study of pre school education' 24 hour World News, Strasbourg, 4 June.

Simons, H. and Elliott, J. (eds) (1990) *Rethinking Appraisal and Assessment*. Milton Keynes: Open University.

Simonton, D.K. (1988) *Scientific Genius. A Psychology of Science*. Cambridge: Cambridge University Press.

Skilbeck, M. (1989) *School Development and New Approaches to Learning. Trends and Issues in Curriculum Reform*. Paris: Organisation for Economic Cooperation and Development.

Skinner, B.F. (1957) *Verbal Behaviour*. New York: Appleton Century Crofts.

Smyth, J. (1989) 'Developing and maintaining critical reflection in teacher education' *Journal of Teacher Education* **40** (2), 2–9.

Snow, R.E. (1973) 'Theory construction for research on teaching', in Travers, R.M.W. (ed.) *Second Handbook of Research on Teaching*, 77–112. New York: Rand McNally.

Southgate–Booth, V., Arnold, H. and Johnson, S. (1982) *Extending Beginning Reading*. London: Heinemann.

Southgate–Booth, V. (1986) 'Teachers of reading. Planning the most effective use of their time', in Root, B. (ed.) *Resources for Reading. Does Quality Count?, 80–98* London: UKRA/MacMillan.

Stenhouse, L. (1975) *An Introduction to Curriculum Research and Development.* London: Heinemann.

Stenning, W.I. and Stenning, R. (1984) 'The assessment of teacher performance: Some practical considerations', *School Organisation and Management* **3** (2).

Stephenson, J. and Weil, S. (1988) *Launch of Higher education for Capability* London: Royal Society of Arts.

Stodolsky, S. (1984) 'Teacher evaluation. The limits of looking', *Educational Research* **13** (9), 11–18.

Strauss, A.L. and Corbin, J. (1990) *Basics of Qualitative Research.* Newbury Park: Sage.

Swartz, R.J. and Parks, S. (1994) *Infusing the Teaching of Critical and creative Thinking into Elementary Instruction.* Pacific Grove CA: Critical Thinking Press and Software.

Taba, H. (1963) 'Learning by discovery. Psychological and educational rationale', *Elementary School Journal* **63**, 308–16.

Thomas, L. and Harri-Augstein, S. (1975) *Report on the Reading to Learn Project.* London: Brunel University Centre for the Study of Human Learning.

Thomas, L. (1976) Learning to learn', *Personnel Management* **37**, 22–24.

Thomas, L. and Harri–Augstein, S. (1984) 'The self organised learner: A converstional science for teaching and learning'. SCEDSIP/COPOL Conference Paper, Kingston Polytechnic.

TIMSS (1997) *Third International Maths and Science Study.* TIMSS International Study Centre,Campion Hall, Boston College, Cheshunt Hill MA 02167 USA.

Tom, A. (1984) *Teaching as a Moral Craft.* New York: Longman.

Torgeson, J.K. (1982) 'The learning disabled child as inactive learner. Educational implications', *Topics for Learning Disabilities* **2**, 45–52.

Trethowan, D.M. (1987) *Appraisal and Target Setting.* London: Harper and Row.

Turner, G. and Clift, P. (1985) *A First Review and Register of School and College Based Teacher Appraisal Schemes.* Milton Keynes: Open University Press.

Turner, G. and Clift, P. (1988) *Studies in Teacher Appraisal.* Brighton: Falmer.

Tuxworth, E.N. (1982) *Competency in Teaching.* London: F.E.U.

Van Manen, M. (1991) *Researching Lived Experience. Human Science Research for an Active Sensitive Pedagogy.* London Ontario: Althouse Press.

Vygotsky, L.S. (1978) *Mind in Society: The Development of Higher Pyschological Processes.* Cambridge Mass, Harvard University Press.

Wang, M.C. and Lindvall, C.M. (1984) 'Individual differences and school environments' in I.F.W. Gordon (ed.) *Review of Research in Education II.* Washington DC: American Education Research Association .

Watson, J. (1996) *Reflection Through Instruction.* London: Falmer.

Weikart, D. (1967) *Preschool Intervention. A Preliminary Report from the PreSchool Project.* Michigan: Ann Arbor.

Weikart, D. (1998) 'Report of an international comparative study of pre school education' 24 hour World News, Strasbourg, 4 June.

Weinstein, C.E., Goetz, E.T. and Alexander, P. A. (1988) *Learning and Study Strategies.* New York: Academic Press.

Wheldall, K and Merrett, F. (1984) *BATPACK, Positive Products.* Birmingham: Birmingham University Press.

Wheldall, K. and Merrett, F. (1985) *Positive Teaching: A Behavioural Approach.* London: Unwin .

Winter, R. (1990) 'Problems in teacher appraisal: an action–research solution' pp. 44–54 in *Rethinking Appraisal and Assessment.* Milton Keynes, Open University.

Wise, A.E., and Darling Hammond, L., Mc Laughlin, M.W. and Bernstein, H.T. (1984) *Teacher Evaluation: A Study of Effective Practices*. Santa Monica, Ca: Rand Corp.

Woodhead, C. (1998) *The Annual Report of Her Majesty's Chief Inspector for Schools in England*. Standards and Quality in Education 1996–97. London: OFSTED, HMSO.

Wragg, E. (1987) *Teacher Appraisal: A Practical Guide*. London: MacMillan.

Wragg, E., Wikely, F., Wragg, C. and Haynes, G. (1996) *Teacher Appraisal Observed*. London: Routledge.

Yorke, M. (ed.) (1995) *Capability in Higher Education. Conference Proceedings*. Liverpool, John Moores University.

Zahorik, J.A. (1990) 'Stability and flexibility in teaching' *Teaching and Teacher Education* **6** (1), 69–80.

Index